More praise for Gordon Chi *Building Community, China*

"Building Community, Chinatown Sty
interested in learning more about how ᴜordon Chin and the
Chinatown Community Development Center successfully dealt with
issues of affordable housing, transportation, and public space, making
San Francisco Chinatown a better place to live."

—Judy Yung, Professor Emeritus of American Studies, University
of California, Santa Cruz, and co-author of *Island: Poetry and
History of Chinese Immigrants on Angel Island, 1910–1940*

"Building Community is an intellectual tour de force by one of
California's most influential organizers, activists, and urban
innovators. Gordon Chin was not merely present at many of the
critical junctures that created the modern Bay Area, his skillful
political organizing and community-building work shaped the history
of the region, from the student strikes through contemporary efforts
to empower and mobilize residents of Chinatown. The book is part
socio-political history, part community development primer, part
how-to guide for community organizers, and part autobiography. And
he writes as he has worked throughout his career—with a clarity
of purpose but in the spirit of collaboration and community, giving
due credit to other individuals and institutions. Though rich with
powerful stories, *Building Community* is much more than a retelling of
history, it is a thoughtfully integrated and conceptually rich narrative
suitable for academic courses in urban studies, history, political
science, ethnic studies, leadership studies, and other disciplines as
well as an imminently readable chronicle of San Francisco history. For
scholars, this book provides a treasure of first-hand accounts and thick
descriptions that will provide the basis for future research."

—Corey Cook, Ph.D., Associate Professor, Department of Politics,
University of San Francisco, and Director, Leo T. McCarthy
Center for Public Service and the Common Good

BUILDING COMMUNITY, CHINATOWN STYLE

BUILDING COMMUNITY, CHINATOWN STYLE

A HALF CENTURY OF LEADERSHIP IN SAN FRANCISCO CHINATOWN

GORDON CHIN

FRIENDS OF CHINATOWN COMMUNITY
DEVELOPMENT CENTER

Web: http://www.gordon-chin-chinatown.com
Email: gordon@gordon-chin-chinatown.com

ISBN: 978-0-9964186-0-7

Manufactured in the United States of America.

Produced by Jay Schaefer Books, San Francisco.
Design by Dennis Gallagher, Visual Strategies, San Francisco.

10 9 8 7 6 5 4 3 2

MAP OF CHINATOWN

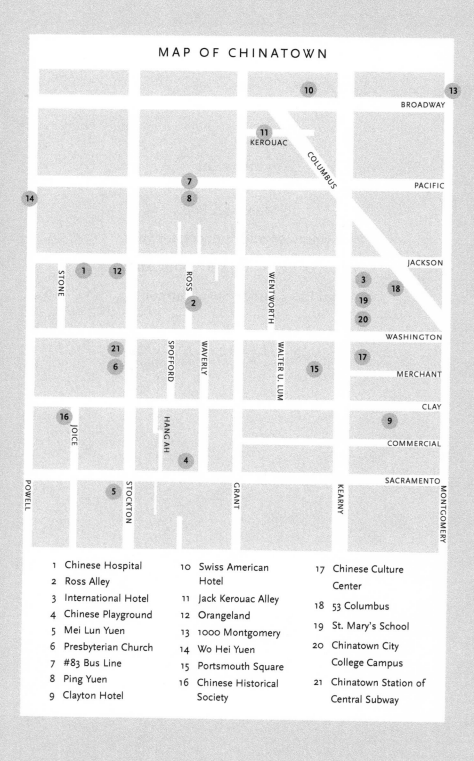

BROADWAY

KEROUAC

COLUMBUS

PACIFIC

JACKSON

STONE

ROSS

WENTWORTH

WASHINGTON

SPOFFORD

WAVERLY

WALTER U. LUM

MERCHANT

CLAY

JOICE

HANG AH

COMMERCIAL

POWELL

STOCKTON

GRANT

KEARNY

SACRAMENTO

MONTGOMERY

1 Chinese Hospital
2 Ross Alley
3 International Hotel
4 Chinese Playground
5 Mei Lun Yuen
6 Presbyterian Church
7 #83 Bus Line
8 Ping Yuen
9 Clayton Hotel

10 Swiss American Hotel
11 Jack Kerouac Alley
12 Orangeland
13 1000 Montgomery
14 Wo Hei Yuen
15 Portsmouth Square
16 Chinese Historical Society

17 Chinese Culture Center
18 53 Columbus
19 St. Mary's School
20 Chinatown City College Campus
21 Chinatown Station of Central Subway

ACKNOWLEDGEMENTS

My sincere appreciation for many wonderful people who helped make this book possible. First and foremost, I want to thank fellow San Francisco Giants fan Tomio Geron for his painstaking research, writing tips, and great support from the beginning of this project.

Much thanks to Jay Schaefer, Dennis Gallagher, and Dean Burrell for their great help in producing a finished product. Writers Judy Yung, Nancy Hom, Genny Lim, and Randy Shaw for their guidance and patience with this first-time writer. Elaine Katzenberger, Sue Lee, and Phil Choy for sharing their advice about books. Alan Wong, Tan Chow, Carlos Zialcita, Tim Ho, Leland Wong, Roy Chan, and Jon Pon for their hours of assistance with photographs. Pat Rose, Winnie Chu, Jeanette Huie, Matthew Lew, and Iva Lee for all their help with book promotion. Norman Fong, Uncle Bob Santos, Seema Agnani, and Rinku Sen for their enthusiastic encouragement. And Dorothy Yee and Cynthia Chin for their love and support throughout this journey.

I also want to thank the many people whom I interviewed for this book for sharing their memories and providing valuable insight on particular issues. Reverend Harry Chuck, Phil Chin, Landy Dong, Wilbert Din, Anni Chung, Vera Haille, Malcolm Collier, Richard Wada, Emil de Guzman, Calvin Welch, Sabrina Gee, and Rose Pak.

And finally, all of the staff and board members of the Chinatown Community Development Center over the past 38 years who have been such a big part of life.

IN MEMORIAM

I have had the honor and privilege of knowing so many community leaders who dedicated their lives to fighting for justice and making San Francisco a better place. They have been great inspirations to me over the past half century, and my memories of them continue to inspire me today. Paige Barber, Sue Bierman, John Boyte, Phillip Burton, Rene Cazenave, Bao Yan Chan, Alan Chin, John Chiu, Kwong Chack Choy, So Chung, Eugene Coleman, Brother Kelly Cullen, Ed Delacruz, Forrest Gok, Howard Gong, Elsie Guerrero, Vera Haille, Hope Hallikias, Isabel Huie, Jim Johnson, Kun Kwong, Him Mark Lai, Tex Lamera, George Lee, Gerald Lee, Y. B. Leong, Enid Lim, Leroy Looper, Watson Low, Peter Macchiarini, Harvey Milk, Etta Moon, Jack Morrison, Margaret Muyco, Rai Okamoto, Betty Ann Ong, Eric Quesada, Al Robles, Mary Helen Rogers, Anita Sanchez, Bill Sorro, Michael Weintraub, Larry Jack Wong, and Sam Yuen.

CONTENTS

INTRODUCTION

EVER SINCE THEY have existed, Chinatowns have been largely misunderstood. While they are often seen by outsiders as just poor neighborhoods or places for cheap food or tourist visits, Chinatowns are dynamic communities that play a key role in economies and in the development of thriving cities. Chinatowns have been home to strong community and religious organizations; strong labor, business, and cultural groups; and political organizations and leaders. Place-based community development organizations, however, have had relatively little written about their role in Chinatowns. This book will describe these place-based groups and how critical they are to a wide range of issues, including transportation, housing, public space, culture, and indirectly, political power. By having such a wide impact, these community development groups are critical in the building of healthy neighborhoods and strong local and national economies, not only for Asian American neighborhoods, but for all American neighborhoods. Just one example of the importance of Chinatown and its community organizations is the growth of leaders such as San Francisco Mayor Ed Lee, who came to prominence after working in Chinatown community organizations.

While the overriding themes of this book are the development of Chinatown and its leadership, this book will also explore related topics that are important to me—Chinatown Community Development Center, the Asian American Movement, and the leadership role that San Francisco has played in the Community Development Movement nationally. And along the way, I will share my thoughts about topics that many would not immediately associate with community development—earthquakes and natural disaster, art and culture, sports and Hawaiian shirts.

I wrote this book for a number of potential audiences. Some of you may have an interest in community development and, in particular, the story of one community organization, Chinatown CDC. You may be working in a grass-roots organization, organizing low-income tenants, youth, or immigrant families, or you are interested in how advocacy organizations deal with complex issues that invariably involve conflict, negotiation, and delicate internal decision making as it relates to dealing with powerful interests.

You may be a professional planner or just interested in urban planning and look at some of my stories as case studies of neighborhood planning. Every neighborhood is unique, but I think you will find examples in this book that resonate with you and the neighborhoods you care about. Like me, you may love San Francisco and be fascinated with how the City works, who its players are, and what goes on in its neighborhoods.

The primary reason I have written this book is to share a little bit of my story and, more importantly, to tell the stories about the people who have given so much to the place I care about. Over the past four decades, the mainstream media have focused attention on San Francisco Chinatown only in the contexts of major events (gang shootings, contentious political campaigns) or high-profile community leaders, with occasional coverage of Chinese food or culture. There is so much about Chinatown that escapes the short-term attention span of the media—the fascinating stories of our families, institutions, and history, which together make up Chinatown. This book is intended to tell a small part of that untold or invisible story.

After a prologue that describes my background and what led me to write this book, the first section recounts the activism that emerged in Chinatown in the late 1960s, the Community Development Movement in San Francisco, and the battle over the evictions from the International Hotel. The sections that follow cover the formation of the Chinatown Community Development Center in 1977 and the issues that confronted both the organization and Chinatown community. Each of these three sections covers approximately a decade in the history of Chinatown CDC. In the fifth and final section, I share my thoughts about subjects beyond Chinatown—the growing Chinese American political leadership in San Francisco, the future of American Chinatowns and the Asian American Movement nationally, and my thoughts about leadership. The sections, which are divided into chapters, are roughly chronological with the sequencing of events based on when the issues first emerged. While the timeline for most of the events in the book ends with my retirement from Chinatown CDC and the election of Ed Lee to a full term as mayor of San Francisco, both of which happened within a few weeks at the end of 2011, occasionally I mention developments that occurred after that time. For more recent updates on community development in Chinatown, visit my website at www.gordon-chin-chinatown.com.

Roger and Lucille "Lucy" Chin were married on September 1, 1943. At the time, Lucy was living with her family on Ross Alley in Chinatown and Roger was serving in the U.S. Army. *(Photo courtesy of Cynthia Chin.)*

The Chin family in Oakland in 1953. L to R: brother, Jeff; mother, Lucy, holding sister, Cindy; father, Roger; and Gordon. *(Photo courtesy of Cynthia Chin.)*

The original Chinese Hospital was built on Jackson Street in 1927, entirely funded by Chinese community contributions. At the time, Chinese were not allowed in either public or private hospitals in San Francisco. *(Photo courtesy of Chinatown CDC.)*

PROLOGUE

San Francisco Chinatown is the place where I was born and my mother before me, the place where my grandmother raised 13 children. I feel very fortunate to have started my life in Chinese Hospital in San Francisco's Chinatown, not only because Bruce Lee was born there (seven years earlier), but also because it symbolizes so much about who I am, what I feel is important about community, and how I have spent most of my life. As I approached retirement in 2011, after three and a half decades as Executive Director of the Chinatown Community Development Center (Chinatown CDC), I began to think about writing a book that would show the connections between the experiences in my life and the development of Chinatown over the last half century. This is that book. It is about building community and nurturing civic leadership, and about people and ideas whose impact has extended far beyond the 20 square blocks that are San Francisco Chinatown.

Just as Harlem has been called the unofficial "Capital of Black America," San Francisco Chinatown was the birthplace of Chinese America and the unofficial capital of Chinese America. It was the only place Chinese could live, even a century after the first Chinese immigrants landed on American shores. It was the place where the first Chinese American institutions— social, economic, cultural, political—were formed. This book offers insights into the types of issues and experiences that have not only transformed the face of Chinatown, but also have helped to groom leaders in community development beyond the Asian American community. The book offers case studies about the importance of "place-based" community development organizations in the building of healthy neighborhoods and strong local and national economies, not only for Asian American neighborhoods, but for all American neighborhoods.

San Francisco Chinatown has survived for one and a half centuries, and continues to survive today despite great challenges—poor and working-class residents needing basic human needs, a struggling employment and business climate, and the most overcrowded urban environment in the nation west of Manhattan. But Chinatown in San Francisco also faces the challenge of identity, given the significant demographic changes occurring in the San Francisco Bay Area—the dispersal of new immigration throughout the region, an aging population, and an aging housing stock and infrastructure. San Francisco Chinatown plays an important historic role in the larger Asian American and Community Development Movements. The preservation and future of all American Chinatowns and other Asian American neighborhoods are vitally important to the nation. My book is about one of those neighborhoods, seen through one person's eyes and experiences.

Some of you may have a broader interest in ethnic communities or a more specific interest in American Chinatowns. This book is what I would call a place-based narrative about San Francisco Chinatown. It is not a comprehensive book about the history of the Chinese in America or Asian Americans. There are many excellent books about particular American Chinatowns, which I will be referencing. One of these is *Hum Bows, Not Hot Dogs,* by my good friend Bob Santos ("Uncle Bob") in Seattle, talking about his life and the story of the International District. In many ways, Uncle Bob publishing his story in 2002 inspired me to write this book.

While most of this book tells the story of Chinatown and San Francisco history starting in the late 1960s with the Asian American Movement and the emergence of Chinatown activism, we need to begin with an understanding of the Chinatown of the post–World War II era in the 1940s and 1950s, my mother's Chinatown.

Seeds of Change

Second generation Chinese Americans like my mother were born and grew up in a Chinatown that had all the problems that continue to exist today—overcrowded housing, inadequate health and social services, and racial discrimination. The Chinese could not own land or buy a home in San Francisco before World War II because of the alien land laws and restrictive covenants. It wasn't until after WWII that some Chinese were able to move into North Beach, Lower Nob Hill, and Russian Hill, although overt housing discrimination would not abate until the 1960s as a result of the Civil Rights Movement and fair housing laws.

The 1950s Chinatown was a small town in character and in social and political structure. It had more American-born Chinese than immigrants, though that would change with the influx of new Chinese immigrants in the late 1960s. San Francisco Chinatown in those days bore resemblance to many historic inner-city African American communities—segregated and lacking public resources or attention, as well as being "self-contained" with locally-owned businesses and community institutions providing the services that government would not. Chinatown residents were not that engaged in citywide civic affairs, either by choice or by force. (Chinese aliens were not given naturalization rights until 1943.) But, change was coming. World War II and the G.I. Bill opened up opportunities to buy a home outside Chinatown, and returning WWII veterans could go to college on the G.I. Bill. Chinese Americans were becoming civil servants in city government and the U.S. Post Office. Chinatown was seeing more homegrown physicians and doctors, bankers and accountants, a professional class to go along with the retail and business sectors.

In San Francisco Chinatown from WWII to the early 1960s, a new generation of American-born Chinese evolved. Yet, despite the emergence of this distinctively Chinese American culture, many Americans still viewed Chinese Americans through the eyes of popular culture imagery. Chinese Americans were stylized (and stereotyped) in films such as *Flower Drum Song*, the 1961 film with Nancy Kwan, which depicted the Forbidden City nightclub where Chinese versions of Frank Sinatra, fan dancers, and comedians entertained San Franciscans—just as white folks went to Harlem to the Apollo Theater and other black nightclubs. "Forget it, Jake. It's Chinatown," the famous line at the end of Roman Polanski's film *Chinatown*, captured how many Americans perceive American Chinatowns—exotic, secretive, and insular places of great mystery, where the Chinese take care of themselves. They are interesting to visit in part because they are "foreign" places.

Whether middle class or poor, family was the foundation for community life in Chinatown. A good example was the Ping Yuen public housing projects on Pacific Avenue: 435 apartments that opened in 1952 to great fanfare as a symbol of the federal government finally recognizing Chinatown as a community with serious needs, one which had also contributed much to the war effort as good Americans. My partner, Dorothy Yee, and her family grew up in the Ping Yuen projects, one of the first families to move into 711 Pacific. My grandmother lived for a few years at the 655 Pacific project.

Chinatown family life in the '50s and '60s included family association banquets and picnics, Chinese School, and religious institutions. It was the place that Saul Alinsky, the renowned community organizing theoretician, once visited in the 1960s and said that Chinatown could not be organized

"Alinsky style" (block clubs and issue-based campaigns) because it was already one of the most organized communities he had ever seen in America. Everyone belonged to something, whether a family association, kung fu club, music club, or worker association. The more appropriate organizing strategy was to build coalitions between the existing social groupings. This rich "social capital" served as a foundation for much of the organizing work in the 1960s and 1970s.

Some of the earliest community organizations also provided services and fought for Chinese American civil rights for more than a century. The Chinese Chamber of Commerce started in 1908 as a community service organization. While there had been Chinese New Year processions from the very early days of Chinatown in the 1860s, it wasn't until the Chinese Chamber took over the parade in 1958 that the Chinese New Year celebration became one of San Francisco's signature cultural events, growing since then to encompass an entire range of New Year activities. The Chamber has a century-long history of advocating for the rights of Chinatown and Chinese Americans. The Chinese American Citizens Alliance (CACA) was first incorporated in 1895 as the Native Sons of the Golden Gate, chartered in 1915 with chapters in most major American cities. It was one of the first Chinese American civil rights organizations in this country. It led a two-decade advocacy effort against the U.S. Immigration Act of 1924, which banned the reunification of Chinese American men with their wives, an issue that finally would be resolved with new legislation granting non quota status to Chinese wives of American citizens.

You can go to any part of Chinatown—any church, family association, restaurant, or coffee shop, the YMCA, Cameron House—and listen to old-timers talk about the families who have been part of their institution for generations and who still give back to their community. This connection between family and community is why I have been so dedicated to Chinatown.

We Called Him "Pop"

Roger "Sick Yong" Chin was our "Pop." Growing up in those days, a lot of Chinese American kids, even if born in this country, only spoke Chinese until kindergarten, and we called our parents "Ma-Ma" and "Ba-ba." I think we started to call our father "Pop" because of the sitcom *My Three Sons* (or was it *Bonanza?*). In any event, he became Pop. And in fact, mom started to call him Pop, too. My Pop was born in China, in the village of Mui Bin in Toisan County of Guangdong Province, on July 10, 1920. He left China at the age of 14, like many Chinese immigrants during the period of the

Chinese Exclusion Act, as a "paper son." That's the process where the overwhelming majority of Chinese immigrants coming to the U.S. used false identities, claiming to be members of the exempt classes (mainly merchants or U.S. citizens) because the Chinese Exclusion Act prohibited the immigration of Chinese laborers. Almost all of the families in Chinatown went by their fake "paper" names. That's why our family name isn't really Chin, but Young (spelled Young, Yong, or Yung depending on what identification document you are looking at). Pop entered the U.S in Seattle as Chin Sick Yong before traveling to Chicago where most of his family had emigrated, including his grandfather.

As a young man in Chicago, Pop became an American. He learned how to speak English. He worked in restaurants by day, gambled a little at night. This seemed to be the lifestyle of a lot of guys in those days. He went to White Sox games at the old Comiskey Park, on the South Side near Chinatown. He told us once that he knew Al Capone (which we really didn't believe). He also said that the Chinatown tongs, the Mafia, and the Blackstone Rangers, then the largest black gang in Chicago, all had a pact not to mess with each other's territory (this one we did believe). Pop loved to explore the country. He used to take the train from Chicago to New York, playing mah-jongg all the way there and back. One time, at the ripe old age of 17, he left for New York without telling anyone in the family. He got an earful about that lark from his grandfather, who was a big man in Chinatown associations.

Pop was inducted into the Army in August of 1942, where he served four years in the 47th General Hospital Corps with two years in Australia, New Guinea, and the Philippines, and received many decorations, including a Bronze Star, before his honorable discharge from Camp Beale, in California. During an Army leave, Pop was supposed to go to Fresno, but he caught the wrong bus and ended up in San Francisco. There, he met Lucille Ng. She served him a glass of water while waiting tables at the Tai Sam Yuen Restaurant next door to the Sun Sing Theater on Grant Avenue. (My grandma, a big Chinese opera fan, would relate how mom described all the big opera stars who hung out at the restaurant. According to mom, most of the guys would hit on her all the time. Not just Chinese opera stars, but American-born Chinese too, including young actors like Sammee Tong, who later appeared in *Bachelor Father*.) I guess Lucy was swept off her feet by Pop, who was a very handsome dude (she thought he was a "Chinese Clark Gable"), and after a whirlwind wartime romance, they decided to tie the knot. But in order to do so, Pop had to go AWOL from the Army for a couple of days. He ended up in the Army brig, only getting out after mom sent the commandant a long letter saying, "It's all my fault!"

Due to racial discrimination and segregation, it is understandable that all my Chinese friends in those days had fathers who were waiters or laundrymen in the daytime and gamblers at night. My dad "ran the numbers" (sold lottery tickets) in West Oakland, so I knew he could take care of himself. He was never a big-time gambler, but there was one time when he was busted in a San Francisco Chinatown gambling parlor. He was, in his words, "small potatoes"—just a pai gow dealer, not the proprietor of the establishment. But, after the bust by the infamous "Chinatown Squad" of the San Francisco Police Department, it was my dad's photo, head down looking really sad, that made the front page of the *Chinese Times* newspaper. My dad said it was only because he was so good looking that his picture was taken. After that, he got a lot of calls from family members in Chicago, wanting to know if he was okay, and many new friends asking if they could borrow some money, since obviously he must have been big time. And that ended my Pop's future as the budding Al Capone of Chinatown.

My dad could look real mean, in a handsome sort of way (must have been that widow's peak that I inherited). Though mom was the disciplinarian, there was this one time I was really afraid of Pop. Coming home from mah-jongg late at night, he would hang up his sport coat (he always wore brown sport coats) behind the bathroom door. When I was around nine or ten, I would occasionally reach into his coat pocket and steal some change as his pockets were full of change. One morning, I reached my little hand into that pocket, but there were no quarters, dimes, or nickels. All my little hand pulled out was a slip of paper on which was written, "Tonite, I beat you up!" *Oh, shit.* I was a pretty dark-skinned kid, but I swear I turned white just staring and staring at that little note. I didn't get that beating, but I never ever went near that jacket again.

The Lucille Ball of Chinatown

My mom, Lucille Ng, was born in San Francisco on October 1, 1918. She was one of thirteen children, only nine of whom survived childbirth. Her dad was Ng Kung Chung, born in China, and her mom was Tam Kim Ling, born in Monterey, California, one of the few Chinese women born in the U.S., as the Chinese Exclusion Act virtually prevented new Chinese immigration to this country, including Chinese women, until its repeal in 1943.

Everyone called my mom "Ah Kum" (her Chinese name) or "Lucy." I never found out how she got the name Lucy, but it seemed fitting since she was known by many as the Lucille Ball of Chinatown—very funny, very outgoing, and very pretty. Since my grandfather seemed to be gone most of the time, working in the fields of the Central Valley, my mom and her siblings had to support the family. The oldest was Uncle George, followed by Aunties Francis ("Bee") and Annie, Uncle Henry, my mom, and Uncles Al and Bill. Everyone began working at an early age, shining shoes, waiting tables, getting leftover food from Chinatown restaurants. This was not uncommon for many Chinatown families in the Depression era. My mom went to Commodore Stockton Elementary School (where later I was a teacher's aide) but had to leave Francisco Junior High in the eighth grade in order to work as a waitress, and she used to tell us about the embarrassment of having the truant officer coming to look for her.

My mom's family was like hundreds of other second-generation Chinatown families—American born, bilingual, working any job they could get, unable to go to college or venture outside the confines of Chinatown due to racial discrimination. As a kid, I remember how cool it was for my brother Jeff and I to sit on Uncle Al or Uncle Bill's motorcycle outside Red's Bar, which today is the oldest bar in Chinatown. My uncles were among Chinatown's earliest versions of Brando-like Wild Ones—very cool. My Auntie Ann and my Auntie Bee both worked in Chinatown gift shops owned by Sinclair and May Louie. Moving up in the ranks over four decades, Auntie Ann managed the Empress Bazaar gift shop on the corner of Grant Avenue and Washington Street, and Auntie Bee managed the Canton Bazaar on the corner of Grant and Sacramento. Helen Fong, my longtime friend and associate Norman's mom, worked with my Auntie Bee for many years before they both passed on. So, my family and Norman's family knew each other long before Norman and I ever met. *What goes around, comes around.*

My dad passed away on December 2, 2006, at the age of 86. Mom passed away on January 15, 2013, at the age of 94. We were happy that they both passed at home, as they would have wanted it that way. And we will be forever grateful for the care they both received from Doctor David Louis who cared for both of them for more than three decades. Pop trained David as a busboy in the early 1970s. David was working his way through school at San Francisco State University, and Pop said he "always had a book in his hands." It wasn't until years later that Pop found out that David had been studying for medical school, later practicing in Oakland in the so-called Pill Hill neighborhood, and it was a wonderful coincidence of fate that David became the family doctor for both our mom and Pop (and for my sister, Cindy). *What goes around, comes around.*

Growing Up

I was born on February 11, 1948, a year after my brother, Jeff. By the time my sister, Cindy, was ready to come into the world in 1952, the family had moved to Oakland, and although we lived just one block from Oakland's Highland Hospital, my mom took a taxi all the way across the Bay Bridge to San Francisco, so my sister too could be born in the Chinese Hospital. My brother, sister, and I are all "Chinese New Year Babies": my brother was born on the first day of the new year, I was born on the second day, and my sister was born on the fourth day, which makes remembering birthdays pretty easy. My mom told us often about hearing all the firecrackers out in the street while she was upstairs in the Chinese Hospital maternity ward, all three times. So, I guess it was inevitable that I would become involved with both the Chinese Hospital and with the annual Chinese New Year Parade.

My family had moved to Oakland when I was three, because Pop could only find work in Oakland, as a waiter by day and running the numbers (selling lottery tickets) by night. He started working in Oakland before the family could move there, and he walked across the Bay Bridge every day to and from work—back when this was possible. After living in a few different apartments in Chinatown, the family was able to purchase a home in East Oakland for the great sum of $10,000, thanks to the G.I Bill.

Growing up in Oakland was cool and like most kids in the '50s and early '60s life didn't seem that complicated. School and sports, *Little Rascals* and *American Bandstand*. Once in a while, Pop would take us to the Roller Derby to see the San Francisco Bay Bombers at the Oakland Auditorium or bowling at the Downtown Bowl in Oakland (back then they still had pin boys resetting the pins). Oakland High ("Go Wildcats") was the most integrated high school in Oakland in those days. I held a trumpet in the Oakland High School Marching Band. I won't dignify it by saying I "played" a trumpet. My sister, Cindy, was an All-City flute player at Oakland High (she once jammed with local jazz flautist Prince Lasha). My brother, Jeff, played some drums, and with my trumpet, we looked really good, much better than we sounded. A love of jazz is something I share with my brother and sister. I am also proud of Cindy's volunteer work with the Oakland Fire Fighters Random Acts of Kindness program—values of giving back that were greatly influenced by both family and our experience at Oakland High School.

Merritt Junior College

After graduating from Oakland High School in 1966, I went to Merritt Junior College on Grove Street (now Martin Luther King Jr. Way) and 51st

Avenue. This was the "old Merritt" before the college moved to the Oakland Hills in 1971. Merritt was my only option, since I goofed off too much my senior year in high school and couldn't get into UC Berkeley (even though all I needed was a B average). Looking back, I am thankful for the experiences Merritt gave me; they formed some of my earliest cultural and political values and perspectives. It was a tumultuous time. Malcolm X was assassinated in 1965 and Watts burned later that year; Martin Luther King Jr. marched on Selma and there were Vietnam War protests across the nation.

Merritt was in every way a working-class school, reflecting its location in Oakland's flatlands. Most kids took the bus there, as I did. It was a great place to be during the mid '60s for young folks like myself who were seeking some sense of identity, not only racial and ethnic identity, but also cultural, political, and spiritual. The vibe at Merritt in those days was fantastic. There was something happening every moment. I used to walk up the street to the old Music City to buy soul 45s. I loved the concerts with jazz artists like Cal Tjader. I saw Eldridge Cleaver speak, I heard Dick Gregory a couple of times, and Shirley Chisholm too (and eventually supported each of them for President). Even though Bobby Seale and Huey Newton had left Merritt by the time I got there, you could not escape the aura and atmosphere of a place where the Black Panther Party was founded. An Oakland High Class of 1966 classmate named Aleta Dwyer Carpenter told me she had a big crush on Huey when she lived across the street from him as a 10-year-old girl. Aleta later became Business Manager at KDIA Soul Radio Station. And many years after that, Aleta became the Director of Property Management for Chinatown CDC.

I took a lot of courses in Afro-American (as it was called then) history. I sat in on meetings of the Afro-American Student Association, then headed by Harriet Smith, and was so thankful that my Asian presence was always welcomed. After all, even though China was an "in thing" with the Movement and everyone had a Red Book, there were no Asian American groups. Yellow Power was very much in its infancy, and the university scene—at Merritt, at UC Berkeley, at SF State—would become the primary places where an Asian American Movement would start in the Bay Area.

I attended meetings at UC Berkeley of a new student group called the Asian American Political Association (AAPA) late in 1967 and early 1968. The AAPA meetings were a great place to explore our identity as Asian Americans, a place to learn about the political process, and if truth be told, a place to meet girls. I remember attending a few meetings, hearing speakers such as Yuji Ichioka, one of the founders of AAPA and one of the first high-profile Asian American activists. Born in San Francisco, he was interned with his family at Topaz internment camp during World War II. He later helped found the Asian American Studies Center at UCLA and is widely credited with creating the term "Asian American" when he was at UC Berkeley. The AAPA meetings were usually chaired by two young UC Berkeley students. One was Jean Quan. The other was Floyd Huen. They later married, started a family, and settled in Oakland, where Floyd became a physician and Jean was elected Mayor in 2011.

I got an early lesson in organizing at one AAPA meeting in 1968, where preparations were being made for a big San Francisco Chinatown demonstration. It was to be cosponsored with other community and student groups, including AAPA's San Francisco chapter and the Intercollegiate Chinese for Social Action.

After Merritt Junior College, I moved to San Francisco to attend San Francisco State College (now California State University, San Francisco). I moved into a small room with my Auntie Bee on Larkin Street.

I did some part-time work, including two weeks on Montgomery Street for a big stock brokerage firm. I was a ticker tape boy. I took stock orders off a big machine and put them into their relevant conveyer belt slots. One morning, I put an order (I think it was for $2 million) in the wrong slot and got yelled at by the manager. I up and left, telling him I didn't need to get up at 5:00 a.m. to take this abuse. And there ended my career with the stock exchange. Hey, I could have been a hedge fund manager! I also worked a day at the Cable Car Drive-In on Geary, but I didn't go back after the manager told me they got held up the night before. Free hamburgers weren't worth it to me. Then I got a part-time job at the U.S. Post Office, a real job—or at least something my folks could understand.

On Strike, Shut It Down!

The San Francisco State Third World Student Strike started on November 6, 1968. It was to become the longest campus strike in U.S. history, ending on March 20, 1969, after an intense and exciting four and a half months. The Strike, as we refer to it now, was a defining moment in our young lives and an important event that changed San Francisco. The evolution of the Strike and the issues that sparked it have been well documented in excellent retrospectives from many who participated in it. From the leadership of the Black Student Union (BSU) to the formation of the Third World Liberation Front (TWLF), the Strike was the catalyst for the Student Movement in the Bay Area. The demands were for ethnic studies, special admissions of minority and low-income students, and the hiring of faculty to reflect the diverse communities of San Francisco.

With all due respect to UC Berkeley's Free Speech Movement, which came earlier in 1964, the San Francisco State Student Strike was different. It was led by students of color with support from the Students for a Democratic Society and other progressive white student groups. This was the awakening of the Black, La Raza, Asian, and Native American students, a coalition of emerging movements and people. The Anti-War Movement was growing daily; Martin Luther King Jr. was assassinated that April 4, 1968, leading to anger across the nation; California had just elected a cowboy actor, Ronald Reagan, as Governor; and the country had elected a "crook" for President. San Francisco State became the venue in which so many social justice passions were played out.

The intense events of those months included the big November 13 demonstration, which brought out the San Francisco Police Tactical Squad for the first time and also introduced S. I. Hayakawa, President of SF State (later to become a U.S. Senator). This demonstration memorialized the shout "Pigs off campus." A second major event was "Bloody Tuesday" on December 2, which witnessed the largest show of support for the Strike, with 5,000 people gathering in the campus Commons, and a major confrontation with the SFPD leading to 32 arrests. On January 23, 1969, the "Mass Bust" occurred, with the arrest of 435 people. The eventual settlement of the Strike was almost anti-climactic, coming in March of 1969 with the establishment of the first Ethnic Studies College in the country.

I remember those big demonstrations on the Commons on November 13 and December 2 and how proud I was to be a part of them. I remember the support of organized labor, churches, and political leaders, and the maturation of many of us young activists who were starting to understand that we as students were not necessarily in the vanguard of the movement. Community leaders joined us at SF State, not without risk.

Later, I watched the news coverage of the November 13 demonstration with my Auntie Bee on her little fifteen-inch black-and-white TV, and she sternly admonished me to stay away from trouble. I don't know whether she talked to my folks about it, but I know she felt responsible for me. And while I loved her very much, I also knew then that I would need to move out on my own, so she wouldn't have to worry.

My buddy Mike Yep and I were in awe watching TWLF press conferences with those dudes sitting in a panel on-stage—Roger Alvarado (Latin

American Student Organization), Benny Stewart and Nesbitt Crutchfield (BSU), Mason Wong and Alfred Wong of the Intercollegiate Chinese for Social Action (ICSA), Filipino activist Ed Delacruz—all of them in their Army jackets and shades. I don't think I ever saw Roger Alvarado without shades on.

The Strike very much reflected a male-dominated sexism, and that too was a lesson of the time. One woman leader of the Strike was my friend Laureen Chew, who was arrested in the Mass Bust and spent 20 days in jail, which she and fellow incarcerated strikers called "The Hole." At the 40th anniversary reunion of the Strike, Laureen said,

> The months of striking, the month-long trial, the years of waiting for an appeal, and the subsequent 20 days I spent in jail as a striker represented my commitment, optimism, and belief that change can and must occur.

I remember the BSU guys, and although I didn't get to meet Danny Glover, there were many African American activists I did meet: Benny Stewart, Nesbitt Crutchfield, Revels Cayton, and Arnold Townsend. Arnold and Benny became leaders in the fight against the redevelopment of the Fillmore neighborhood in San Francisco with the Western Addition Community Organization (WACO) fighting alongside famed tenant leader Mary Rogers. Benny went on to head the Marin City Community Development Corporation. Arnold, still active in the Western Addition, has long been involved with KPOO Radio and as a minister of the Without Walls Church.

I remember meeting Filipino activists Ed Illumin and Ron Quidachay, and learning from their involvement with the battle over the International Hotel. Ed would later join the San Francisco Human Rights Commission as a Housing Specialist, and Ron would become a judge with the San Francisco Municipal Court and Superior Court.

Mason Wong, a former Marine, was someone from my personal past. He lived on Ross Alley, where my mom grew up and where I spent my first three years. My mom knew Mason's dad, Wong Chu Mo, who owned Kum Hon Restaurant on Jackson Street and who everyone knew as Chinatown's preeminent Chinese film star and comedian. The coolest acronym for any program I have ever heard came when Mason Wong and the ICSA formed a volunteer tutorial program to keep Chinatown street kids in school. The program's full name was "Free University of Chinatown Kids, Unincorporated."

The San Francisco State Strike was also when I met Dorothy Yee, the love of my life. There we were, out on 19th Avenue as the picket line spiraled around. She looked at me and shouted, "On Strike!" I looked back and replied, "Shut It Down!" And we have been together ever since.

In retrospect, the San Francisco State Student Strike was not only about establishing ethnic studies. It was also about the relationship between the university as an institution and our communities. Most students attending SF State lived in San Francisco. Few lived in campus dorms, of which SF State had far fewer than other universities. It was a working-class school, especially for students of color. After class, we went back on the M streetcar to our communities in the Mission, Western Addition, Chinatown, or the Richmond District. Many had already become active in those communities—African American students in the fight to oppose redevelopment and displacement in the Western Addition, Asian and Latino students active in youth work in Chinatown and the Mission. We wanted the university to help our communities as well.

The First Ethnic Studies Classes

Even though the Strike lasted a total of four and a half months, the equivalent of one semester, most of us lost a full year of classes because the settlement did not come until much later. It was exciting to be part of the first-ever Ethnic Studies program in the nation in the fall of 1969. The Asian American Studies (AAS) department started with a slate of 17 classes. I was enrolled in at least four of them—"Beginning Cantonese" taught by Mary Yang, "Chinese American History" taught by Phil Choy and Him Mark Lai, "Asian American Culture and Identity" taught by Jeff Chan, and "Chinese American Community" taught by George Woo.

Jeff Chan's class was really interesting, as it explored the cultural context of being Chinese American and Asian American. It was a great introduction to emerging Asian American writing and Asian American arts. We had some great guest speakers, including Frank Chin, one of the first high-profile Asian American writers. My favorite guest speaker was Dr. Herb Wong, a great DJ with KJAZ, the renowned Bay Area jazz station. He was very cool, keeping his shades on during the entire class.

I took George Woo's Chinatown Community class for two semesters. In the second semester, in 1970, we had to research a paper on an issue of our choosing. I did mine on Chinese Hospital, which was in the midst of the greatest challenge it had faced since it was built in 1927. The old Chinese Hospital on Jackson Street was cited by the State for not meeting seismic standards. At the time, the Chinese Hospital was building a new outpatient facility next door. After a great deal of planning, they decided to ask the State to allow them to convert the new outpatient facility into a new hospital. It was no easy undertaking in terms of design and construction or permits and approvals, but it was done. Incidentally, this is one of the first Chinatown issues Rose Pak was instrumental in.

In the course of researching my paper I got to interview both Dr. Rolland Lowe, one of Chinatown's outstanding physicians, and Linda Wang, then a Medical Social Worker at the Chinese Hospital. Both of them would later become, like me, very involved in Chinatown housing. Linda was co-chair of the Chinatown Coalition for Better Housing, and both Linda and Rolland were co-chairs of the International Hotel Citizens Advisory Committee.

I enrolled in an innovative new program developed in 1970 by the Asian American Studies Department and the College of Behavioral and Social Science. Officially, it was called Coordination of College and Community Resources, but everyone referred to it as the Nine Unit Block Program. Students enrolled in three BSS courses to support a 20-hour-per-week field placement in a community organization, and were given a small stipend. I chose the Chinatown Youth Center from the 15 Asian American nonprofit options. Although the program only lasted one year due to lack of funding, it was one of the most important and innovative attempts to connect the college with the community.

Many student participants in the program went on to long-term leadership positions in San Francisco, such as Fred Lau (who became Chief of Police), Anita Sanchez (San Francisco Civil Service Director), Jeff Mori (who went on to head the Japanese Community Youth Council), Steve Nakajo (who became Executive Director of Kimochi Kai), and Filipino leaders Ed Illumin and Ed Delacruz with West Bay Filipino Services. Without Asian American Studies and the Nine Unit Block Program, I do not think I would have gotten my BA from San Francisco State in 1972. As it was, it took me four years to complete two years of upper-division studies.

Perhaps even more important than changing an institution, the Strike changed us as individuals. The convergence of so many things in our young lives that year led many of us to dedicate our lives to serving our communities. The Strike helped define an era in San Francisco. It was also a seminal experience for me and an important touchstone in my life. Those two years helped me determine who I was and what I might become. I wasn't sure yet exactly what that would be, but I knew it would have something to do with Chinatown. Those weren't two years spent on campus. They were two years doing a lot of new stuff—protesting at SF State, discovering Chinatown, learning about other communities of color, and meeting hundreds of wonderful friends in all of these places.

641 Balboa Street

During the Strike, I moved out of my aunt's place and in with some of my new friends from San Francisco State. We lived in a two-bedroom flat at 641 Balboa Street (at 8th Avenue in the Richmond District), which became my crash pad, a casual and ever-changing living arrangement so common in the '60s. The original 641 Balboa gang included Phil Chin, Landy Dong, Mike Yep, and Alan Chin. Phil and Landy both drove U.S. Postal trucks. Phil grew up on Bannam Alley in North Beach, next door to Heather Fong, who would become San Francisco's first woman Police Chief. Landy's family ran a laundry on Union Street. Alan had just become Executive Director of the Chinatown/North Beach Youth Council. He grew up on Clay Street, where his mom operated the Tong Yee Heung Peanut Store. I remember many nights helping Alan "dump peanuts," as we called it, from these huge sacks into water vats in exchange for a great home-cooked dinner with his family. We were all shocked and saddened when Alan passed away from cancer in 1974 at the young age of 28.

While at 641 Balboa, Mike Yep was my closest buddy and a youth worker like me, and we hung out together at the Chinatown Youth Council and later at the Police Activities League (PAL) youth center as volunteer youth counselors. Alan, Phil, Landy, and Mike all came up through the Cameron House Youth Program, and it is no accident that so much of the early leadership of Chinatown nonprofit organizations had Cameron House roots.

641 Balboa became a hangout for young student activists who had all grown up in Chinatown or North Beach. At various times over the next two years, John Wichman, Jon Pon, Terry Chow, Wayne Barcelon, Chester Ng, and Malcolm Collier lived there. John worked at Cameron House and later as a drug counselor, and was a great conga player. Malcolm taught anthropology and Asian American Studies at SF State and was a great photographer. Jon was one of the first city planners I ever met, working with Alice Barkley at the Community Design Center and later with the City Planning Department. Wayne was an architectural student, later joining Darlene Jang (with whom I went to Oakland High) to form the firm of Barcelon and Jang. Terry drove a MUNI bus for a couple of years and then became one of the first Chinese in the Glaziers Union.

At times there were six or seven of us crammed into the two-bedroom place, sleeping on couches and chipping in $25 each per month for rent. The landlady was Mrs. Sit, mother of Ruby Hong. Ruby was the Principal at Commodore Stockton Elementary School (before it was renamed to Gordon

J. Lau Elementary in 1998). She and her sister, Judy, had the unenviable task of knocking on our door and telling us to keep the noise down, especially when we had a big party going on.

Fred Lau also used to hang out at 641. He talked all the time about working out, so he could apply for the SFPD. Fred made the *SF Chronicle* with a famous photo of him stretching on some kind of rack to make himself taller—he was one inch short of the 5'9" SFPD height requirement. The height limit was later successfully challenged by the Officers for Justice as being discriminatory against Asian Americans. Fred was able to join the force, only the third Chinese American to do so (after Herb Lee and Don Tong). He later rose up through the ranks and was appointed Chief of Police by Mayor Willie Brown in 1995.

On most Tuesday night meetings, the 641 Balboa gang would hang out at George Woo's house on Francisco Street. We always looked forward to these evenings after the Chinatown Youth Council meetings—youth leaders such as Warren Mar and Ray Fong would be there with activists like Alice Barkley, Mason Wong, Danny and Alice Wong, Laureen Chew, and Malcolm and Irene Collier. Of course, George did most of the talking. He talked about the Chinatown establishment, about Chinatown gangs, about China, about food. He turned us on to Sun Tzu's *The Art of War*, the famous military treatise that guided Mao Tse Tung and is read by military and political strategists alike. Some of George's favorite sayings still resonate with me:

> Organizations will come and go, but the community will always be here.

> You may not agree with the politics of other elements in the community, but you should respect them as a part of the community.

> If you are serious about Chinatown, you need to commit yourself to the long term.

Learning about Government

While those three years of my life doing Chinatown youth work were very exciting (sometimes too exciting) and a lot of fun, I started to become more interested in the intensifying affordable housing and community development issues, notably the I Hotel Eviction and the fight for the Mei Lun Yuen housing project. I developed an interest in government from listening to folks like Larry Jack Wong and Alice Barkley on the early evolution of many Chinatown agencies and programs. I also started to read more about federal urban policy in my urban studies classes at SF State. I had grown out of the attitude, shared by many young activists, that book learning was secondary to learning on the streets. After all, if many of our fights were against government policies, then I needed to learn about government.

Two experiences from 1971 to 1974 taught me a lot about government and a little about politics: working at the San Francisco Human Rights Commission in 1971, and working as an intern at the office of U.S. Congressman Phillip Burton from 1972 to 1974. Until then, my major government job had been at the U.S. Post Office. I wanted to learn how local or federal policies and programs were developed, how legislation worked at City Hall or Washington, and how the political process is used to get something done.

In 1971, I got a job at the Human Rights Commission (HRC) working with the City Wide Youth Council. Youth councils from all over the City were represented, including the Chinatown Youth Council. It was a great learning experience in how City government works. I learned that to get anything passed in City commissions, it was not enough to just have the right policy—you also had to have a good sense of the political ideology of particular commissioners. Under the leadership of Bill Becker, HRC had a much higher profile than it has ever since. In some ways, the HRC was a counterpoint to the established order, even though it was a City agency.

In 1972, I decided to continue on at San Francisco State and enrolled in the graduate school of the Social Welfare Department. I wasn't that keen on becoming a social worker, but I was attracted to the department's community organizations program, which was tailored to social workers interested in community organizing. My advisor, Tim Sampson, was a well-known organizer who had worked in the early 1960s with the Welfare Rights Organization, a national organization training welfare moms to fight for their rights in many American cities.

I chose to do my social work field placement at the office of Congressman Phillip Burton. SF State was more open to such legislative placements than other social welfare schools. Fellow graduate student Zoraina Harris and I chose Phil Burton because he was one of the most influential people in the City and a leading advocate in Congress for social justice, particularly regarding income support for poor, elderly, or disabled Americans. The Burton office was a happening place with folks like Willie Brown and Nancy Pelosi visiting regularly.

Congressman Burton was a rising star in the liberal wing of the Democratic Party, known for his tough talk, "death stare," and love of politics. In 1972, Phil Burton had just pushed through the historic Black Lung legislation for coal miner benefits and had become a national advocate for the poor and disenfranchised. He was just embarking on two major legislative campaigns that would make history. The first was to establish the first urban park system in the National Park Service, the Golden Gate National Recreation Area (GGNRA). The second was Supplemental Security Income (SSI), an expansion of safety net welfare benefits for low-income seniors and disabled Americans, to complement the Aid to Families with Dependent Children (AFDC) welfare program for low-income families. Congressman Burton was a strategic mastermind in the art of crafting legislation with broad bipartisan support, and SSI won with an interesting coalition of support, including President Nixon and Senator Pat Moynihan.

The Burton field office was headed by Doris Thomas, who was an expert on immigration, and Ed Sarsfield, who would later go on to head San Francisco's Social Services Department. Ed was great at teaching young interns how policy and legislation worked. He was an avid reader and encouraged us to read stuff like the annual Brookings Institute Federal Budget Priorities book and Moynihan's *The Politics of a Guaranteed Income*.

The years from 1972 to '74 were a fascinating period to be in a congressional office, particularly in Phil Burton's office, which was so involved in developing a liberal perspective and strategy in the midst of an historic transformation of federal policy under the Nixon administration. This new policy was known as the "New Federalism." It redirected federal programs and funding into a series of revenue sharing block grants to cities and states, allowing for greater local decision making. Prime examples of the New Federalism were the Concentrated Employment and Training Program (CETA), and block grants for criminal justice and education funding. Most important to me was the Community Development Block Grant (CDBG), which sent HUD funding for affordable housing and economic development. CDBG came to San Francisco in 1974 and became the most important funding source for many early Chinatown projects.

One final and lasting memory I have of being at Phil Burton's office was the day Ed Sarsfield, in one of his wonderful impromptu lectures, talked at length about how he firmly believed that someday San Francisco would see the Chinese and gay communities at the forefront of political leadership in City Hall. Mind you, this was in 1973, and I, being a cynical 25-year-old, said "Yeah, right."

Telling Our Stories

Many books have been written about San Francisco Chinatown. They are books about Chinese American history, personal journeys seeking identity as Chinese Americans, and about Chinese culture, both real and mythological. Outstanding books by authors such as Judy Yung, Lara Jo Foo, and William Poy Lee tell stories in ways that teach us about the community where they came from. Bonnie Tsui's *American Chinatown* shares many wonderful stories from real people in San Francisco Chinatown and other Chinatowns. And recent books by San Francisco–based authors, such as David Talbot's *The Season of the Witch* and Gary Kamiya's *Cool, Gray City of Love*, offer glimpses into Chinatown's history and place in the City.

As much as I have enjoyed these books and others, many stories of San Francisco Chinatown have yet to be told, particularly of contemporary history over the last half century. We owe it to the legacy of the late pioneering Chinese American historian Him Mark Lai to tell our Chinatown stories, as often as we can, from as many perspectives as we can. They can be personal stories, family stories, histories of important Chinatown institutions, chronicles of key events, or analyses of critical issues the community has experienced. Our Chinatown histories need to be documented, and our stories need to be told.

The Asian American and Community Development Movements in San Francisco, 1968–1977

The San Francisco State Third World Student Strike sparked numerous confrontations between students and the San Francisco Police Department. The Strike spanned four and a half months in 1968, the longest student strike in American history. *(Photo Courtesy of Alan Wong.)*

Strike leader Laureen Chew was incarcerated for three weeks during the 1968 San Francisco State Third World Student Strike. She is currently Associate Dean of the College of Ethnic Studies at San Francisco State University. *(Photo courtesy of Alan Wong.)*

The August 17, 1968, Chinatown demonstration was the first organized demonstration involving community leaders and student activists. Gordon Chin is pictured here under the sign reading "Some of our best slums are Chinese" in front of friend Alvin Ja. *(Photo courtesy of UC Berkeley Ethnic Studies Library. Original photo in the article by Kem Lee.)*

The struggle to save the homes of the International Hotel tenants lasted over a decade until their eviction in 1977 and the building's demolition in 1978. *(Photo courtesy of Chris Huie.)*

The August 4, 1977, eviction of the I Hotel tenants was one of the most dramatic moments in San Francisco history with 200 San Francisco police officers facing off against more than 1,000 supporters of the tenants. *(Photo courtesy of Chris Huie.)*

George Woo (L) and Alan Wong (R) were two important mentors to many young Asian American activists attending San Francisco State during the 1968 Third World Student Strike and becoming involved in San Francisco Chinatown. *(Photo courtesy of Alan Wong.)*

On September 12, 1972, 200 seniors from the Chinatown Coalition for Better Housing and Self-Help for the Elderly marched on the HUD Regional Offices in San Francisco in support of the Mei Lun Yuen housing project, the first time Chinatown senior residents had demonstrated against a federal agency. *(Photo courtesy of Rev. Harry Chuck and Cameron House.)*

The Chinese Playground served as Chinatown's only playground for more than 75 years. At one-third of an acre, it is a symbol of the fact that Chinatown residents have less open space than residents of any other San Francisco neighborhood. *(Photo courtesy of Chinatown CDC.)*

On August 1, 1979, Chinatown TRIP and community leaders celebrated the inauguration of the #83 Pacific bus line, the first expansion of public transit service in Chinatown in over four decades. L to R: Mrs. Chang Jok Lee, Mr. George Lee, Phil Chin, Peter Nardoza, Sue Lee, Supervisor John Molinari, (person unknown), and Tom Matoff. *(Photo courtesy of Chinatown TRIP.)*

CHAPTER 1

Ten Years That Woke Up Chinatown

ON AUGUST 17, 1968, an historic demonstration was held on the streets of Chinatown with a couple hundred community activists and students holding signs reading "Chinatown is a Ghetto" and "Tourists out of Chinatown." The demonstration was aimed at many neglected issues that were now being addressed by student activists—affordable housing, employment and youth programs, and better health care. It was the first organized Chinatown demonstration to link social justice activism with student activism. Community leaders included San Francisco Supervisor Jack Morrison and Chinatown religious leaders Larry Jack Wong, Ed Sue, and Harry Chuck. The demonstration started with a march from Il Piccolo, Alice Barkley's café on Waverly Place, through Grant Avenue, and ending at Portsmouth Square.

At Portsmouth Square, Larry Jack Wong shouted out, "No longer can the Chinese Six Companies speak for all of us! No longer can City Hall ignore us. We will continue to march until we get something done!" The Chinese Six Companies, considered the "Chinatown Establishment," was composed of the major fraternal and district associations in the community and often claimed to speak for the entire community. Alice Barkley spoke about the horrendous housing conditions in Chinatown. George Woo (spokesperson for the Wah Ching, one of the largest youth gangs in the community), Mason Wong (San Francisco State Student Strike leader), and Bill Lee (student body president of Galileo High School) all spoke about the needs of Chinatown youth.

After the march, the headline in *East West* newspaper, Chinatown's only English-language weekly, proclaimed "Demonstration Ends Chinatown Passivity!" On its editorial page, *East West* highlighted the historical significance of the August 17 demonstration:

> A new force has exerted itself in the leadership of Chinatown....
> They came because they care about Chinatown and her people...
> We believe that this is the first united front, a melding of militant
> youth with the post-collegiate young professionals to challenge the
> Establishment of Chinatown.

Community leader Larry Jack Wong advised us young folks to look decent for the march, not like some crazy, hippie radicals. Some of the students put on coats and even ties, but I was not one of them. I was only a participant, certainly not a leader in the demonstration, but somehow it was my picture that came out on the front page of the *East West* newspaper. I thought to myself, *Cool*. I recalled my dad's picture on the front page of the *Chinese Times* after that gambling raid. I guess it was just being at the right place at the right time for two really good-looking guys.

Chinatown from 1968 through the early 1970s was undergoing great change—in population, leadership, and organizations and its relationship to the rest of the City. Immigration, particularly from Hong Kong, was exploding due in large part due to the 1965 Immigration Act, which favored family reunification and placed Chinese immigration on par with other countries. Youth gang activity (due to a large influx of immigrant youth) was growing, and Chinatown experienced increasing gang violence. Immigration into Chinatown and San Francisco created the dire need for expanded social, health care, and mental health services, both from government and community agencies, and the formation of new social service agencies.

From that first Chinatown demonstration, built on the passion of the Civil Rights Movement and the youthful energy that came out of the San Francisco State Third World Student Strike, many young Chinese Americans were exploring their "new community." Even for youth who were born and raised in Chinatown or San Francisco, the world and how they perceived Chinatown was changing. Challenging the Establishment became a lifestyle. Mentors such as George Woo, Alice Barkley, and Larry Jack Wong encouraged us to question authority—but respectfully. I recall attending a few Chinatown Economic Opportunity Council (EOC) meetings along with other young folks acting as the conscience of the community. EOC was one of President Johnson's War on Poverty agencies, with a stated value of having "citizen participation" in the form of local community boards to direct programs and funding. In Chinatown, the local EOC board was controlled by members appointed by the Chinese Six Companies, which to activists was considered the Chinatown Establishment.

GEORGE WOO

I met George Woo during the San Francisco State Third World Student Strike in 1968. To me, he was (and still is) a larger than life character, with his full beard, stocky build, and his rough way of talking. He was a professional photographer, at one time with *Sunset* magazine. He was also a kung fu teacher and fully bilingual and biliterate. It was George who first introduced me to Rose Pak, who in the early 1970s was a young reporter with the *San Francisco Chronicle*.

George was one of the few Chinese American activists at the time who had strong relationships and a degree of trust with the Chinatown gangs. He was a great influence and mentor to many of the gang members. George wasn't into citywide or electoral politics much. Instead, he was more into community politics. He taught us the importance of relationships and the need for young activists to make long-term commitment to community, and how to think about Chinatown strategically if we were serious about social change.

The Chinese Six Companies was the self-proclaimed leader of Chinatown, holdovers from another era who were desperately trying to hold on to power in a rapidly changing community. The Chinese Six Companies was organized as a board of district associations, each representing a different emigrant county in Guangdong Province. (It grew to include eight counties). The Six Companies has remained an all-male organization for more than a century and a half, even as many family associations (based on common family surnames) have become gender integrated. In the 1960s and 1970s, family associations as a whole were considered by most liberal members of the community as a part of the Chinatown Establishment, but this characterization today is primarily directed at the Chinese Six Companies. The old guard was not afraid to red-bait leftist organizations such as the Intercollegiate Chinese for Social Action (ICSA) or Red Guard. In the words of Foo Hum, a Six Companies leader in 1968:

> To me, there are very few problems in Chinatown, if any... There is a problem in this community, a few Caucasian beatnik educators took a few native-born Orientals and inspired them with Mao Tse Tung Red Books, and that sort of thing.

At the time, Chinatown did not have as strong a network of community nonprofit organizations as it has today. But it was blessed with a few social and religious nonprofit institutions that had served the community well, including Cameron House, which was established as a Presbyterian Mission in 1874. The Chinatown YMCA, founded in 1912, and the Chinatown YWCA, in 1916, each provided essential services for youth. The Chinese Chamber of Commerce, formed in 1912, provided services to small businesses and sponsored cultural events such as the Chinese New Year Parade.

The Chinese population in Chinatown and citywide grew after two key historic events—in 1943 with the repeal of the 1882 Chinese Exclusion Act and again in the late 1960s with the passage of the 1965 Immigration Act. The repeal of the Chinese Exclusion Act (the first law to exclude a racial group) and subsequent immigration laws allowed returning Chinese American veterans to bring their foreign-born wives into the country, over 5,000 in number. The Displaced Persons Act also allowed more than 6,000 Chinese foreign students and scholars to remain in the U.S. after their visas had expired. The 1965 Immigration Act replaced the former quota system, which was heavily weighted to European immigrants, and allowed up to 20,000 Chinese immigrants into the United States annually.

The 1960 Census reported a total citywide Chinese population of approximately 75,000, roughly 10 percent of the total San Francisco population. About 50,000 Chinese Americans resided in the larger Chinatown area of about 60 square blocks (including parts of North Beach and Nob Hill). The 17-block Chinatown core area (bounded by Kearny, Stockton, Sacramento, and Broadway Streets) housed roughly 20,000 residents. Chinatown leaders criticized these statistics as woefully undercounted, a charge many immigrant and non-English speaking communities have levied historically. The Chinatown core area continued to experience severe overcrowding with residential densities of over 10 times the average for San Francisco (885 persons per acre in Chinatown, compared to the San Francisco average of 82 persons per acre.) In fact, for the past half century, San Francisco Chinatown was the most crowded neighborhood in the country west of Manhattan.

The War on Poverty: From Protest to Programs

In the late 1960s and early 1970s, Chinatown saw the blooming of many new 501(c)3 nonprofits. We were coming out of a period when the only funded nonprofit agencies were part of the Economic Opportunity Council (EOC), which administered the War on Poverty started in the Johnson administration. And while the early EOC programs were dominated by the Chinese Six Companies, new programs would emerge under the leadership of Presbyterian Minister Larry Jack Wong, then the highest-ranking Chinese American at EOC. Larry Jack was the "inside" guy who helped move EOC to do more for Chinatown. Many community folks were involved in program planning in this seminal period when so many new organizations were started: George Woo, Alice Barkley, Alan Wong, Germaine Wong, Herb Wong, Bert Tom, and Buddy Choy to name a few.

A lot of community leaders got their start in Chinatown youth work. The first Director of the Chinatown Summer Youth Program was Herb Wong, followed by Franklin Fung Chow. Among Herb's youth leaders that first year were Albert Cheng (who later headed the Chinatown Youth Council and created the "In Search of Roots Program"); Ling Chi Wang, who became the first Executive Director of Chinese for Affirmative Action and later headed UC Berkeley's Asian American Studies Department; and Genny Lim, who became a writer and poet.

The Community Action Program of the EOC, under the leadership of Larry Jack Wong, led to the creation of many new Chinatown programs, including Self-Help for the Elderly. Self-Help started at #3 Old Chinatown Lane, a narrow dead-end alleyway, on August 16, 1966. It was one of the first major outcomes from the War on Poverty, providing meals, housing assistance, social services, and transportation to Chinatown's growing senior population. Sam Yuen was ably assisted by dedicated social workers, from Vera Haille to Anni Chung, who became Executive Director in 1981, leading Self-Help's growth over the past three decades into a large multipurpose agency with new services, including mental health, housing, substance abuse, in-home support, and employment.

Among the many other new organizations established in this crucial period from the late 1960s to early 1970s was the Chinese Newcomers Services Center (serving recent Chinese immigrants), Chinatown/North Beach Family Planning, and On Lok, which became a national model for elderly care. Chinese for Affirmative Action (CAA) was formed in 1969 as a Chinese American civil rights organization. I worked at CAA one year during the directorship of Henry Der as an employment rights worker.

The City's new Northeast Mental Health program brought programs in early childhood development, senior aftercare, and drug treatment in the early 1970s. The community involvement in establishing a community-based mental health system after most California state mental health hospitals were closed in the 1960s provided good context for many young activists, myself included, to influence a public institution as it was being created. Many new Chinatown child care centers and programs were started in the 1970s, including Kai Ming Head Start and Wu Yee, headed by Norman Yee, who is now a San Francisco Supervisor.

LARRY JACK WONG

Larry Jack Wong was a Presbyterian Minister at Cameron House, and one of the first Chinatown activists who played a leadership role on the inside of government with the Economic Opportunity Council. Larry would be a guiding force and mentor for so many early Chinatown activists, including George Woo, Alice Barkley, Buddy Choy, and Harry Chuck. They were my mentors, and Larry Jack was theirs, bringing a larger perspective about social justice in America back to Chinatown when he returned from McCormick Theological Seminary in Chicago. At McCormick, Larry Jack's roommate was Andrew Young, who would later emerge as a key leader in the Civil Rights Movement and a disciple of Martin Luther King Jr. Young would go on to many leadership roles, as Mayor of Atlanta, Congressman, and UN Ambassador. It would have been absolutely fascinating to be a fly on the wall of that seminary dorm room, listening to the conversations of those two young men who are American heroes in my book— Andrew Young and Larry Jack Wong.

Two organizations that Chinatown CDC would work closely with throughout our history were the Asian Law Caucus (ALC), formed in 1972 to provide legal services, and Asian Neighborhood Design (AND), established in 1974 to provide community design services to nonprofit organizations citywide. I had monthly lunches with ALC Executive Director Peggy Saika and AND Executive Director Maurice Lim Miller, and we learned a lot from each other during those talks.

All of these new nonprofit organizations provided a great expansion of services to Chinatown residents, families, seniors, youth, and children. They represented the start of a decade in which much of the new Chinatown leadership and Asian American leadership in San Francisco would come from the nonprofit sector. They also created an opportunity to get "real jobs" (that is, jobs that paid) in community work for people who would emerge as civic and political leaders. With the emergence of a growing number of young activists and social services workers in these budding nonprofit organizations, a community was evolving of people who worked in and for Chinatown. In addition to the historic community organizations such as Cameron House and the YMCA, these new nonprofits would serve as a base for leadership and activism that would continue for the next half century.

The second floor offices at 250 Columbus Avenue was where a lot of young activists hung out. Located on William Saroyan Place, 250 Columbus housed the Chinatown office of the Community Design Center and also the Chinatown/North Beach offices of the San Francisco Neighborhood Legal Assistance Foundation (SFNLAF). Many of us would visit the Community Design Center to see Alice Barkley, Phil Chin, or Jon Pon when they worked there. SFNLAF, which was part of the national Legal Assistance Corporation (sadly dismantled by the Reagan administration), was where many Chinatown issues found legal support and advice.

So where else did folks hang out? The Chinatown YWCA started a basement coffee house for community workers to chill out, and On Lok spearheaded a new Chinatown/North Beach District Council, which held monthly lunches for community agencies to share information, introduce new staff, and coordinate on key issues. In addition to going to George Woo's house on occasion, activists hung out at Alice and Dick Barkley's Il Piccolo cafe on Waverly Place, and years later, George Woo started his own restaurant at the China Trade Center. We hung out at a lot of restaurants and coffee shops, at Sun Wah Kue on Washington Street (enjoying roast beef), and a lot of places on Jackson Street—the Jackson Café, Kum Hon, Song Hay, and of course, New Lun Ting, which everyone knew then and now as "Pork Chop House." You could get rice and gravy for 35 cents there.

A Hotbed of Chinatown Issues

While many San Franciscans will remember high-profile community issues such as the International Hotel Struggle and Chinatown youth gangs, the early 1970s ushered in many important and at times contentious issues that would impact the future of community leadership, internal community politics, and policy perspectives for many years to come.

In 1969, CAA organized Chinese parents and students to successfully sue the San Francisco School District in *Lau v. Board of Education* under the 1964 Civil Rights Act for unequal treatment of non-English-speaking students. Lucinda Lee Katz was one of the plaintiffs in the historic Supreme Court case *Lau v. Nichols* in 1974, the hallmark of bilingual education. The ruling became national precedent, paving the way for bilingual education in thousands of school districts in the country. CAA provided the early leadership for *Lau v. Nichols* and bilingual education, working closely with The Association of Chinese Teachers (TACT), which was founded in 1969 as an advocate for the education needs of Chinese American teachers, students, and parents.

One of the most intense battles was the fight by Chinese parents against school busing. In 1971, a group of Chinese immigrant families organized under the banner of "Concerned Chinese Parents" to protest the San Francisco Unified School District's desegregation plan, which was a result of a lawsuit brought by the NAACP. The *Brown v. Board of Education* decision to desegregate schools was first rendered in 1954 and reinforced by the Civil Rights Act in 1964. Numerous angry community meetings were held in Chinatown and at the San Francisco Board of Education. One of the most memorable images was when Superintendent Thomas Shaheen was chased out of a Chinatown meeting, beset with people jumping onto his car (which was driven by Lillian Sing, then an activist and now a Superior Court judge) as he was trying to leave. I happened to see this ugly scene as I was working at the time as a teacher's aide at Commodore Stockton Elementary School. The Chinese busing protests, led by parents who wanted their kids to attend neighborhood schools, would spark the opening of many private "freedom schools" in Chinatown, some of which stayed in operation for five years. The issue would also catapult attorney Quentin Kopp, conservative spokesperson for the Chinese parents group, into a long career in politics, first as San Francisco Supervisor and later as State Senator.

The Chinese Hospital was in the midst of the most challenging tasks it had faced since it was built in 1927. The old Chinese Hospital on Jackson Street was cited by the State for not meeting seismic standards. At the time, the Chinese Hospital was building a new outpatient facility next door. After a great deal of planning, hospital officials asked the State to allow them to convert the new outpatient facility into a new hospital. It was no easy undertaking in terms of design and construction or permits and approvals, but it was done. (This was one of the first Chinatown issues in which Rose Pak played an instrumental role.) Saving Chinese Hospital was a major victory for Chinatown. The Chinese Hospital was first built in response to the virtual absence of private or public medical services for San Francisco's Chinese residents. The Chinese Hospital was built through community leadership and community donations and has always occupied a special significance as one of Chinatown's first indigenous institutions.

The Chinese Cultural Foundation (CCF), founded in 1965 by banker Jun Ke Choy, incorporated the Chinese Culture Center in an effort to acquire the site of the former San Francisco Hall of Justice on Kearny Street for a Chinese arts and culture museum. The Hall of Justice had been vacated in 1956 when the City built a new Hall of Justice in the South of Market area (you may see the old Hall of Justice in reruns of the *Streets of San Francisco* with Karl Malden). The foundation was unable to finance the acquisition and develop the site when the City put it up for sale for $850,000, but it was able to negotiate the incorporation of a new Chinese Culture Center on the third floor of a proposed new Holiday Inn.

Another issue that led to some tension in the formative years of the CCC was the concern of Asian American neighborhood arts advocates that CCC was only concerned with "elite" Chinese culture and Chinese art, with little regard for an emerging Asian American arts movement. The Neighborhood Arts Movement was growing in the late 1960s, led by artist activists such as Bernice Bing, who believed that the major arts institutions (symphony, opera, ballet) and larger museums received most of the City arts funding at the expense of smaller, neighborhood arts organizations.

Chinatown Youth Work

For youth workers such as Mike Yep and myself who were struggling to catch up lost credits at San Francisco State while also doing community work in the post-Strike era, the aforementioned Nine Unit Block Program was a great help. As part of that program, Mike and I did our Chinatown field placement at the Chinatown/North Beach Youth Council, which was located in the former Hungry i nightclub in the basement of the International Hotel on Jackson Street, and headed by Executive Director Albert Cheng.

The Youth Council was composed of representatives from 40 Chinatown youth groups, from social service agencies such as Cameron House and the YMCA to gangs such as the Wah Ching. "Team 40" became leaders in Chinatown youth activism in the 1970s. They were mostly American-born Chinese youth, 13 to 18 years old and primarily attending Galileo High School (when they were not at Mike's pool hall). Mike Yep and I went on a few camping trips with Team 40, usually coordinated by former youth worker Dennis Flanders. You could tell that young Team 40 workers like Warren Mar, Ray Fong, Chauncey Low, Greg Lau, Albert Yip, Leland Wong, and many others would go on to other leadership roles in the community.

Before being hired with the Chinatown Youth Council, Mike and I worked for the Summer Youth Program, supervising youth activities and youth employed for the summer with various agencies. The fight for summer jobs was an enlightening education in organizing and navigating delicate relationships between San Francisco neighborhoods. With the advent of the War on Poverty and the Economic Opportunity Center, San Francisco had prioritized five "high need" neighborhoods for assistance in minority concentrated areas: Hunters Point, the Western Addition, the Mission, Chinatown/North Beach, and Potrero Hill. Every year, the process of deciding how many Summer Youth jobs would go to each of these areas was an exciting experience, with each area bringing out the troops at public meetings. At times things got really heated, with the occasional racial epithet thrown around. We all made it out alive, and to this day I can look back at some great friends from all over San Francisco who first met there.

In 1970, the Chinatown Youth Services and Coordinating Center was formed to deal specifically with Chinese youth delinquency. While Chinatown had long-established youth agencies—including Cameron House, the YMCA, and the YWCA—these agencies were generally not dealing with hard-core street kids. The 1965 Immigration Act brought hundreds of Chinese immigrant youth to Chinatown, most of them non-English speaking and lacking in education, whose only employment prospects were in low-wage Chinatown restaurant jobs. Most became alienated from their families, and many turned to gangs and a life on the street to survive.

Mike Yep and I volunteered for the Chinatown Youth Services Center, which involved going to the Youth Guidance Center to advocate for alternatives to incarceration, primarily for kids aged 12 to 14. This program was headed by Tom Kim, who had trained in the Mission with the Real Alternatives Program, the San Francisco model for alternatives to youth incarceration. Mike and I were especially involved with youths who hung out at the Police Activities League (PAL) at the Victory Hall building on Stockton Street, then owned by the Chinese Six Companies. As volunteer counselors, we took kids camping and to San Francisco Forty-Niner games and helped them deal with parental conflicts and the youth justice system.

Things were getting hot in Chinatown. Between 1974 and 1977, there were 27 Chinatown gang-related murders, most notoriously the Golden Dragon Massacre in September 1977, which claimed five lives. Many of the murders preceding the Golden Dragon remain unsolved. Included in these was the murder of Barry Fong Torres, the executive director of the Youth Services Center. The older brother of Ben Fong Torres of *Rolling Stone* fame, Barry Fong Torres was shot at home when he answered the door one evening in 1972. I remember the horror many staff, board members, and volunteers experienced afterward, and a tearful meeting the next day facilitated by Dr. Rolland Lowe, then board chair. The board closed down the offices for a couple weeks to let things chill out, then later turned the direction of the Youth Services Center away from direct gang intervention and working with younger junior high age youth in prevention programs. I kept on for a while as a volunteer with PAL, but started to think about doing other community work.

Researching Chinatown

Two important 1969 Chinatown studies set the foundation for major neighborhood planning and change that was soon to come. In June, the Community Design Center, headed by Alice Barkley, released the report titled "Chinatown, An Analysis of Population and Housing." In November, the "San Francisco Chinese Community Citizen's Survey and Fact Finding Committee Report" was published. Popularly known as the "Baccari Report," for coordinator Alessandro Baccari, the report concluded a one-year research effort and made recommendations in 14 areas.

The Community Design Center report, done at the request of the Chinatown Housing Committee, was the first comprehensive analysis of Chinatown's population, demography, housing conditions, and land ownership. Chinatown was "largely isolated socially from the rest of the city," the report stated. The report addressed seven major questions about Chinatown housing, including land ownership and usage, rental structures, housing conditions, subdivisions of units, overcrowding, and the effects of immigration.

Looking back today, the questions posed and the conclusions of the Community Design Center report in 1969 were very perceptive, influencing the early discussions and planning for Chinatown CDC years later. The questions posed in 1969 remain important ones that Chinatown continues to deal with today, nearly a half century later.

The Baccari Report spanned the period from June 1968 to August 1969, with publication in August 1969. Alessandro "Al" Baccari, head of the project, was known then (and to this day) as the historian on all things Italian American and North Beach in San Francisco. The report was the most comprehensive survey of Chinatown community needs and issues ever conducted, with a committee of 67 people, plus 300 on subcommittees. The final report was 834 pages, with a 227-page summary. Like the Community Design Center report, the Baccari Report offered many good ideas, many of which later came to fruition in some form. The greatest impact may very well be the refutation of the notion that the Chinese can take care of their own, an attitude that was prevalent in much of the first half of the century and that so many Chinatown leaders embraced themselves. "They've got a hell of a lot of problems," Baccari said of Chinatown. "Little by little... the financial district has chipped away at Chinatown and has converted the acquired land to business properties." I will not repeat the hundreds of facts, opinions, and suggestions, but here are just a few of the housing recommendations:

- Preserving historic character in any building rehabilitation.
- Master leasing of single-room hotels for senior housing.
- Making revisions to Chinatown height limits.
- Creating a Special Assessment District to help finance rehabilitation.
- No massive relocation of residents, as in the Western Addition redevelopment.
- Facilitating smaller buildings of 25, 50, 75 units on smaller sites.

CHAPTER 2

Fighting for San Francisco Neighborhoods

THE COMMUNITY DEVELOPMENT Movement in America started in the early 1960s in places like the South Bronx, Bedford-Stuyvesant, the Lower East Side, and hundreds of poor and distressed inner-city neighborhoods in Detroit, Philadelphia, Cleveland, and Washington, D.C. These areas had the poorest of the poor, provided inadequate education and city services, had few locally-owned businesses and very little investment. Community Development Corporations (CDCs) started up in rural America as well, serving some of our poorest Americans in the Mississippi Delta, the barrios of the Southwest, the coal mines of Appalachia, and the fishing villages in coastal Maine. CDCs spanned quite a spectrum of activity and place-based entities.

In San Francisco and other West Coast cities, the description "community development corporation" was used almost interchangeably with "housing development organization" or "neighborhood organization" or even "minority organization." Calvin Welch came up with "community-based housing organizations" to distinguish what we do from private developers and to be inclusive of our tenant organizations as well as developers. I use the term "community development" because it encompasses other roles we play and other interests besides affordable housing, such as parks and playgrounds, social services, and transportation to name a few. The earliest CDCs in San Francisco were the Hunters Point CDC and the Mission Housing Development Corporation, both created as components of the only Model Cities areas in San Francisco.

In San Francisco, the Community Development Movement can trace its genesis to the fight against displacement of poor and working-class San Franciscans, either by private or publicly-sponsored development. The International Hotel was (and remains) the most graphic symbol of private development displacing poor people (to be discussed in the next chapter).

But in terms of sheer scale, nothing compares to the displacement of thousands of San Franciscans in the Western Addition and South of Market due to actions of the San Francisco Redevelopment Agency in the 1960s and 1970s. It was the fight against "urban renewal" that was the defining context for much that would occur in the Community Development Movement in the next two decades.

Redevelopment was part of a grand vision of some San Francisco planners to solidify San Francisco's role as the financial capital of the West, complemented by rapidly expanding downtown office development and the Bay Area Rapid Transit system. This vision was largely advocated by the Joseph Alioto mayoral administration from 1968 to 1976 and implemented by Justin Herman, the Executive Director of the San Francisco Redevelopment Agency from 1959 until his death in 1971. By the time Justin Herman and the Redevelopment Agency were done, more than 14,000 homes were lost (with only 5,000 later replaced) in the Western Addition and South of Market areas.

Known more commonly as "The Fillmore," the Western Addition area experienced an expansion of the African American population to over 43,000 by 1950, largely as a result of the migration of African Americans from the South to work in the WWII–related ship-building industries. The Fillmore was also called "The Harlem of the West" with a jazz district where Billie Holiday, Miles Davis, and Duke Ellington often performed. It was a neighborhood with growing African American institutions, churches, and small businesses. After redevelopment, the Western Addition lost 883 businesses, most of them African American owned and operated, never to return.

Throughout this shameful history of redevelopment, community resistance was led by the Western Addition Community Organization (WACO), which included many church leaders and resident activists, including Mary Helen Rogers, "Speedy Woods," Arnold Townsend, Benny Stewart, and others who were active in the Black Student Union at San Francisco State. Indeed, the Western Addition struggle with urban renewal was a significant factor in the passage of the National Uniform Relocation Act in 1970, which guaranteed a measure of tenants' rights and financial assistance in any displacement caused by federally funded development.

The Western Addition has always been an ethnically diverse area that included Japantown, San Francisco's first Japanese American community. Japanese Americans who lost their properties during the WWII internment had rebuilt the community after the war, only to see redevelopment displace a large part of it less than two decades later. The new Japantown was centered around a newly-constructed Kintetsu Mall, and the new Geary Boulevard expressway dissected the community. Activist groups such as the Committee Against Nihonmachi Evictions (CANE) fought for low-income tenants and against displacement of residents and small businesses.

Meanwhile, planning visions for extending San Francisco's downtown southward across Market Street had germinated beginning in the 1950s, coming from much of the City's business elite community. It was a vision built around San Francisco as the financial center of the West and the growth to accommodate that role. It was called "Yerba Buena" and would be anchored by a new convention center in what was then a largely blue-collar, industrial area. The South of Market, or "South of the Slot" as old-timers called it, was home to over 4,000 residents, primarily white men living on fixed incomes in single-room hotels. They were retired longshoremen, merchant marine workers, and union laborers who settled there after retirement.

The primary opposition to Yerba Buena came in 1969 from the Tenants and Owners Opposed to Redevelopment (TOOR), led by two heroes in the San Francisco Community Development Movement—80-year-old George Woolf, who was the first president of the Alaska Cannery Workers before retiring in the South of Market, and Peter Mendelsohn, a retired merchant seaman who at the time was 65 years old. Following on the heels of WACO's lawsuit against the Redevelopment Agency and the U.S. Department of Housing and Urban Development, TOOR sued and won an injunction in 1970, stopping Yerba Buena redevelopment until a satisfactory relocation plan was prepared.

The injunction gave TOOR the leverage they needed to enter into negotiations with the Redevelopment Agency. After TOOR was able to leverage opposition to the overall Yerba Buena Convention Center plan, they continued to refine what eventually became a final settlement in May 1973. The settlement led to the creation of a new nonprofit controlled by TOOR as the primary development vehicle for the replacement housing—the Tenants and Owners Development Corporation (TODCO). It was led for the past three decades by another veteran San Francisco activist (and friend) John Elberling.

The American Dream Starts with the Neighborhoods

Most every day, as I am waiting for the N Judah streetcar near my house, I start my day by looking up at the wall of the Harvey Milk Community Center and seeing this quote by former San Francisco Supervisor Harvey Milk: "The American Dream starts with the neighborhoods..."

The Community Development Movement has come to encompass many other movements for social justice: movements for affordable housing, for tenant rights, for the urban environment, for community organizing and empowerment. A common thread between all of San Francisco's housing and land use oriented movements is the passion San Franciscans have for our neighborhoods, and the quality of life in these places where we live, work, and play. Thank you, Harvey, for helping me start each day by reinforcing my passion for our neighborhoods.

By the early 1970s, San Francisco would have a handful of CDCs, each started through very different circumstances. They were joined by many new community organizations that were all involved in issues of place-based neighborhood planning and land use advocacy or community and tenant organizing. Citywide, San Francisco "Community Congresses" were organized starting in 1975 to bring together these and many other neighborhood organizations to develop a common agenda and form new working alliances and coalitions. The Council of Community Housing Organizations would form in 1979 as our umbrella organization, ably led for the next three decades by two dedicated leaders, Calvin Welch and Rene Cazenave.

In San Francisco Chinatown, our struggle for land and for place started with the International Hotel, but there were three other Chinatown campaigns that were lesser known, but no less important. The fight for Chinatown's new Mei Lun Yuen housing project, the organizing to save our Chinese Playground, and the leadership of Chinese bus drivers for better transportation.

These seminal fights would form the foundation of leadership for the Community Development Movement in San Francisco Chinatown and lead to the establishment of Chinatown Community Development Center in 1977. As young activists in San Francisco, we found ourselves at the confluence of movements—the Community Development Movement trying to save our places in inner cities across the country, and the Asian American Movement fighting for rights and justice in many of these same communities. We were Asian American activists whose call to action had changed from "On Strike, Shut it Down!" to "We Won't Move!" And nowhere would that call out be heard more often or heard more loudly than at the International Hotel.

CHAPTER 3

The Fall of the I Hotel

THE FIRST TIME I was ever in the International Hotel I went to see Bill Cosby in the old Hungry i nightclub, which was located on the Jackson Street side of the building. I believe it was in 1967 because I wasn't sure I could get in, being 19. I suspect that only old-time San Franciscans would readily associate the Hungry i with the International Hotel, as that famous cornerstone of the Beat Movement closed its doors in 1968, around the time the I Hotel tenant activism was heating up.

After 1968, I spent much of the next couple of years in the I Hotel, but still not as the housing activist I was to become. At the time, I was a youth worker with the Chinatown Youth Council, which took over the old Hungry i nightclub space. It was great being in that space with memories of the greats who once played there—Cosby, Lenny Bruce, Mort Sahl, Woody Allen to name a few. I still remember the message scribbled on the wall of the old dressing room, signed by Nina Simone, something about Banducci not paying enough. I was there the night when Asian American author Frank Chin and his cast were rehearsing Frank's play "Chicken Coop Chinamen," when Frank was called out by some Chinatown dudes who didn't like *anyone* using the word "Chinamen."

If there was one historic moment, one iconic symbol for the Asian American Community Development Movement in America, it would be the International Hotel. The struggle for the I Hotel, spanning nearly half a century, has meant so much to many of us, in some ways becoming a touchstone for many different social movements in this country, such as Filipino community empowerment; the preservation of American Chinatowns; the fight against displacement, gentrification, and downtown expansion; and the Student Movement. The I Hotel was all of these and more. The infamous I Hotel Eviction is commemorated by events and news stories every year on the August 4th anniversary.

The I Hotel Eviction was the most high profile of many anti-eviction movements in Asian American communities during the late 1960s—including the Committee Against Nihonmachi Evictions (CANE) in San Francisco's Japantown, People Against Chinatown Evictions (PACE) in Honolulu Chinatown, and the Fight to Save the Milwaukee Hotel in Seattle's International District. These fights shared much in common—to protect vulnerable senior residents, oppose displacement and urban renewal, and involve student activism. In San Francisco, the International Hotel was also the first home base for many new Asian American "left wing" organizations, including the Asian Community Center, I Wor Kuen, Wei Min She, Chinese Progressive Association, Kearny Street Workshop, the Katipunan Ng Mga Demokratikong Pilipino (KDP), and Everybody's Bookstore. All of these groups contributed to the International Hotel's legacy as something much bigger. It linked local struggles and local stories to a national narrative and a national Asian American Movement seeking to protect their own place in America.

What is commonly referred to as the "International Hotel Struggle" is really three distinct decade-long episodes, each important in their own way, each with their unique stories and lessons. The fight to save the I Hotel started around 1968, when the first eviction order was issued, and lasted a decade until the eviction on August 4, 1977. A second period in the extended struggle spanned 15 years after the eviction and demolition in 1979, during which numerous unsuccessful development plans were put forth. And a final period started around 1994 with the planning and development of the new I Hotel until its completion in 2005. I will share some of my memories of each of these periods, but first, it is important to remember what the I Hotel was before all this happened.

The International Hotel was a center for the Filipino community since it opened at 848 Kearny Street in 1873. That's right, there was an International Hotel for nearly a century before the 1977 eviction. In fact, there was a Manilatown community that extended some 10 blocks down Kearny to Market Street. It was a community of many residential hotels (like the I Hotel, the Victory Hotel, the Bell Hotel), barber shops such as Tino's, restaurants like Mabuhay, pool halls like the Lucky M, and dance halls like Club Mandalay. It was Filipino fraternal associations, Filipino residents, Filipino businesses, and a Filipino community long before the Financial District even existed in San Francisco. East of the I Hotel was the San Francisco waterfront, the center of the maritime industry, the San Francisco Bowery, and the Produce District.

I don't know what life was like in Manilatown in those days, but thanks to my many talks with an old friend, the late Al Robles, I was able to imagine the life of a manong coming home after working for months in the fields of the Central Valley to San Francisco and the International Hotel and many similar hotels on Kearny Street. Besides being one of San Francisco's most cherished poets, Al also ran the Manilatown Senior Center for Self-Help for the Elderly. Originally housed at the I Hotel, Al kept the spirit of Manilatown alive even after the eviction from the basement of the Clayton Hotel (Chinatown CDC's first housing project) on Clay and Commercial Streets.

A great example of that spirit was the Manilatown String Band, which was led by International Hotel tenant Frankie Alarcon. This was a fantastic band of manongs that brought a big smile to my face every time I heard them play. One smart thing Al did was to work out a program with the Jewish Community Center to bus in a group of older Jewish ladies to the Manilatown Center once a month to dance with the older Filipino manongs. These parties were a blast! Al told me that these "taxi dances" happened at the I Hotel and other Kearny Street hotels throughout the thirties, forties, and fifties. Around then, Chinatown's Forbidden City and Skyroom nightclubs were happening places too, and the whole Manilatown/Chinatown scene was perhaps reminiscent of white folks going uptown to Harlem. Wow, I must have been born in the wrong decade!

A Ten-Year Fight to Save Their Homes

The I Hotel prior to 1968 housed some 182 tenants in 184 single rooms, consisting of about 52% Filipino, 20% Chinese, and 28% other nationalities. The old International Hotel was the de facto capital of Manilatown. At the time, Manilatown was the largest urban Filipino neighborhood in the country with as many as 30,000 residents. Most were older manongs who worked in the fields and in canneries up and down the West Coast and Alaska for six months out of the year, but who still called San Francisco, Manilatown, and the International Hotel their home. All of that changed in October 1968.

It was then that the first eviction notice was posted at the International Hotel, ordering residents to vacate by January 3, 1969. This sparked the first I Hotel protest march and demonstration on November 27, 1969, which started to galvanize local political support. San Francisco Supervisor Jack Morrison and Assemblyman John Burton helped get this first eviction notice suspended. The I Hotel was then owned by the Milton Meyer Company, headed by major Democratic patron Walter Shorenstein.

In March of 1969, a suspicious fire led to the death of three elderly tenants, and the mobilization of university students in support of the I Hotel. After the mysterious fire, which sparked allegations that the I Hotel was "unfit for occupancy," other community supporters got involved. The Washington, D.C.–based Center for Community Change (CCC) secured a $50,000 grant from the Ford Foundation to help with repair costs and to guarantee rent payments. Ed Illumin, whom I met during the San Francisco State Strike, was working with CCC during this period as did Filipino activist Art Naldoza. The Center for Community Change retained architect Alice Barkley to oversee a plan for repairs. Students from many Bay Area universities, myself included, spent countless hours in one of San Francisco's first "sweat equity" efforts. All of these supportive efforts—student demonstrations, legal representation, political support, technical assistance, funding support—resulted in the "Peace with Lease" period of the struggle. A new three-year lease was signed through June 1972. This three-year reprieve came to an end when the lease transitioned into a month-to-month lease. Again the threat of eviction loomed. Again the tenants and their supporters mobilized. The International Hotel Tenants Association (IHTA) was formed in the spring of 1972 and inaugurated by a march on Walter Shorenstein's office in May.

In October of 1972 came the surprising news that Milton Meyer had sold their interest in the International Hotel to the Four Seas Corporation, based in Thailand. This sparked a new round of eviction notices and demonstrations, this time in front of Four Seas's offices in San Francisco. Four Seas was headed by Supasit Mahaguna, who controlled a large share of the liquor distribution network in Southeast Asia. Besides renewing eviction efforts, Four Seas also started to aggressively pursue legal processes for demolition of the I Hotel, ultimately obtaining a demolition permit in March of 1975. Much of 1975 and 1976 saw the demolition permit issue played out in San Francisco courts, commissions, and at City Hall.

A new eviction order from Four Seas in December 1976 led to San Francisco Sheriff Richard Hongisto and Deputy Sheriff James Denman being charged with contempt of court for refusing to proceed with eviction. Hongisto was convicted in January 1977 and sentenced to five days in prison. He would serve those five days later that April, but not before he posted the formal eviction notice on the International Hotel on January 11, sparking one of the largest public demonstrations for the I Hotel on January 16, with 7,000 people protesting. Everyone was there—labor, churches, Glide Memorial Church, People's Temple, and university and high school students from all over the Bay Area.

Perhaps the strategy that gained most attention and controversy during this period was what was to be known as the "Buy Back Plan" or "Moscone Buy Back Plan." Mayor George Moscone proposed that the San Francisco Housing Authority purchase the International Hotel under eminent domain, utilizing $1.3 million of Community Development Block Grant funds, and then sell the building to a new nonprofit to be formed by the IHTA. The San Francisco Housing Authority voted to pursue eminent domain proceedings on December 23, 1976.

The Buy Back Plan became the context for newer internal developments with the International Hotel. The very idea of a "public/private" solution to save the I Hotel involved a number of "professional" supporters who knew something about affordable housing—the Center for Community Change; local attorneys and architects like Alice Barkley, Edith Witt, and David Prowler with the San Francisco Human Rights Commission; planner Chester Hartman; Brad Paul with the National Trust for Historic Preservation. I doubt that all these folks ever met as a group, but the International Hotel Struggle had galvanized a number of people willing to help identify strategies that could really work, and work within the political system as we knew it.

At the same time, the Buy Back Plan was hotly debated within the IHTA and within the community of organizations that were housed in the I Hotel. International Hotel tenant leader Felix Ayson came out strongly against the Buy Back Plan, which was supported by then IHTA President Joe Dionnes. The internal split led to Emil de Guzman becoming new IHTA President, a post he would hold through the eviction and beyond. The Buy Back Plan also became an issue of heated ideological and philosophical debate amongst the leftist organizations supporting the I Hotel. *Was it right that the tenants should have to "buy back" their homes? Was it all just a trick by the capitalist system? Wasn't affordable housing a human right? Was Mayor Moscone a hero or villain?* The internal debate in 1976 and 1977 about the Buy Back Plan was perhaps the most prominent example of such internal debate and conflict that permeated so much of the last few years of the International Hotel Struggle prior to eviction. It seemed like the term "sectarian politics" was part of every conversation about the I Hotel, and for many young activists like myself, at times we were working within the system, at other times against it. It was confusing, but it was also an exciting education.

The San Francisco Superior Court rejected San Francisco's eminent domain action in May of 1977, ruling that the City could not use its eminent domain powers to take private property for the purpose of transfer to another private party. Brad Paul helped get the I Hotel placed on the National Registry of Historic Places in June. A revised Buy Back Plan was proposed by local housing activists Joel Rubinzahl and Vivian Fei Tsen (who later became Chinatown CDC's first Housing Director), which called for the Housing Authority to retain ownership of the building (after eminent domain), but then lease (not sell) it to the IHTA. Mayor Moscone rejected this idea and reiterated his support for the original Buy Back Plan. However, none of the legal maneuvers to overturn demolition, impose eminent domain, or delay eviction succeeded in preventing what happened in the wee hours of Wednesday, August 4, 1977.

August 4, 1977

It started around 11:00 p.m. the night of Tuesday, August 3, continuing into the wee hours of Wednesday, August 4. Two thousand people linked arms as a human barricade to protect the International Hotel tenants. Chanting and singing could be heard blocks away from the I Hotel. The streets were blocked off. A large contingent of media was present from local and national news, as well as hundreds of people who were not part of the human barricade, but who either wanted to monitor what the police would do or who just wanted to be there. Tenant leaders like Felix Ayson and Emil de Guzman shouted out chants or instructions from second-floor windows.

Then, pointing down Kearny Street, Felix shouted out, "They are coming," and the chaotic eviction was underway. Chanting and singing, "We shall not be moved," the human barricade waited for the police and sheriff's department, led by Sheriff Richard Hongisto, to arrive. The San Francisco Police Department came in full force, including the Mounted Patrol. It must have been the first time in a long time that horses were seen in Chinatown or Manilatown. The San Francisco Fire Department moved in a ladder truck on the Columbus Street side of the building, lowering police and sheriff officers onto the roof of the I Hotel. They entered the building after encountering some resistance from supporters on the upper floors. Tenants had barricaded themselves in upstairs rooms, and one by one were removed from their homes and escorted out through the main entrance on Kearny Street, greeted by shouts and cheers from their supporters. Some supporters engaged in direct confrontation with police, but the human barricade was overwhelmingly non-violent.

For a long time, I regretted not being there. But while I was at most of the major demonstrations, I was not a regular in the human barricade that stood in front of the I Hotel for the days and nights leading up to the eviction. I saw my role differently, working on strategies to save the building if the eviction happened, which anticipated possible demolition. There is nothing I can add to the stories, testimonials, and emotional memories of those who were there that night.

My friend David Prowler recalls:

> I went down there, and there were thousands of people in front of the hotel, chanting. I remember that there were so many walkie-talkies—this was before cell phones. There were so many walkie-talkies in that area that there was no communication. They just all jammed each other. The police couldn't communicate. The sheriffs couldn't communicate. And then this fleet of police cars and sheriffs cars with sirens and lights, coming up Kearny Street. Kearny Street was closed. And it was like an invasion.

Estella Habal was a Filipina leader, along with Emil de Guzman, with the KDP who would later write *San Francisco's International Hotel*, the definitive book about the International Hotel Struggle. About the night of August 4th, Estella wrote that everyone was singing "We Shall Overcome" as they waited for the San Francisco police and sheriffs:

> "We shall not, we shall not be moved. We shall not, we shall not be moved, just like a tree standing by the water. We shall not be moved." So we sang that over and over again. It gave us strength and courage, actually because it's a united singing. The sheriff is pulling people away, and part of the drama that non-violent resisters create is to show that unity.

The Day After the Eviction

The day after the eviction was very surreal to many of us who were around. Still tears, a lot of quiet looks, everyone asking ourselves questions: *Why? Why did this need to happen? Where are the tenants? What can we do now?* Everyone was so upset that the building had been trashed, doors smashed in, garbage everywhere, and many tenants were heartbroken that many of their personal belongings, photos, and keepsakes were gone (despite assurances from Four Seas and the City that these would be kept safe). In early September, many tenants were scattered in various relocation sites. The single largest group of tenants moved into the Stanford Hotel at 245 Kearny (and Post Street), which was much closer to Downtown than to Manilatown/Chinatown. The Stanford became the new base for the International Tenants Association, but most of the tenant leadership had dispersed, some moved into other residential hotels, others back to the Philippines. I spent a lot of time at the Stanford in the months following the eviction. After all, the tenants were gone, but the International Hotel still stood, and we had to save the building from demolition. We couldn't give up.

The San Francisco Board of Supervisors led by John Molinari and Dianne Feinstein put Proposition U on the November 8, 1977, election ballot, asking if San Francisco should buy the International Hotel and preserve it under management by the San Francisco Housing Authority. Unfortunately, with no campaign experience or resources to counter Four Seas's well-funded campaign, and with low voter turnout, Prop U lost by a wide margin.

The International Hotel was empty, and everyone was waiting to see what would happen with the demolition. The City was maintaining the position that demolition could not occur until all the appeal processes were exhausted. This did not prevent an ugly incident in September when the owner of Grange Debris Box Rental in San Rafael, hired by Four Seas, brought a bulldozer and wrecking crew to the I Hotel site and started the demolition, without a valid demolition permit and despite many verbal warnings by the San Francisco Police Department to cease. Grange finally stopped his bulldozer after San Francisco Police Officer Dennis Meixner pulled his firearm, aimed it at Grange and threatened to "blow your head off." This was one cop who was cheered by the tenants and supporters.

Grange was determined to fulfill his demolition contract with Four Seas, and came back twice that September, confronted by supporters on September 19 when he tried a subterfuge by bringing his bulldozer from the back of the building on Columbus Avenue. The IHTA and their attorneys, Bill Carpenter and Sue Hestor, could not get the courts to stop the demolition. The San Francisco Building Inspection Department did suspend the demolition permit for a few months, but it was reinstated by the Superior Court, and by February 1979, the International Hotel was gone.

The Chinatown Block Study

The post-demolition period of the International Hotel was a difficult time, at times very sad and demoralizing, and the question of "What do we do now?" was asked by everyone who was involved. But, communication decreased dramatically with so many tenant leaders and activists having moved on, or simply being exhausted, leaving a vacuum in collective strategy. Still, we could not give up.

The Chinatown Block Study was co-sponsored by the International Hotel Tenants Association (IHTA), the Chinatown Coalition for Better Housing (CCBH) and Chinatown CDC. It came about in discussions with Brad Paul, then with the National Trust for Historic Preservation. Brad had helped get the International Hotel put on the National Registry of Historic Places. Even though the National Registry designation was not enough to preempt demolition, Brad and the National Trust funded a study to explore strategies for both preserving the building and ensuring that affordable housing could be planned, indeed required, on the site in the event of demolition. The study began in December of 1978 and was completed in December 1979. The status of demolition remained a fluid issue in those years with Prop U and continued political support to explore whatever measures were possible to preserve the building. Indeed, Mayor Moscone and other city officials supported the Chinatown Block Study, perhaps because there was so much public anguish over the eviction.

We retained the planning firm of John M. Sanger and Associates to do the study (often called "The Sanger Study"), which looked at four different scenarios and strategies—two plans to preserve the International Hotel building, and two plans for new construction on the larger I Hotel block. The preservation alternatives looked at rehabbing the I Hotel as a Single Room Occupancy Hotel (SRO) as it had been historically, and at conversion of the I Hotel into senior apartments. (This latter alternative was deemed infeasible early on, as it would have greatly reduced the number of units in the building). The two-block-wide alternatives included one that would preserve the International Hotel building and add new buildings around it, and another plan (assuming demolition of the I Hotel) for all new construction and new uses on the block bounded by Kearny, Jackson, Columbus, and Washington Streets.

I spent many nights at the Stanford Hotel with former tenants, one of whom I knew as "Seaweed" (who reminded me a lot of my Uncle Henry), a small and wiry former cannery worker, and Tex Lamera, who later got into the new Wharf Plaza Senior Housing Project. Although the IHTA was in disarray, tenant leaders Etta Moon and So Chung took on the responsibility of getting tenant input into all the Chinatown Block plan alternatives.

Needless to say, the preservation alternatives did not succeed in preventing the eventual demolition of the International Hotel by the end of 1978. To this day, all of us involved still believe the preservation plan involving Historic Tax Credits was feasible and would have worked, but having a feasible plan was not enough to change the court's decisions on eminent domain and demolition. Nevertheless, the Chinatown Block Study was critically important in establishing continued "moral authority" of the International Hotel, and reinforcing planning policy that affordable housing must be part of *any* future development on the International Hotel block. We will pick up the story of the next phase of the International Hotel story in chapter 19.

CHAPTER 4

Saving Chinese Playground

SINCE ITS CONSTRUCTION in 1927, the Chinese Playground on Sacramento Street has served as Chinatown's only playground for children and youth for over half a century. At only one-third of an acre, Chinese Playground has been a graphic symbol that Chinatown residents enjoy less open space per capita than any other San Francisco neighborhood. This dire need for open space and recreation was not recognized by the City until the late 1960s when Chinatown was designated as a "high-need neighborhood" in San Francisco's Open Space Element. Over its history, Chinese Playground was where neighborhood kids went after school and on weekends as their only place for outdoor recreation. I came to know Chinese Playground mostly through the memories of friends and families. My mother played there with her brothers and sisters in the 1930s and 1940s. My partner, Dorothy, and her siblings went to the playground on most summer days.

The "old" Chinese Playground didn't have much in the way of play structures, certainly not by current playground standards. It was basically one set of swings and one set of slides, one basketball court, and two tennis courts (which doubled as volleyball courts) and was staffed by a recreation director in a small 300-square-foot clubhouse. The tennis courts gained some attention as the place where the late Tom Kim taught so many Chinatown youths the game of tennis, including the famous "Louie sisters," who achieved professional status in the 1960s. Bill Lee in his book *Chinese Playground* talks about this playground as a gathering place for Chinatown youth gangs. To be sure, that happened, particularly late at night. But, Chinese Playground was a small place that was used by almost everyone in the community at all times of the day. In the mornings there were the tennis players and tai chi exercisers; in the afternoons, child care agencies and kids from Commodore Stockton Elementary School; and in the evenings, teenage youth (who were not all in gangs). While Chinese Playground didn't come close to meeting the needs of a Chinatown whose population grew rapidly after WWII, still it was an important central place for neighborhood youth and children. It was "our playground."

The Mandarin Towers Condominium Project

In 1968, the Mandarin Towers was developed on Stockton Street as Chinatown's newest and largest market-rate condominium project. With its 16 floors rising to 186 feet, it was by far the tallest building in Chinatown and was approved by the City Planning Commission in 1964, miraculously without requiring a single parking space. It was not surprising then that soon after, real estate and development interests, including Chinese businessmen H. K. Wong and Lim P. Lee (who were previously involved with the comprehensive Chinatown Baccari Report), put forth a proposal for the City to build a nine-story parking garage two blocks away from the Mandarin Towers at the site of the Chinese Playground. They proposed that a seven-story, 450-space parking garage be built on the site. The proposal offered to "replace" the Chinese Playground on the roof of the new garage. The proponents of the garage, while not directly linked to the Mandarin Towers development, argued that Mandarin Towers and other existing or proposed Chinatown developments had resulted in a great demand for a new parking garage.

The garage proposal had been percolating since 1966, and the developers needed to go through a number of City approval processes. City policy mandated that any new public underground garage could only be allowed under a City park, not under a playground. The City Recreation and Parks Commission, under the presidency of Walter Shorenstein, obtained this legal opinion from the City Attorney, and the Commission twice rejected the Chinese Playground garage plan.

Neighborhood residents and activists led by the Reverend Harry Chuck of Cameron House were up in arms and immediately organized opposition to the ill-conceived plan under the banner of "The Ad Hoc Committee Against Building the Garage at Chinese Playground." A petition opposing the plan gathered over 5,000 signatures in three weeks, citing five key issues:

1. Chinese Playground is Chinatown's only playground;

2. The garage will only benefit special interests at the expense of the community;

3. The garage will result in traffic and pedestrian safety problems for children;

4. The community was not consulted on the garage plan; and

5. Chinatown's juvenile delinquency problem would get worse without the Playground.

Opposition to the garage plan became widespread. "Business has rights, yes, but so do the people," said attorney Gordon Lau at a June 1969 public meeting on the garage. City agencies expressed serious concern, and many Chinatown groups circulated a petition in opposition, including the recently formed Red Guard. Community leaders Harry Chuck, Alice Barkley, and Lau were effective advocates against the garage. When it came up for final approval before the City Planning Commission and Board of Supervisors, the plan was easily defeated.

The Committee for Better Parks and Recreation in Chinatown

The leadership that came together to save Chinese Playground decided that if such outrageous ideas as putting a parking garage on Chinatown's only playground could receive serious attention by the City, then it was time to organize a group to advocate for Chinatown's open space and for Chinatown's children. The Committee for Better Parks and Recreation in Chinatown was formed in 1968. Among its early leadership were Sister Beverly Karnatz, Stan Yee, Doreen Der, Donna Yick, and Vera Haille. The Community Design Center, whose Chinatown district office was headed by Alice Barkley, provided technical assistance. The "Chinatown Park Rec Committee," as it came to be known, worked with the Community Design Center to develop plans for a new and improved Chinese Playground. With help from the landscape firm of Eckbo, Dean, Austin, and Williams, the Committee involved community seniors, children, and youth to help design their own playground, resulting in a renovated Chinese Playground in 2006, renamed by the Recreation and Parks Commission as the Willie Woo Wong Playground after the local Chinatown basketball legend. The Chinatown Park Rec Committee continued advocacy for improvements to Chinatown's public spaces and expanding open space with new parks and mini parks.

Members of the Committee were some of Chinatown's first environmental activists during the late 1960s and early 1970s, when housing activists received much more public attention with the International Hotel Struggle and organizing for the Mei Lun Yuen housing project. I credit the Chinatown Park Rec Committee with providing a broader vision of community development. It not only embraced affordable housing as core needs and

REVEREND HARRY CHUCK

The Reverend Harry Chuck was an early mentor for myself and hundreds of Chinatown youth in his roles as Youth Director and later Executive Director of Cameron House. Harry was the catalyst in Chinatown's fight to save Chinese Playground from being developed into a parking garage, leading to the formation of the Committee for Better Parks and Recreation in Chinatown. Harry and Linda Wang were the first co-chairs of the Chinatown Coalition for Better Housing, which led the community fight to support the Mei Lun Yuen housing project developed by the Presbyterian Church in Chinatown.

Young activists looked up to Harry because he was also really "cool." He was known as a Chinese Frank Sinatra for his mellow singing voice. I learned a lot from Harry, especially his calm demeanor and the importance for leaders to listen. His passion for social justice extended well beyond Chinatown. He was one of the first Asian American religious leaders to speak out for same-sex marriage, telling his congregation, "The time is now to open our church doors and our hearts."

strategies, but also open space, recreation, and community centers. That vision guided the early direction of the Chinatown Resource Center when it was formed in 1977.

In the 1970s, the Chinatown Park Rec Committee planned and advocated for some of the first "mini parks" in San Francisco on the East and West portals of the Broadway Tunnel, funded by the 1974 San Francisco Proposition J Open Space bond. The total redesign of the Helen Wills Playground on Broadway and Larkin Streets was conceived and advocated for by the Committee in the late 1970s, as was a new children's playground at Portsmouth Square. And in 1978, the redesign and reconstruction of the Chinese Playground continued with the construction of a new clubhouse and tiny tot play area. Throughout, the Chinatown Park Rec Committee embraced "participatory design" to involve Chinatown residents in determining what kind of parks and playgrounds they desired. These involved focus groups and workshops with Chinatown seniors, youth, and children in the planning process.

Long before the Environmental Justice Movement emerged in the early 1980s, which highlighted the toxic conditions and health risks that residents of minority and low-income communities all over America faced daily, there has been a long history of environmental activism in communities of color like San Francisco Chinatown.

Open space and recreation, clean air, sunshine, and a quality environment are all values that Chinatown's environmental activists share with the
mainstream Environmental Movement. Nonetheless, such inner-city urban
environmentalists are not often identified with being part of the Environmental Movement associated with larger-scale environmental challenges,
such as global warming, saving the redwoods, and Bay Area water quality.
But, the struggle for a quality Chinatown environment, often at odds with
powerful economic interests, has been no less heroic. The founding members of the Chinatown Park Rec Committee may not have been the first
environmentalists in Chinatown, but they were the first organized volunteer
advocacy group to fight for a quality environment in the most densely-
populated neighborhood in America west of Manhattan.

CHAPTER 5:

The Mei Lun Yuen Affordable Housing Project

THE FIGHT FOR Mei Lun Yuen did not have the profile of the International Hotel Struggle, moving at its own pace with many meetings in Chinatown, flaring up publicly during particular intervals at City Hall and eventually in Washington, D.C. But, both struggles were very important and indeed complementary, each representing different approaches to community development, affordable housing, empowerment, and social justice. In simple housing policy terms, if the I Hotel represented the need to preserve existing housing, Mei Lun Yuen represented the need to build new affordable housing.

Mei Lun Yuen in Chinese means "Garden of Beautiful Neighbors," which is somewhat ironic when you learn the 10-year history of this affordable housing project. The story of Mei Lun Yuen starts in September 1970, when a 21-member Citizens Advisory Committee was appointed to the HUD #701 Chinatown Housing and Recreation Study conducted by the City Planning Department. ("701" referred to the HUD Planning funding category.) Co-chaired by the Reverend Harry Chuck of Cameron House and Planning Commissioner Mortimer Fleishhacker, the #701 Study was the first comprehensive report and analysis of housing and open-space needs in the Chinatown community. It undertook a comprehensive review of both community needs and recommendations for follow-up. In the area of affordable housing, the Study recommended both rehabilitation and new construction strategies for Chinatown, specifically evaluating 39 potential new construction sites in the larger northeast area of San Francisco. The Study's top priority site was on the southwest corner of Stockton and Sacramento Streets, adjacent to the Stockton Street Tunnel. Before being named Mei Lun Yuen, the site was referred to as "Stockton/Sacramento."

Mei Lun Yuen, eventually completed in 1982, was Chinatown's first new affordable housing development. The Ping Yuen public housing projects were built in 1952–1953 by the San Francisco Housing Authority, which continues to own and manage the project. Mei Lun Yuen was the first non-profit-sponsored development, as such, owned by a community institution. Moreover, Mei Lun Yuen was Chinatown's first experience with a HUD-financed development, under its now defunct Section #236 Program. It was a construction subsidy program, where HUD directly subsidized construction and provided rental subsidies in order to maintain affordability for residents. Mei Lun Yuen became somewhat infamous for being the very last #236 project in the United States. It took almost a decade from start to finish, experiencing almost every conceivable challenge along the way.

Chinatown Coalition for Better Housing

Before the Chinatown #701 Study was completed, members of its Housing Committee began to discuss forming a permanent housing advocacy association. They formed the Chinatown Coalition for Better Housing (CCBH) in June 1972, with co-chairs Harry Chuck and Linda Wang, who was a medical social worker at Chinese Hospital and chaired the #701 Housing Committee. It was composed of both young community activists and students such as myself, Phil Chin, and Donna Yick and Chinatown senior residents who were organized by Anni Chung of Self-Help for the Elderly. CCBH was a great learning experience for me and other young activists just getting involved in Chinatown at the time. We were learning as we were doing, learning "real stuff" about making change. Our political perspectives about working within the system—and/or challenging the system at the same time—were still evolving.

As young activists, we learned a lot by watching how leaders such as Harry and Linda operated. They complemented each other very well. In Linda's words: "Harry and I played different roles. He was the good guy, and I was the bad guy. His thing was to be very conciliatory, and I always took the position of pushing. It was a nice complement of different styles."

In Harry's words: "Whenever we dealt with somebody like the Redevelopment Agency who we didn't like, she would jump all over the guy. Then I would come in and say, 'Well, what do you think we can do? We've got to get going on this.'"

We also learned a great deal about how the affordable housing system worked. It involved financial and political interplays between local and federal government. We learned that getting affordable housing built required knowledge of planning and zoning, construction, development financing, architecture, and the political process. We learned a lot of this from Alice Barkley, who at the time headed the Chinatown office of the Community Design Center. Alice was also an activist who, with her husband Dick Barkley, ran the Il Piccolo coffee shop in Chinatown—an early hang out for many Chinatown activists. I remember many, many CCBH meetings at Culbertson Hall in Cameron House, and also many Steering Committee meetings at Linda Wang's house or Alice Barkley's house.

After the completion of the Chinatown #701 Study and the decision to pursue the Stockton/Sacramento site as an initial project, the Chinatown Coalition for Better Housing was formally recognized as the community advocacy group to lead the community process for the project, including having a major say in selecting the project sponsor. I distinctly remember two resident members who were part of the sponsor selection subcommittee—Mr. Huck Chow and Mr. Y. B. Leung. Mr. Leung later became a co-chair of CCBH, and I remember frequent visits to his apartment on Stockton Street, hanging out with his young children.

The Presbyterian Church in Chinatown

Cameron House, a mission of the Presbyterian Church in Chinatown, has a renowned history as a place of refuge for Chinese girls and women escaping from the slave trade in the late 19th and early 20th century, led by Presbyterian missionary Donaldina Cameron and later Lorna Logan. Cameron House evolved into a multipurpose community center in the 1950s, primarily a place for youth. Cameron House's summer program has been highly regarded all over the Bay Area as a safe and enriching program for youth, and its youth leadership program can count as its graduates many Chinatown leaders over the past four decades. The Reverend Harry Chuck was the Executive Director of Cameron House and also preached at the Presbyterian Church during the planning and community advocacy for Mei Lun Yuen in 1973.

When the Presbyterian Church decided to seek the sponsorship of Mei Lun Yuen as a nonprofit developer in 1973, there was no assurance, stated or implied, that it would be selected as the sponsor, notwithstanding the leadership that Harry Chuck and Cameron House had devoted to advocating for the project. But, the Presbyterian Church was eventually selected to be the sponsor, with a strong recommendation from CCBH, because there was a great sense of trust in the Church given its strong leadership and proven commitment to Chinatown for over a century. CCBH and the Redevelopment Agency then recommended that the Presbyterian Church team up with Arcon/Pacific as its joint venture partner, given Arcon/Pacific's stronger financial capability.

This partnership structure was amended in 1977 after Arcon/Pacific discovered that the underground garage could not be built to the size and capacity they desired. Since this was to be a major source of the project's profit, they asked to bow out as owner/sponsor, but remain as developer to build the project. So the Presbyterian Church became the sole owner/sponsor of Mei Lun Yuen, embarking on what was to become an experience of a lifetime. Many challenges awaited the Presbyterian Church as "brand new" sponsor of a major affordable housing project, which Chinatown was closely watching and anxiously anticipating. They met every challenge with patience and determination, with a committed Mei Lun Yuen Housing Committee that likely met a couple hundred times over the project period.

The Mei Lun Yuen Board was led by Cynthia Joe, the one person who held things together when "the going got rough." In Cindy's words: "I gave my youth to this project." Cindy at the time was a chemist with the federal Government Services Agency (GSA), not a professional housing developer, but she cared deeply about affordable shelter for the poor and senior citizens. Cindy continues to lead the Mei Lun Yuen Board over four decades since the project began, finding time along the way to serve on the San Francisco Planning Commission.

Marching on City Hall

The Mei Lun Yuen project was the first issue that truly involved Chinatown senior residents in advocating for their own needs and their own interests. They were organized by a young social worker, Anni Chung, who learned from Self-Help for the Elderly Executive Director Sam Yuen, an early pioneer who believed that seniors not only should be served, but their leadership needed to be supported and nurtured. Anni and others, like Vera Haille, embraced that philosophy of empowerment as well.

That organizing commitment was critical in getting early local support for Chinatown housing and the Mei Lun Yuen project before the Planning and Redevelopment Commissions and the Board of Supervisors. The first major hearing took place in March of 1972, before the Board of Supervisors hearing on the designation of Chinatown as a high-need neighborhood, an important early policy decision that would guide future advocacy efforts. It was the first time City Hall regulars ever saw hundreds of Chinese seniors get off buses and march up the steps to the City Hall rotunda. Many similar hearings were to come on various other decisions—local funding

CYNTHIA JOE

Cynthia "Cindy" Joe was born and raised in Chinatown. She grew up in the Cameron House Youth Program and became a part-time Girls Worker before attending Presbyterian Westminster College. She received a degree in chemistry and began a long career with the federal General Services Administration. I met Cindy during the Chinatown Coalition for Better Housing advocacy for the new Mei Lun Yuen housing project, which was sponsored by the Presbyterian Church in Chinatown. Cindy became the chair of the Church's Mei Lun Yuen Housing Committee in 1972, despite having no housing or development experience. She considered it her "calling" to lead the church into

providing affordable housing for the poor. Cindy would continue to lead Mei Lun Yuen through innumerable challenges of funding, approvals and litigation until the project was completed a decade later in 1982.

Cindy became a housing activist, chairing the Chinatown CDC board during the early 1980s when land use and development conflicts dominated much of the agenda. She was known citywide as a passionate advocate and was appointed by Mayor Willie Brown to the City Planning Commission in 1997. To me, Cindy has personified the meaning of "citizen" leader. She just did it because it was the right thing to do for Chinatown.

commitments in 1972–1973 and environmental impact report approvals in 1973–1974—before Mei Lun Yuen could move forward at the local level.

One of the Chinatown senior leaders who gained some notoriety at City Hall was Mrs. Huie Dak Lan, who was in her mid or late 70s at the time and active with Self-Help for the Elderly. She became known not only because she spoke in Chinese, but because she spoke passionately and loudly. This was not something you saw many elderly Chinese do in public. She was not afraid to speak out, and even if you didn't know what she was saying, you could just feel what she was saying. She was an earlier version of more recent Chinatown senior leaders like Ping Yuen leader Mrs. Chang Jok Lee and Community Tenants Association leader Mrs. Bao Yan Chan—all strong women, all strong Chinatown tenant leaders. Ms. Huie Dak Lan said many times that she knew that the Mei Lun Yuen project would not likely be built in her lifetime, but she was fighting not only for herself and Chinatown seniors then, but also for all those who would come after her. Years later I would hear Mrs. Bao Yan Chan say something very similar about the International Hotel, but I was glad that Mrs. Chan did see the new I Hotel before she passed in 2006.

Marching on the Federal Government

On September 12, 1972, 200 seniors marched from Chinatown to the HUD Regional Offices at the Embarcadero Center. There were no buses this time, and it was quite a scene to see this procession of elderly Chinese, predominantly women, march those six blocks midday to the San Francisco Financial District. It was the culmination of a long campaign from City Hall to Washington, D.C. Signs shouted the message "Chinatown Needs Housing," "HUD, Are You Listening?" "Mei Lun Yuen, Now!"

Previously, the Presbyterian Church had worked extremely hard on the HUD Section #236 process, working closely with the City of San Francisco, which did its part with numerous local approvals and funding commitments, including an approval for $518,000 in August of 1972. However, HUD was the final decision maker for federal funding, and despite crossing so many local hurdles and maintaining progress on the project planning, ultimately HUD would have to approve the Final Funding Commitment. The HUD Region Nine Administrator at the time was James Price, who informed the Presbyterian Church that there were too many applications for too little funding, and that Mei Lun Yuen was deemed a "low priority" project in the region. CCBH co-chair Linda Wang and Alice Barkley traveled to Washington, D.C., the very next day, September 13, and the March on HUD was in part a send off to Linda and Alice, so that Chinatown's crying need for Mei Lun Yuen would be heard in Washington. While HUD did not overturn the regional HUD decision, Linda and Alice's trip to our nation's capital was important and successful in maintaining strong support from San Francisco's Congressional delegation, which would become absolutely critical in the ensuing months. On September 14, 1972, Mayor Joseph Alioto also wired HUD Secretary George Romney, asking for speedy "Cuban" financing for Mei Lun Yuen.

Then in May of 1973 President Richard Nixon froze all federal HUD housing funding. He did not do this through the normal give and take of the federal budget process, subject to debate and negotiation with Congress. Rather, he just instructed the Office of Management and Budget not to spend the money, including funds that had already been authorized through Congress. This brazen act became known as the "Nixon Housing Moratorium." Mei Lun Yuen, which at the time was focused on strengthening its project to be competitive with other regional housing projects, now faced the daunting challenge of fighting the Nixon administration's policies and politics. There was a procedure for projects to receive an exemption from

SAM YUEN

Sam Yuen was the first Executive Director of Self-Help for the Elderly. After emigrating from China, Sam's family ran a grocery store in Greenville, Mississippi. Sam was not a professional social worker. Before he started with Self-Help, he worked at the Post Office, which was one of the things that struck me as so cool about him. He was just a regular guy, didn't condescend to anyone, treated everybody with respect and a smile. He was one of the first Chinese "senior citizens" I met who could speak English, and he was street smart, knowing what he knew and what he didn't know. He knew to rely on

key leaders such as Vera Haille and Anni Chung, whom he nurtured and mentored.

Vera and Anni considered Sam "brilliant" for his approach to social services. He would talk to hundreds of Chinatown seniors each week, learn about their unique needs, and then create a new program at Self-Help to meet that need. Sam was not a fiery advocate like George Woo, nor a keen strategic thinker like Larry Jack Wong, but his strong character and calm leadership provided another role model for many of Chinatown's younger activists, myself included.

the funding moratorium, and this was what the Presbyterian Church and CCBH worked on next.

A key supporter in this effort was San Francisco's Congressman, Republican William Mailliard. I remember Harry Chuck bringing me in at least a couple times to meet with CCBH and the Chinatown seniors, and many of us found out then that Harry Chuck was a Republican! (I don't think this was some closely guarded secret, though it wasn't something Harry shouted about.) Harry had a good relationship with Congressman Mailliard and San Francisco Supervisor John Molinari, another Republican and a strong supporter of Mei Lun Yuen. Somehow, perhaps in tandem, they were able to garner the support of Republican Senator Hiram Fong of Hawaii, who at the time was the chair of the Senate Housing Committee. Mei Lun Yuen received its moratorium exemption on June 27, 1973, just four days before the end of the 1973–74 fiscal year, which was a very real deadline to keep the Mei Lun Yuen project alive.

Opposition from Nob Hill

Throughout the local planning review of Mei Lun Yuen from 1972 to 1974, it was evident that there were some folks from Nob Hill who did not like the project. Their opposition focused on one issue or another that have come to typify "Not In My Backyard" (NIMBY) opposition to affordable housing—loss of views, traffic congestion, and an increase in crime. But the Planning and Redevelopment commissions and the Board of Supervisors (with a few exceptions) had maintained their strong support up through the passage of the project's EIR in April of 1974. It was after that approval when litigation reared its ugly head. Condominium owners at 840 Powell Street and 850 Powell Street, one block up the hill from Mei Lun Yuen, filed the first of what would be a dozen lawsuits challenging aspects of the EIR and other approvals. They were joined later by the Nob Hill Association, which included many of the luxury hotels and high-end owners in the area. Over a two-year period, all of these lawsuits were defeated in court by attorneys for the project and the San Francisco City Attorney's office.

For us activist supporters of Mei Lun Yuen, it was a frustrating time. Not only did we have to fight the Nixon administration (and become dependent on Republican friends to do so), we had to take a back seat to all the lawyers while being anxious to do something. Then, something happened that gave us something to do. The Nob Hill Neighbors group filed a petition to the City Planning Department to essentially downzone the Nob Hill area from heights of 200–240 feet down to 40 feet. The Nob Hill Neighbors were more of a resident-based group than the Nob Hill Association, including both homeowners and renters, and they had done some good things to improve Nob Hill. They were also overwhelmingly white in their membership.

Ordinarily, community activists in one neighborhood have a basis of mutual respect, if not support, for their peers in an adjoining neighborhood. The mistake that Nob Hill Neighbors made with their rezoning application was in defining the Nob Hill area as extending all the way down to Stockton Street. Well *Stockton Street is Chinatown!* As if attacked by some invading force seizing our land, you can imagine our reaction. Not only were Chinatown residents and organizations not notified of this action, but it was evident to us that many Chinese residents of Nob Hill didn't know about it either. It became clear that the inclusion of Stockton Street in the Nob Hill zoning application was done to specifically target the Mei Lun Yuen project. The showdown came at the City Planning Commission hearing on site in Nob Hill at the Grace Cathedral on February 7, 1977, which was attended by more than 500 people. The majority of the audience was Chinese. Most of them were not Chinatown residents but residents of Nob Hill, which had become predominantly Chinese by the 1970 Census. Many came under the banner of "Concerned Chinese Nob Hill Citizens," a group that Sue Lee,

Michael Louie, myself, and other activists who lived on Nob Hill formed to demand that whatever plans were put forth for Nob Hill involve all of its residents. Subsequently, Nob Hill was rezoned, without Stockton Street. And in future years, Chinatown organizations, including Chinese Neighborhood Improvement Resource Center (CNIRC), worked collaboratively with both the Nob Hill Neighbors and Nob Hill Association on many issues of mutual interest, but with a spirit of mutual respect.

The Geen Mun Neighborhood Center

A final challenge faced by the Mei Lun Yuen project was not as life threatening as the HUD moratorium or the litigation or the Nob Hill downzoning, but it was an interesting episode on how things sometimes work out in ways you don't expect. The redesign of Mei Lun Yuen, eliminating the public garage, resulted in the addition of some 15,000 square feet of retail space on Stockton Street. However, the project budget would only cover a rough build out of the space, basically a concrete shell. With a very tight time frame due to the redesign, there were no firm retail tenants committed to financing all the necessary tenant improvements, and HUD had threatened not to close the Mei Lun Yuen project until a commercial tenant committed to a two-year prepayment on its lease. And of course, while this little snag was happening, the general contractor for Mei Lun Yuen was reminding the church that each delay was making it harder for them to keep to their price guarantee.

But a completely unrelated project of Chinatown CDC came up with a solution. One of the five founding sponsors of the Chinatown CDC was the Chinatown Coalition for Neighborhood Facilities (chaired by community leader George Ong). The coalition was later incorporated as the Chinatown Neighborhood Center (CNC) in 1977, chaired by architect Tom Hsieh, with the mission of developing a new multipurpose Chinatown community center. The vision was for an incubator type place for smaller agencies or outreach offices of larger agencies. Chinatown CDC was providing staff support to CNC. I headed CNC's Site Committee and Anni Chung chaired its Program Committee. With Chinatown CDC support, CNC was able to secure incremental commitments of Community Development Block Grant funding over a four-year period of $395,000 by 1980.

After the site search process for CNC was completed, it was becoming clear that the organization could not purchase a building in Chinatown, much less renovate it, for $395,000. So, Chinatown CDC helped facilitate a discussion between the Chinatown Neighborhood Center and the Presbyterian Church about a master lease of the Mei Lun Yuen retail space, in some ways killing two birds with one stone (lease). The Chinatown Neighborhood Center was renamed the "Geen Mun Center" and opened its doors in 1983 with 10 Chinatown social service agencies as tenants, including Chinese Newcomers Service Center, two child care centers, and a senior meals site for Self-Help for the Elderly. The Presbyterian Church, now able to satisfy HUD demands for a retail tenant and for a lump sum rent prepayment, signed a 10-year master lease with CNC one week before their general contractor price guarantee was about to expire.

Long Live Mei Lun Yuen!

The Mei Lun Yuen project, completed in 1982, was composed of 150 senior housing units in a 12-story tower and 35 three- and four-bedroom family townhouse units surrounding a central courtyard. The project includes community and resident meeting space, underground parking, and a community center on the ground floor. It has been managed by the John Stewart Company since it opened. When it came time to rent up the project, over 5,000 seniors applied for the 150 senior units, setting a record for San Francisco affordable housing projects. Mei Lun Yuen is a wonderful project that has withstood the test of time, garnering numerous architectural awards after its completion. But the real story of Mei Lun Yuen is the indigenous leadership and community organizing, the story of the Chinatown Coalition for Better Housing and the Presbyterian Church in Chinatown, a story that spanned a decade and planted seeds of learning and experience that continue to inspire Chinatown activists to this day.

Unless you were intimately involved, you will not think of Mei Lun Yuen as emotionally charged, life-changing, or as iconic as the I Hotel. But it was for many of us. It was the other side of the coin from the I Hotel, different in style and politics, but both were important episodes in our lives. In the words of my good friend and fellow football fan Phil Chin, "Mei Lun Yuen was the Super Bowl of community projects. It was a season no one expected us to win, and we came out champs."

Harry Chuck gets the last word here: "I don't look at it as political. I see my work with Mei Lun Yuen as a response to injustice. We were fighting a war in Vietnam, spending money overseas killing Asians, and here we were denying local Asians badly needed housing. This is a justice issue that had to be focused on."

CHAPTER 6

Those Chinese Bus Drivers

I LOVE HANGING out with bus drivers and especially the Chinese bus drivers I am happy to call my friends. I have learned a lot from MUNI drivers who see so much real life from behind the wheel of those diesel coaches and trolleys. One of my favorite driver sayings is, "It's very hard to drive both the outside of the bus and the inside at the same time." Watching out for cars, pedestrians, and bikes on crowded San Francisco streets while monitoring fragile seniors, mothers with strollers, and rowdy school kids on the inside can be really challenging. I have often thought about this when faced with delicate balancing acts between sensitive community or political dynamics on the "outside" of a community organization, and divergent opinions on strategies and decisions while running the "inside" of the group. Another thing I have learned from bus drivers is that in games of dominoes or cards, while getting the right tiles or cards is important, just as important is "talking the game"—knowing how to bluff, when to hold them, and when to fold them.

It wasn't that long ago, in the 1950s, when it was rare to see Chinese American or Asian American workers in the building trades, in uniform protective services, and especially in union jobs. As in many big cities, certain jobs were dominated by particular ethnic groups—Irish cops in San Francisco for instance. Historically, racial discrimination kept minority residents—African Americans, Latinos and Asian Americans, and women—out of the better paying jobs. Things changed somewhat after WWII created a labor demand with many (white) American men working in the armed services. African Americans, many who moved to the Bay Area from the South, found work in blue-collar industries such as the Hunter's Point shipyards, in federal agencies such as the Post Office, and in City departments like the Municipal Railway (which for much of the past three decades has been 60–80% African American). With the 1960s came affirmative action as a result of the Civil Rights Movement, which opened up more civil service opportunities to minority workers, although never achieving parity with their population.

In the early 1970s, some of my friends, including some of my roommates at 641 Balboa, started applying to be bus drivers. Landy Dong was hired as a MUNI driver in December 1973 and Phil Chin followed in January 1974. Also in that class of 1974 were my roommates Mike Yep and Terry Chow, Phil's brother Frank, Alvin Ja, Randy Tom, Clifton Tom, and Robert Wong. All these new MUNI drivers had grown up in Chinatown, and many were active in community and social justice groups like the Chinese Progressive Association, Chinatown Youth Council, and Leeway's. All told, the number of Chinese bus drivers in San Francisco grew to 20, a minuscule number out of a MUNI driver workforce of more than 2,000, but still significant symbolically.

This background is important because we too often stereotype "community activists" as either flaming radicals or people who work in nonprofit organizations. There is a rich history in this country and in San Francisco of people of color activism in blue-collar industries and in the labor movement (at times fighting organized labor). The early Chinese bus drivers of San Francisco were as much a part of the social justice environment of the '60s as anyone else. That 1974 class was the beginning of increasing efforts for affirmative recruitment and hiring of Chinese Americans for all kinds of City employment. Much of this effort was led by CAA and many of those 20 new Chinese drivers made it a point to help recruit others. By 2012, the percentage of Chinese bus drivers at MUNI was approaching 30%, second only to African Americans. There has also been a significant increase in Filipino drivers. And in 2008, Irwin Lum became the first Chinese American elected as president of the Transport Workers Union, Local 250 A, supported by Larry Martin (then head of the International Union of Transit Workers) and elected by a broad cross section of the MUNI driver workforce.

The Transport Workers Union has historically been one of the strongest, most progressive unions in San Francisco. The San Francisco General Strike of 1934, under the leadership of Harry Bridges and the Longshoremen Union, was a cornerstone of San Francisco labor history. It was a violent period in the City, but it highlighted the leadership role of the San Francisco labor movement on the West Coast and nationally. There has not been a general strike since then, but there have been two major labor events. One was the strike of 1974, initiated by SEIU and supported by the Transport

Workers Union. The other was the City Strike of 1976, started by City craft unions, and also supported by the Transport Workers Union.

The Strike of 1976 lasted for six weeks, leaving San Franciscans with no bus service, no trolley car service, and no cable cars. With the great proportion of San Francisco residents and workers dependent on public transportation, hardship was felt throughout the City. No group felt this more than the City's seniors, who had no means to go to a doctor or hospital or to meet other daily survival needs. In Chinatown, whose 10,000 senior residents are nearly half of the population, the shutdown of the public transportation system was devastating.

The Chinese bus drivers, though few in number, organized. Phil Chin approached Anni Chung at Self-Help for the Elderly and raised the idea of starting an "escort service," using their own cars to take seniors to General Hospital and anywhere else they needed to go. Self-Help also needed transportation for its many home health aides serving seniors. He got his roommates at 641 Balboa—Landy Dong, Mike Yep, and Terry Chow—behind the idea, later joined by Randy Tom, Clifton Tom, and Robert Wong. It was an organized effort, sort of a private shuttle service, with Phil serving as the "dispatcher" for six or seven set routes, organizational skills that Phil and Landy developed from their many years driving U.S. Postal trucks. These guys loved to drive, and they knew the "Streets of San Francisco." I don't think they ever gave a name to the Chinatown Escort Service (that's what I called it), but the service for Chinatown seniors continued to the end of the Strike.

None of these guys had the licenses, permits, or insurance coverage to do any of this—they just did it anyway. I believe that this impromptu service was one of the first such "paratransit" programs in the City. Self-Help for the Elderly later organized a Senior Escort Service for young volunteers to escort seniors within Chinatown. Other nonprofit senior and disabled organizations worked to create a movement to institutionalize paratransit programs citywide. Those Chinese bus drivers in 1976 were a part of this movement.

Chinatown TRIP

In the months following the 1976 City Strike and the Chinatown Escort Service, activists Phil and Landy started to talk about what else they could do to help Chinatown. They hooked up with Wil Din, who at the time worked at United Airlines and lived in Polk Gulch. Wil was a plaintiff in a lawsuit filed by Chinese for Affirmative Action against United Airlines over the lack of minority hiring. Phil, Landy, and Wil talked a lot about Chinatown's many transportation needs—pedestrian safety, better bus service, parking, and traffic circulation.

Around 1976, MUNI, headed by Curtis Green at the time, started the Planning, Operations, and Marketing Program (POM) as a comprehensive review of service and routes citywide. Phil and Landy recall some early meetings at the Chinese Methodist Church and their disagreement with some MUNI recommendations for Chinatown, which would have reduced the #15 Kearny line service and #41 Union line service in order to augment service on Stockton Street. Phil, Landy, and Wil decided to put their critique in writing and develop their own suggestions. And once again, they organized despite the risk of losing their MUNI jobs.

They started to talk to other Chinatown activists and agencies about MUNI's plans and their own ideas. One activist they talked to was Sue Lee, who was an employment counselor at the Chinatown Resource Development Center (CRDC). Sue was active in organizing Chinatown immigrant adult students, who like seniors were very transit dependent. Eventually, MUNI retracted its Stockton Street recommendations and gave attention to a suggestion from the Chinatown group. That idea was to extend the #55 Sacramento Street line (which went from the Financial District, through Chinatown, and ended at Clement and 6th Avenue in the Richmond District) all the way to 33rd Avenue to serve the growing population in the Outer Richmond. This was implemented years later in conjunction with the change of the #55 line into a trolley line, the #1 California. So, folks in the Richmond (Chinese and non-Chinese alike) can thank some Chinatown activists for having the foresight to push for transit services that benefited both neighborhoods.

Around this time, Phil, Landy, and Wil got serious about forming an organization to advocate for Chinatown transportation needs. They pulled together a larger group, including Sue Lee, George Woo, city planner Jon Pon, architects Wayne and Darlene Jang, Michael Louie, and transportation planner Chi Hsin Shao. Phil Chin came up with the long name "Chinatown Transportation, Research, and Improvement Project," with the catchy acronym, Chinatown TRIP.

The #83 Pacific Bus Line

Chinatown TRIP built on the momentum from the POM "victory" over MUNI and the extension of the #55 Sacramento line. They worked with MUNI to add the then #82 line onto Stockton Street, reducing the headways (the time between arriving busses) from three minutes to two minutes. Their big project success came with the #83 Pacific line, one of the first projects that our Chinatown Neighborhood Improvement Resource Center worked on in the first year. And to this day, it's one of the best things we have done.

For decades, Chinatown residents who had wanted to travel west had to choose between the #55 Sacramento line and the #41 Union line, which were parallel but eight blocks apart. The #55 served primarily Nob Hill, the #41 served primarily Russian Hill, and both were meant to serve Chinatown in between. Chinatown TRIP advocated for a new east/west bus service between Sacramento and Union Streets, to go up Pacific Avenue.

The #83 Pacific was what was known as a "community service" line or, as MUNI drivers call it, a "short run." Unlike main lines serving major thoroughfares, community service lines are much shorter routes serving a particular neighborhood. In the northeast sector of San Francisco, the only community service line that existed prior to the #83 had been the #39 Coit line, which took tourists from North Beach up the hill to this San Francisco landmark Coit Tower and back. Chinatown TRIP said, "We want a short run too!" Their proposal was for a short run that would start in the Financial District on Battery Street, go up Pacific Avenue to Van Ness Avenue, where it would loop back down Pacific—a route of about one and a half miles.

Initially, MUNI was cool to the idea of the Pacific Avenue short run. They said that Pacific was too narrow for a new bus line. So, one day when Landy Dong was due to start his daily shift, taking his full-size bus from the MUNI Kirkland Bus Yard in Fisherman's Wharf to his #55 Sacramento route, Landy said to Mike Yep, "Let's go for a ride." Instead of heading straight for Sacramento Street, Landy took his motor coach up Pacific Avenue, wanting to check out whether Pacific was really too narrow for a new bus line or not. Landy and Mike tested it out for themselves and afterwards they agreed: "No problem." In fact, if a full-size motor coach was doable, then a short run (with smaller buses) should be even easier. Case closed.

With support from the Chinatown Resource Center, Chinatown TRIP circulated petitions in all of the affected neighborhoods and the Financial District. Strong support came from Supervisor John Molinari. The #83 Pacific was inaugurated on August 1, 1979. It was one of the first new bus lines in San Francisco in decades, this one conceived and advocated for by Chinatown TRIP.

Many other transportation projects would follow. But for me, it all started with Chinatown TRIP, one of the only volunteer minority transportation advocacy groups in the country. Their early leadership inspired a commitment to transportation as an essential community value, as important as housing and open space in comprehensive community planning. And it all started with those Chinese bus drivers.

Fighting for Chinatown's Land and People, History and Identity, 1977–1987

The brutal rape and murder of a young woman resident on August 23, 1978, sparked the Ping Yuen Residents Improvement Association to demand better security, staging the most successful rent strike in the history of the San Francisco Housing Authority. *(Photo courtesy of Chinatown CDC.)*

The Clayton Hotel at 656 Clay Street was the Chinatown CDC's first residential hotel acquisition and rehabilitation project. At the 1982 ribbon cutting were (R to L) Supervisor Nancy Walker, Mayor Dianne Feinstein, Executive Director Gordon Chin, and Housing Director Howard Gong. *(Photo courtesy of Chinatown CDC.)*

The Chinatown CDC renovated the 65-room Swiss American Hotel on Broadway Street in 1984. It has a colorful history, a place where comedian Lenny Bruce once lived and where the San Francisco Beat Museum is located today. *(Photo courtesy of Chinatown CDC.)*

In 1980, Ross Alley was the first Chinatown alleyway project of the Chinatown CDC, the Chinese Chamber of Commerce, and the Committee for Better Parks and Recreation in Chinatown. *(Photo courtesy of Chinatown CDC.)*

On March 31, 2007, Jack Kerouac Alley, which connects Chinatown and North Beach at Columbus and Broadway Streets, was dedicated by Chinatown CDC along with key community partners Vesuvio Cafe and City Lights Bookstore. *(Photo courtesy of Chinatown CDC.)*

From 1981 to 1984, 17 families in the 1000 Montgomery Building were threatened with eviction by a group of attorneys who sought to convert the residences into law offices. Pictured in this *San Francisco Examiner* photo were (L to R) tenant leaders Mary Stemburger, Cruz Luna, and Mary Ghirardini. *(Photo courtesy of San Francisco Examiner.)*

Although the original 17 families at 1000 Montgomery were displaced, the developer went bankrupt in 1985 and the building was acquired by On Lok Senior Services, which, with the help of Chinatown CDC, renovated the building into senior assisted housing in 1989. *(Photo courtesy of Chinatown CDC.)*

Chinatown CDC Housing Staff in the 1980s. L to R: Daryl Higashi, Cathie Lam, Agnes Lee, Michael Neumann, Elaine Joe, Gordie Lam, and Gordon Chin. *(Photo courtesy of Chinatown CDC.)*

Participating in one of many City Hall hearings and demonstrations on the Orangeland project were Gordon Chin (center in raincoat) and, to his right, Asian Law Caucus attorney Edwin Lee. *(Photo courtesy of Asian Law Caucus.)*

From 1983 to 1985, the Orangeland project at Stockton and Jackson Streets was one of most hotly contested development projects in San Francisco. *(Photo courtesy of Chinatown CDC.)*

CHAPTER 7

Starting an Organization

THE IDEA OF forming a new Chinatown organization started in late 1974 with discussions started by members of five volunteer groups, usually over a meal, coffee, or a game of mah-jongg. This early brainstorming involved myself and Phil Chin from Chinatown Coalition for Better Housing (CCBH), Stan Yee from Committee for Better Parks and Recreation in Chinatown (CBPR), and later, Sue Lee and Michael Louie from Chinatown TRIP and Anni Chung from Chinatown Coalition for Neighborhood Facilities (CCNF). Many of us lived in the Polk Gulch area around Larkin Street, and we saw each other often. Each group was very busy on its own issues. CCBH had the I Hotel and Mei Lun Yuen, CBPR was planning for the new Chinese Playground and advocating for a new Chinatown park, and TRIP was advocating for a new Chinatown transportation study and bus line. All of us were volunteers in these groups and had day jobs.

In the mid 1970s, with so many important issues and projects underway, it was becoming clear that our volunteer efforts could be much more effective if we had some permanent staff support and a place to meet. The discussion of starting an "umbrella group" to support the five volunteer organizations started modestly. We would have been happy to get funding for one staff member and a storefront office, but we worked to create a more ambitious concept and proposal. We envisioned an organization that could facilitate coordination between the five groups, ensuring, for instance, that the CBPR's goal of a new Chinatown park and CCBH's goal of new housing were not competing for the same sites. We sought to create a planning vision for Chinatown as a whole community that was greater than the sum of our respective parts. And we believed that forming a united front coalition would enhance the power of each group at City Hall.

We submitted a proposal for a two-year grant of $80,000 to the San

Francisco Foundation late in 1976 and were stunned and elated when the foundation approved the grant in its entirety. We were new to the foundation world and appreciated this early show of support. I believe that the track record we established over a number of years as volunteer organizations was an important factor in establishing our early credibility. We were a new nonprofit 501(c)3 organization, but we had been doing good work for nearly a decade. The grant from the San Francisco Foundation started the more formal process of determining the initial organizational structure, staffing, budget, facilities, and overall mission and early program goals.

In 1977, we had to come up with a name for the San Francisco Foundation proposal, and we didn't have a lot of time to decide on one. We somehow ended up with The Chinatown Neighborhood Improvement Resource Center, but most people referred to us as the Chinatown Resource Center. The next two chapters will briefly chronicle the first decade of the Chinatown Resource Center and the housing development arm we created in 1981, the Chinese Community Housing Corporation (CCHC). In 2000, we formally merged the two organizations as the Chinatown Community Development Center (Chinatown CDC), but the two corporations had always functioned as parts of one organization, and I served as Executive Director of both since day one.

April 1, 1977

I have always loved the fact that we incorporated and became a formal organization on April Fools' Day, 1977. I think it says something about my sense of humor as well as about an organizational culture that has been sustained since day one. That attitude is summed up in a phrase that I have repeated a few times: "We should not take ourselves too seriously, but we should take our work very seriously." While I will always remember that I became an Executive Director on April Fools' Day, on my first day on the job I felt like Robert Redford in *The Candidate* ("Now what do I do?"). My starting salary was a whopping $16,000 a year, which was about what I was making at the Post Office if you count the overtime.

I remember how jazzed I was at having the honor of being the leader of something so new. It was a big change from a lifestyle of working so many part-time jobs, going to school, and getting into so many activist activities. I felt grounded in doing one job, albeit one that I knew little about. I tried to explain to my mom what I was doing and what type of organization I was doing it for. She did not get the community development stuff, but she did understand that it had something to do with making Chinatown better, which made her proud and made me feel good. My dad actually understood it better than mom. When my folks operated the Kim Ling Restaurant in the 1960s in Oakland's Fruitvale District, some of their most frequent lunch patrons worked around the corner at the Spanish Speaking Unity Council, including the late Henry Mestre, who was executive director. When I told him about my new job, my father said, "Oh, you doing what Henry doing." I said, "Right." He said, "So how come you don't wear a suit like Henry?" This was a question I had no answer for, but *What goes around, comes around.*

One of the first tasks I had was to find a home for this new organization. Our first office was in the Chinatown YWCA on Clay Street, which was a great hang place for young folks and community volunteers, playing basketball in the gym, spending evenings in their basement coffee house. In January of 1977, we moved into a one-room space on the mezzanine of the YWCA, rent-free, with the understanding that this was to be temporary until we could find a permanent site. On Lok was planning its first senior care center on the site of the former St. Francis Day Home at 1441 Powell Street, and they offered us its use in May 1977, another rent-free deal. As the building was a fixer-upper—no heat, crumbling paint, and old plumbing—we fixed it up with a lot of volunteer help. My roommate Malcolm Collier nailed in what seemed like miles of metal flashing along the walls to keep the mice out, and at our open house, then-Redevelopment Director Wilbur Hamilton asked why the stairway didn't have any rails. In November of 1978, we moved into our first "real" office in the heart of Chinatown at 615 Grant Avenue, near California Street. We had to pay rent this time for the third floor, which was about 2,000 square feet. We stayed at 615 Grant until moving to the Tower Hotel in 1981.

The initial board of directors of the Chinatown Resource Center was composed of five individuals who each represented one of the grass roots sponsors:

- Chinatown Coalition for Better Housing (CCBH)
- Committee for Better Parks and Recreation in Chinatown (CBPR)
- Ping Yuen Residents Improvement Association (PYRIA)
- Chinatown TRIP (TRIP)
- Chinatown Coalition for Neighborhood Facilities (CCNF)

Our first board chair was Phil Chin, an active member of both Chinatown TRIP and CCBH, and Phil's leadership was essential to guide a very

SUE LEE

Marilyn Sue Lee was the first staff person I hired for Chinatown CDC in 1977, as Program Director. We had both been members of the Chinatown Coalition for Better Housing, and we had both been born in Chinese Hospital. Sue was also an early member of Chinatown TRIP. She grew up in the Richmond District but had strong roots in Chinatown. Her grandmother had a grocery store on Pacific Avenue for many years. Sue has had many leadership positions in San Francisco—as an aide for Supervisor Nancy Walker, one of San Francisco's first progressive district supervisors; as Executive Director of the San Francisco Small Business Commission; and currently as Executive Director of the Chinese Historical Society of America.

Once Sue embraces an issue, she is tenacious in her commitment, as she was as one of the founders of the Richmond District Neighborhood Center. In the 1970s, Sue lived on Clay Street with a group of roommates (one of whom was budding film director Wayne Wang). When it was threatened in San Francisco's first wave of condominium conversions, she organized the tenants and waged a fight at City Hall. She got then Supervisor Dianne Feinstein to visit the building. Eventually, the conversion was defeated.

new and young staff. The board later expanded to nine members, adding other community-wide perspectives. This expansion reflected our nascent involvement in issues such as land use planning and zoning, monitoring private development, promoting historic preservation, and community reinvestment, which complemented the five founding groups focused on housing, open space, public housing, transportation, and neighborhood facilities.

The first staff I hired was Sue Lee, as Community Organizer, who was previously an employment counselor at the Chinatown Resource Development Center. Sue oversaw our community organizing program and was lead staff for transportation and public housing. The second staff hired was Jennie Lew as community planner, who had just graduated from MIT in planning and architecture. Jennie was lead staff for open space and land use planning. Following Sue and Jennie were planner Babette Jee, who oversaw our Chinatown Historic Survey and many neighborhood improvement projects, and Agnes Lee as our Community Organizer working with tenants in the Ping Yuen public housing projects. Managing the office operation was Pauline Chew.

For that first year, we were a small and effective staff who survived our start-up phase, unheated office, and generally bare bones operation, not to mention an inexperienced Executive Director. It was an exciting time since everything we did was so new, and as new staff, we didn't know what we didn't know. Having been volunteers for so long, it took some adjustment to being paid staff; having to adhere to administrative, legal, and financial systems in running an organization; fundraising and reporting to funders; and being accountable to a board of directors whom we had worked along-side as volunteers and friends for such a long time.

A Decade of Learning and Relationship Building

The first decade of the Chinatown Resource Center was a period of constant learning, reading and being exposed to some great teaching, and relation-ship building. Since my earlier involvement with CCBH in the early '70s, many of us young activists learned a lot about housing from Alice Barkley, who at the time ran the Chinatown Field Office for the UC Community De-sign Center. I had also begun to read a lot about housing and community development and took a few urban studies courses at SF State in the early '70s from urban studies professionals like Dick Legates. While working at the Human Rights Commission, I learned a lot from dedicated and experi-enced housing activists like Edith Witt. And I enjoyed many early visits with progressive activist Calvin Welch, who was a great source of learning about housing and land use. You probably could not find four people as different as Alice, Dick, Edith, and Calvin, but I benefited greatly from all of them, from their knowledge, and more so from their passion for community-based development.

In Chinatown, we established new relationships with many sectors of the community. None was more important than the Chinese Chamber of Commerce led by President Stephen Fong and consultant Rose Pak. Ste-phen, Rose, and the Chamber supported the Chinatown Resource Center in many of our earliest projects, helping build good will and relationships with the business community. George Woo had first introduced me to Rose Pak when she was still a reporter for the *San Francisco Chronicle,* before she started as the general consultant to the Chinese Chamber of Com-merce. That was the start of Rose and I becoming very good friends over the next three decades. Rose taught me and the Chinatown Resource Center a great deal about Chinatown family associations and the intricate internal political structure we activists had referred to as the "Chinatown Establish-ment." Like George Woo, Rose taught us not to stereotype any part of the community, and even more importantly, how to work together on issues of mutual importance.

The Chinatown Resource Center and the Chinese Chamber of Commerce started working together to advocate to the City for street repairs and repaving, improved street lighting, and alleyway beautification projects, which were all "safe" community issues that helped build our early credibility as an organization, dispelling some of the perception that we were too "radical." Our first decade would see the Resource Center, Chinatown TRIP, and the Chinese Chamber partner on many important transportation projects.

The early 1980s saw a new generation of Chinatown Resource Center staff. The organization was established with more funding stability from Community Development Block Grant (CDBG) and foundation support and the HUD Neighborhood Development Program. In 1981, Enid Lim joined the staff as Community Liaison and for the next two decades became just as much the "public face" of the organization as I was. Also in 1981, Marilyn Chu became Planning Coordinator, joined in 1983 by Alton Chinn as Community Education Specialist and Eva Cheng as Community Organizer. Alton and Eva had come to the organization with a great deal of community experience, Eva with Self-Help for the Elderly and Alton as a reporter for *AsianWeek* newspaper. Social worker Doreen Der would come on as Program Director in 1985.

Planning for Chinatown

On day one of the organization, Chinatown CDC inherited the program of our five founding organizations, which already had established priorities and projects needing staff support. We developed contracts with each of the five groups to determine what we would do for them in the forthcoming year, a process that was challenging at times, but very important in order to maintain some balance and sense of fairness that we were not giving too much help to one group over another.

The Committee for Better Parks and Recreation in Chinatown's top priority was the planning and advocacy for a new Chinatown Park. The #701 Chinatown Housing and Recreation Study had recommended in 1971 that acquisition and development of a new Chinatown park was critical for a neighborhood with only two acres of public open space. The #701 Study had recommended a private garage and parking lot on Vallejo Street/Churchill Alley as the priority site for the new park, on the border between Chinatown and North Beach. Much of the early 1980s was devoted to pursuing this site, with the Committee succeeding in getting City funding commitments toward eventual acquisition. The Churchill site faced opposition from North Beach merchants who did not want to lose parking, so the Committee and the San Francisco Recreation and Parks Department shifted focus to another site, the Cathay Mortuary on Powell Street, which would eventually be acquired by eminent domain by the City in 1987.

In the early 1980s, the Chinatown Coalition for Better Housing continued its campaign for Mei Lun Yuen and support for the International Hotel. One other important Chinatown housing issue at the time was the efforts of the San Francisco YWCA to convert their building on Powell Street from a 170-room hostel for visiting young women to an 84-unit senior housing facility. Famed architect Julia Morgan designed the YWCA Residence Home in 1932. The YWCA appointed a Community Task Force in 1972 to explore the idea of senior housing, which included CCBH members Linda Wang and Phil Chin. The YWCA applied for a HUD Section #202 funding in September 1976. HUD issued its initial funding approval one year later, and the renovation of the YWCA was completed in 1982.

Throughout the 1980s, the Chinatown Resource Center also worked to ensure that other Chinatown needs were addressed in the new Community Development Block Grant (CDBG) program. We helped other Chinatown groups apply for CDBG's Neighborhood Initiated Improvement Program to implement small-scale play structure and beautification projects for many Chinatown schools and child care centers. The CDBG program was an important learning experience for all of us. We learned about government policy and programs, but we also learned a lot by observing the strategies and styles of community leaders from other San Francisco neighborhoods.

We used the community engagement process of CDBG to organize our neighborhoods through collaborative planning, and we started to understand the importance of community unity in a political context. A prime example of the importance of the CDBG program was the new Geen Mun Neighborhood Center, located in the Mei Lun Yuen housing project, which opened on September 1, 1982. Chinatown CDC managed the construction of the center and helped the Geen Mun Center secure a total of $875,000 in CDBG funding for acquisition and renovation costs over five years.

The early 1980s saw many important transportation projects get started building on the momentum of the new #83 Pacific bus line. The City agreed to undertake the first Chinatown Transportation Circulation Study and the Chinatown Resource Center provided Chinatown community outreach for the reconstruction of San Francisco's Cable Car system in 1982. In 1981, the #1 California MUNI Line was converted from a diesel bus line to an electric trolley line. San Franciscans living in Chinatown or working in the Financial District would remember that the former #55 Sacramento diesel bus line would be loaded to capacity with Financial District workers every rush hour, often bypassing Chinatown riders when it got to Chinatown. Financial District workers would often be asked to volunteer to "get off the bus" when the diesel busses would stall trying to make it up the steep Sacramento Street slope. It was TRIP's idea to advocate for the electrification of the line and extending it to the Outer Richmond District. Electrification, with its network of overhead wires, was not the prettiest site with new overhead electrical lines, but a practical solution to benefit thousands of MUNI riders.

Planning also began in 1982 for the Stockton Tunnel Improvement Project, advocated for by Chinatown TRIP to make the Stockton Tunnel (the main connection between Chinatown and Union Square) safer, cleaner and more attractive. For decades, the Stockton Tunnel was an eyesore, dark and dingy, often leaking water from the ceiling. Moreover, it was dangerous for pedestrians with no safety railings between the walkways and the roadway that spanned two city blocks. TRIP pushed for the City's successful application for $210,000 in Federal Jobs Bill funding for new safety rails, new lighting, and waterproofing for the tunnel. The Stockton Tunnel project, like the #83 Pacific bus and the #1 California line, were ideas started in Chinatown that benefited and garnered substantial support from other San Francisco neighborhoods—the Financial District, Nob Hill and the Richmond District—and we would come to embrace inter-neighborhood coalition building as a core organizational value.

When the Stockton Tunnel Project was finally completed in 1984, we held a wonderful ribbon cutting ceremony in Chinatown, joined by many leaders of the Union Square Merchants Association, who came "through the tunnel" to join us in Chinatown. On May 10, 1969, when America celebrated the Centennial of the "Gold Spike" at Promontory Summit in Utah and the joining of the Central and Union Pacific Railroads that completed the Transcontinental Railroad, the key role of the Chinese in building the railroad was ignored. We thought about this when we celebrated the new Stockton Tunnel and the "joining" of Union Square and Chinatown. *What goes around, comes around.*

Community-Based Research for Chinatown

From 1977 to 1981, Chinatown CDC developed a foundation of community-based research about important community-wide issues that would guide Chinatown planning for the next decade, building upon early 1970s community studies such as the Community Design Center's Chinatown study, the Baccari Report, and the #701 Chinatown Housing and Recreation Study. The Community Development Block Grant program taught us that we needed updated documentation of Chinatown needs and analysis of potential solutions. In our first three years, we planned and completed a number of research projects that were Chinatown "firsts": a Land Use Survey, a Property Speculation Study, a Community Reinvestment Survey, a Historic Survey, and a Single Room Occupancy (SRO) Study.

These studies, as well as numerous neighborhood improvement projects in our early years, provided an analytical framework that would inform much of our planning and public policy for the next decade and beyond. The Chinatown Land Use Survey would be a foundation for the Chinatown Rezoning Plan a decade later. The Community Reinvestment Survey would lead to our sponsorship of the first Chinatown Community Reinvestment Conference with 22 financial institutions, in April of 1981, to encourage community lending. The Chinatown SRO Study would inform our Chinatown housing preservation and housing policy work, establishing a housing policy basis for the eventual SRO Preservation Ordinance. In conjunction with our five founding groups, we also advocated and organized support for critical City-sponsored studies. In 1978, Chinatown TRIP successfully advocated for the Chinatown Circulation Study, which would become the most comprehensive study of Chinatown's transportation needs and strategies for improving public transit, parking, and traffic circulation. The Resource Center and the Committee for Better Parks and Recreation in Chinatown jointly sponsored the first Chinatown Alleyway Study.

Our community research was greatly assisted by our being selected as one of 20 community development organizations for HUD's new Neighborhood Development Organizations program in 1978. Frankly, we were a little surprised at being chosen since we had only existed for two years. But, HUD was impressed with the solid track record our five founding grass roots sponsors had built up over the previous decade. Sue Lee became our NDO Program Project Manager, and we received HUD funding between 1979 and 1982. The NDO Program had an interesting component requiring each organization to provide on-site technical assistance to two other community organizations. The two organizations we were assigned were Operation Life, a welfare rights organization in Las Vegas, planning for a new community center to serve welfare moms, and the International District Improvement Association ("INTERIM") in Seattle with a plan to improve their Danny Woo Community Garden. This was the start of a great relationship with

INTERIM and other organizations in Seattle.

But, the HUD NDO program had initially embroiled us in a high-profile controversy by assigning us to provide technical assistance to an organization in Cleveland. We were starting our preparation to fly to Cleveland when we were told that an article appeared in the local Cleveland newspaper in which Commissioner Voinovich harshly criticized Mayor Dennis Kucinich for bringing in some "Chinese consultants" from San Francisco to work with a community group linked to Kucinich. Voinovich and Kucinich were running against each other for mayor, and we became a historic footnote in this campaign. I told HUD, "No way are we going to Cleveland" to be met at the airport by throngs of media, not to mention picket signs. This was one of many lessons I would learn about how politics can affect our work. I still have never been to Cleveland. Maybe they are still looking for me.

The Center for Community Change (CCC) was an important national relationship in the first decade of Chinatown CDC. Based in Washington, D.C., CCC was a national technical assistance and public policy organization founded by progressive activists and union leaders in 1968. CCC provided technical assistance and research about federal policies and programs such as the CDBG, the Community Reinvestment Act, and housing trust funds. In September 1981, the Center sent a whole team of staff to San Francisco to do an organizational assessment of Chinatown CDC I had the honor of serving for a decade on the CCC board of directors and the privilege of meeting some great people, such as Civil Rights leader Julian Bond and former President of the National Council of La Raza, Raul Yzaguirre.

In 1984, I was selected to participate in the Development Training Institute (DTI) National Internship Program. DTI was an important resource in my personal leadership development, providing an enriched environment for sharing experiences, challenges, and innovative strategies with 30 executive directors of community development organizations from across the country. In the first decade of the Chinatown CDC, these national experiences—the HUD Neighborhood Development Program, sitting on the board of the Center for Community Change, and the Development Training Institute—gave me a broader perspective about our work in Chinatown with the inspiration which comes from being part of a national movement.

CHAPTER 8

Becoming Housing Developers

THE IDEA FOR a new community-controlled nonprofit development entity in Chinatown was first proposed by the #701 Chinatown Housing and Recreation Study in 1972. While the Chinatown Coalition for Better Housing was working hard to advocate and organize for the new Mei Lun Yuen housing project, it was also exploring new projects and proactive affordable housing strategies for Chinatown. Over a four-year period starting in 1974, CCBH advocated for the City to set aside CDBG funding for new Chinatown housing, succeeding in establishing a Chinatown Site Acquisition pool of $2 million by 1978. CCBH leaders Harry Chuck and Linda Wang argued that since Chinatown was not a Redevelopment Area, the community's affordable housing needs were not being met.

The #701 Study had recommended a number of possible new sites in the greater Chinatown area, and CCBH discussed potential acquisition and development alternatives with both the San Francisco Redevelopment Agency and the San Francisco Housing Authority. These meetings were not fruitful, and CCBH felt that its strong advocacy work to get the $2 million for Chinatown was not complemented by an equally strong commitment from City agencies for full community involvement in planning for new housing. As a result of distrust of City housing agencies, CCBH embraced the idea of a community-controlled Chinatown nonprofit housing organization.

CCBH asked CRC staff to further evaluate the Housing Development Corporation idea, and identify program priorities and structures for such a new organization. We reviewed the recommendations of the Chinatown #701 Study and the report from the UC Berkeley School of Planning team headed by Tim Dean, and Jennie Lew and I developed a concept paper in October of 1977 outlining four program strategies: Site Acquisition, New Construction, Rehabilitation, and Housing Services. The Mayor's Office of

Community Development approved a start-up grant of $125,000 for this new organization, which we called the Chinese Community Housing Corporation (CCHC).

CCBH leaders Linda Wang and Harry Chuck and advisor Alice Barkley helped identify potential board members for CCHC, which we created as a totally separate entity from the Chinatown Resource Center. The initial CCHC board reflected a good balance of community activists and professionals in the housing, real estate, and architectural fields. The first board chair was Wayne Hu, and members included community leaders Linda Wang, Anni Chung, George Woo, Dr. Rolland Lowe, Ted Dang, Phil Choy, and Al Woo, former San Francisco Planning Director Allan Jacobs, and Bob Thompson, who was former attorney for the International Hotel Tenants Association.

The foundation for a successful community-based nonprofit housing entity was established by the advocacy efforts of CCBH and by the spirit of the International Hotel and Mei Lun Yuen struggles. In creating a new housing organization, we were creating not only internal capacity to do housing development, but also a program to implement a broader community housing strategy for Chinatown. We learned from the International Hotel experience that fighting for the preservation of existing affordable housing was just as important as building new housing. We learned from Mei Lun Yuen that fighting for new affordable housing was not enough. What would be the point of building new housing if during that same time the community lost many more housing units due to private housing displacement? Our new affordable housing roles must be integrated into a more comprehensive community housing strategy, which meshed with our roles as advocates, organizers, and planners.

We knew that we could not solve Chinatown's housing problem as housing developers. We could not buy and rehabilitate all 900 buildings in Chinatown. Nor could we acquire and finance new development sites to meet the needs of a population that exceeded 20,000 people. What we could do was integrate our housing development strategy, developing partnerships with private owners, with other developers, and with financial institutions. Those partnership goals directed our Chinatown housing program for our first decade, and before the organization would acquire our first housing development in 1981, we engaged in many housing activities with that spirit of partnership.

Early in 1979, about a year after CCHC was started, the boards of both the Chinatown Resource Center and the Chinese Community Housing

WAYNE HU

Wayne Hu was an important inspiration and advisor to the Chinatown CDC in its formative years. He was the first board chair of the organization's housing arm, the Chinese Community Housing Corporation (CCHC). As a real estate appraiser and developer, Wayne provided professional advice and guidance on both affordable housing policy and projects. A true "Chinatown kid," Wayne developed leadership skills at both Cameron House and the Chinatown YMCA. He has served in many Chinatown leadership positions, including heading the Chinese New Year Parade for over two decades, a role he inherited from his father, Jackson Hu. Wayne has been active in San Francisco civic affairs his entire life and was appointed by Mayor Art Agnos in 1988 to be a member of the San Francisco City Planning Commission.

Corporation started discussions about restructuring the two organizations. CCHC had been established as a separate and independent nonprofit organization with its own board of directors and staff. Indeed, the Chinatown Resource Center established it as a spin-off, since it was not the original intent of the CRC to become housing developers. However, it became evident that the idea of a totally independent entity needed to be revisited. The concern was not about CCHC staff capability, but about the need for greater strategic coordination and community accountability. The boards were seeing that too much of the visioning, community relationships, and political savvy were dependent on the Chinatown Resource Center staff.

A joint CRC/CCHC Board Task Force was established in the spring of 1979, co-chaired by Buddy Choy from the CRC Board and George Woo from the CCHC Board. The eventual restructuring resulted in the linkage of the two organizations, with me serving as Executive Director of both entities. This structure remained until 2000 with the formal merger of both CRC and CCHC into the Chinatown Community Development Center (the name we will use for the rest of this book.) The restructuring was important in establishing a comprehensive vision and an identity and mission that integrated the community roles of advocacy, organizing, and planning with the development roles of financing, construction, and management under one roof.

Even before we were able to hire new housing development staff, we tried our hand at a housing project. We master leased the vacant second floor of an existing hotel at 523 Grant Avenue in 1979 to provide 12 units of residential hotel housing and for office space for staff. Architect Babette Jee and many volunteers from UC Berkeley renovated the residential and office space with no government or foundation resources. (I still remember the terrible job I did in spackling the stairway.) We scrounged supplies and used furniture for the community room, and Asian Neighborhood Design built furniture for all the units. From the 523 Grant Avenue experience we learned that this "sweat equity" stuff wasn't as easy as we thought. We had to bring in a contractor to repair the electrical system and install new kitchen appliances, for example. We gained a great appreciation for the process of construction and construction management.

Our first generation housing staff included Housing Director Fei Tsen, Rehabilitation Loan Coordinator Cathie Lam, Property Manager Agnes Lee, and Housing Assistant Elaine "Pinky" Joe. They were followed by a second generation, which included Property Management Director Gordie Lam and Construction Manager Mike Neumann. This expanded team was led by Housing Directors Howard Gong from 1982–85 and Daryl Higashi from 1985–94. Agnes and Cathie were both skilled organizers. Gordie was an ordained Presbyterian Minister. Mike had been a contractor in Santa Cruz and a stand-up comic of sorts. Howard Gong was nicknamed "Harvard" for his ability to debate any issue you could think of. Daryl brought the spirit of Aloha having grown up in Hawaii, working as a nonprofit developer in Honolulu before making his big leap across the Pacific Ocean to join the organization.

The first buildings we acquired were the 1204 Mason Street Apartments and the Clayton Hotel on Clay Street. Housing Director Fei Tsen led the acquisition process for these projects, with assistance from realtor Ted Dang. 1204 Mason occupies a unique location on the corner of Mason and Washington Streets, across the street from the San Francisco Cable Car Barn and kitty corner from the Chinese Recreation Center. After rehabilitation, 1204 Mason was dedicated by Mayor Dianne Feinstein in October of 1982. 1204 Mason is also a building with a wonderful history. The building manager in 1981 was 61-year-old Elsie "Consorcia" Guerrero, a delightful Filipina who came to the U.S. from Hawaii in 1945 and later raised her five children at 1204 Mason over two decades. We renamed 1204 Mason as "The Consorcia" after Elsie's passing in 1996.

In 1983, Chinatown CDC staff and board members negotiated the first Chinatown Rehabilitation Loan Fund with San Francisco Federal Savings, which earmarked a $10 million loan pool for low-interest renovation loans to property owners. This partnership was one of the first outcomes of the Chinatown Community Reinvestment Conference we sponsored the year before to educate community lenders about the Community Reinvestment Act, which became law in 1977. The conference was the first substantive dialogue with financial institutions on ways they could embrace community lending. With San Francisco Federal Savings, we had improved more than 150 units of existing housing in over two dozen buildings in Chinatown and North Beach. The most notable project was the Min Yee Building on Grant Avenue owned by the Loong Kong Tien Yee Association. The three upper floors of the building—the association headquarters and two residential floors—had been vacant for a decade and a half, after a devastating fire in 1966. We provided technical assistance to Loong Kong and helped package the $900,000 loan to SF Federal, which resulted in 20 new studio apartments. This partnership with a Chinatown family association was an important experience in learning the process of being a technical assistance provider to a private owner. The Min Yee Building was also important symbolically in showing our commitment to working collaboratively with Chinatown property owners.

Wharf Plaza I and II was the first housing development partnership we formed with private developers. Gerson Bakar and the Pacific Union Company were major Bay Area developers. Gerson had met with CCBH in 1977 to gain support for the project, which was connected to the new multi-block Levi Plaza project on the Northern Waterfront as a headquarters for Levi Strauss, housing, and commercial space. In lieu of incorporating affordable housing into the project, which was encouraged in the Northern Waterfront Plan, Gerson and Pacific Union had acquired a former Bank of America warehouse and an adjacent site on Francisco and Bay Streets, and proposed to build affordable units there. The Chinatown CDC, under the leadership of Fei and Board Chair Wayne Hu, and with the support of the Mayor's Office of Community Development, became a limited partner in the new 220-unit Wharf Plaza Project, which eventually opened in June of 1982 as the single largest Section 8 project at the time in San Francisco.

The Council of Community Housing Organizations

As Chinatown CDC gained experience in housing development, we learned that progressive housing policy advocacy was essential to ensure sufficient resources to develop, acquire, and renovate affordable housing. By the end of our first decade, the Affordable Housing Movement in San Francisco was well underway. Many new nonprofit housing developers had formed in San Francisco and the greater Bay Area supported by new intermediaries such as the Local Initiatives Support Corporation and networks including the Non

FEI TSEN

Vivian "Fei" Tsen was the first Housing Director for Chinatown CDC in 1979, developing the organization's initial affordable housing strategy. When I first met Fei in the early 1970s she was a housing consultant with Community Economics based in Berkeley and struck me as a prototypical Berkeley hippie, albeit of an Asian American variety, with her granny dresses and horn-rimmed glasses. Fei has since been an accomplished Bay Area planner and housing consultant for more than four decades.

As a member of the San Francisco Redevelopment Commission, Fei spearheaded planning for the Yerba Buena Center's award-winning Children's Play Area. She has been active in scores of planning and environmental organizations, including SPUR and the Greenbelt Alliance, and in 1988 was named as a Loeb Fellow of the Harvard University Graduate School of Design. Fei has been an active board member of Chinatown CDC, serving as Board Chair from 2011–13, leading the Gordon Chin Leadership Campaign in my honor.

Profit Housing Association of Northern California. Banks were becoming active partners in the financing of affordable housing. Local government was starting to see nonprofit developers not only as advocates, but also as part of the affordable housing delivery system. But, the establishment of this new industry did not just happen overnight, not without a great deal of community advocacy and organizing.

In 1978, the Council of Community Housing Organizations (CCHO) was formed as a San Francisco coalition of community organizations concerned about affordable housing. The new network was not limited to nonprofit developers, but included tenant and community organizations as well. From the outset, CCHO was led by a strong board of community representatives and staffed by longtime activists Calvin Welch and Rene Cazenave. One of CCHO's earliest campaigns was to redirect San Francisco's Community Development Block Grant (CDBG) funding away from the San Francisco Redevelopment Agency and into nonprofit, community organizations.

Since the CDBG Program had started in 1975, San Francisco's annual CDBG allocation from HUD was $30 million a year, of which a large percentage (between 25–35%) each year was allocated to the Redevelopment Agency. In 1980, CCHO filed an Administrative Complaint to HUD arguing that funding allocations were not benefiting low- and moderate-income residents as required by the CDBG legislation.

As a result of the CCHO complaint and a concerted advocacy and organizing effort, San Francisco's CDBG allocations over the next decade increasingly reduced funding to the Redevelopment Agency. Funding for nonprofit CDCs increased, recognized as a program component of the CDBG program, and San Francisco established an annual commitment of $5 million for site acquisition and housing rehabilitation. This was a historic redirection of resources and served as a benchmark for the Community Development Movement across the country.

Working alongside the San Francisco Tenant Movement, which succeeded in achieving rent control (albeit a more moderate version than tenants sought) in San Francisco in 1979, CCHO and allies also pushed through in 1981 the first office/housing linkage ordinance in the country. Called the Office Housing Production Program (OHPP) it required large new office buildings to develop affordable housing or pay an in lieu fee to mitigate the new housing demand these new office buildings were generating. The OHPP would result in more than $40 million in housing financing over the next decade.

By the end of the 1980s, the Community Development and Affordable Housing Movements were fully established in the San Francisco. The Council of Community Housing Organizations had emerged as a respected and at times powerful player in San Francisco public policy, with strong relationships with the tenant and environmental movements, and to some extent, organized labor. The political context in San Francisco had changed as well, with the advent of district elections of San Francisco supervisors in 1976, which provided greater access to neighborhood issues and organizations.

In our first decade, the Chinatown CDC had developed a track record in housing rehabilitation and had acquired and renovated six housing projects providing 275 units of affordable housing in Chinatown, North Beach, and the Tenderloin. We also assisted private property owners with rehabilitation and technical assistance. Chinatown was experiencing great momentum from the completion of other important Chinatown housing projects in 1982, including both the Mei Lun Yuen and the Chinatown YWCA Senior Housing project. By decade's end, we were recognized as a strong, creative, and effective organization, but we were also tested by many challenging issues. None of these issues would challenge us as greatly as the horrific events that would occur in Chinatown's Ping Yuen housing project in August of 1978.

CHAPTER 9

The Ping Yuen Rent Strike

AFTER 10:00 P.M. on August 23, 1978, Julia Wong was brutally raped and murdered at the Ping Yuen North public housing project in Chinatown. The 19-year-old resident, barely 5 feet tall and 100 pounds, was coming home from her job at a Chinatown garment factory. She had to walk up a dark stairway that night as the elevator was not working, which was a frequent occurrence. Julia was accosted and raped in the stairwell on the sixth floor of the 12-story building on Pacific and Stockton Streets, and then thrown over the railing into the courtyard below. Since she appeared to her rapist to be still alive, he went down to retrieve her body, which he then carried back up to the sixth floor to be thrown off once again. Her perpetrator had gone into Ping Yuen North after a night of drinking on the nearby Broadway strip. This was what the San Francisco Police Department reported after its investigation and subsequent arrest of a suspect, who lived in a hotel on Broadway.

The horrific murder of Julia Wong shocked all of Chinatown, particularly the residents of the Ping Yuen projects. They experienced crime but nothing this violent had happened before. Residents knew the rise in crime was not caused by Ping Yuen residents or other Chinatown residents. They believed crime usually came after closing time at the many bars in the Broadway area. The Ping Yuen projects were not secured by any gates or fences. To young activists like me, the murder of Julia Wong was as devastating, sensational, and senseless as the murder of Chinatown Youth Services Director Barry Fong Torres in 1972. It was something that affected us all very personally (especially myself, as my family members lived there). For many years after the murder, the outside wall on the fifth floor of Ping Yuen North was marked with a red "L" as a reminder of the horror which occurred there. We asked the same questions that we knew had no simple answers: *How did this happen? Could we have done anything to prevent it? What can we do to make sure it doesn't happen again?* Our lives and the lives of the residents of Ping Yuen would never be the same, and Ping Yuen had changed dramatically since those happier days in 1951 when all of Chinatown celebrated the construction of the new Ping Yuen housing development, the first government housing built in Chinatown.

Prior to the building of Ping Yuen, Chinatown's physical infrastructure had remained largely unchanged since it was rebuilt after the Great Earthquake and Fire of 1906. Chinatown housing was mostly single room occupancy hotels built for bachelors. Chinatown needed larger apartments to accommodate the growth of Chinese American families, who had limited options to purchase or rent outside of the community due to racial discrimination. Residents had waged a decade-long campaign for the new housing during WWII.

One of my favorite pictures of old Chinatown shows a scene on Pacific Avenue in 1951. Pacific Avenue was closed off to traffic between Kearny Street and Grant Avenue, and the street was wall-to-wall people. The open air walkways of the sixth floor of the Ping Yuen project were jam-packed with lucky new residents looking down at the crowd. Banners proudly proclaimed the *Dedication Ping Yuen* (Chinese for "Tranquil Garden").

Chinatown leaders felt that new government housing was not only a critical community need, but also symbolically important in its recognition of the Chinese American contribution to the war effort. Chinese Americans participated in the armed forces and in the war effort at home, working in the Hunters Point Shipyards, in civil defense, and in raising funds for war relief efforts. Chinatown and Chinese Americans were loyal and patriotic—and they proved it. I tell young Chinatown activists and veteran Chinatown activists who believed that the Movement started with the I Hotel that the fight for Ping Yuen in the 1940s was really Chinatown's first affordable housing campaign. The completion in 1951 of the Ping Yuen East project at 655 Pacific was followed in 1952 by Ping Yuen Central at 711–795 Pacific and Ping Yuen West at 895 Pacific. These three six-story complexes with 240 new apartments were joined by the construction in 1962 of Ping Yuen North, a twelve-story high-rise apartment complex of 194 apartments at 838 Pacific, bringing the total for all four Ping Yuen projects to 434 units, which at the time comprised the majority of family-sized apartments in the community.

The Ping Yuen Residents Improvement Association

Founded in 1966, the Ping Yuen Residents Improvement Association (PYRIA) is the oldest of the five grass roots groups that founded the Chinatown CDC. We established an early relationship with this group, working with them on various improvement projects using CDBG funding. One of the earliest projects that we worked on with Ping Yuen was planning for their first community center. We identified a former storage room at Ping Yuen North for conversion into a community center and headquarters for the association, a place for meetings and events and programs including food giveaways and youth tutoring. We gained approval from the San Francisco Housing Authority and $134,000 in CDBG funding. A second project was the renovation of a new child care center at 799 Pacific. We secured $50,000 from CDBG for the child care center renovation, which was completed in 1981 and served 24 infants and 32 preschool children.

These projects helped build a solid relationship with PYRIA. We worked with tenant leaders, including George Lee, Mrs. Chang Jok Lee, Louise Yee, Watson Lee, and many other members of the PYRIA board, which became more active in the late 1970s due in large part to these early improvement projects. Further, the San Francisco Housing Authority knew that they had to do more in Ping Yuen, since Chinatown organizations were already supporting the tenants, including the Chinatown CDC, Self-Help for the Elderly, the Asian Law Caucus, and the San Francisco Neighborhood Legal Assistance Foundation. These community relationships would prove important as events unfolded in 1977 and 1978.

When the murder of Julia Wong happened, the Ping Yuen tenants got together and decided they needed to take action. On August 25, two days after the crime, the tenants issued a press release demanding that Housing Authority Director Carl Williams beef up security by hiring armed guards in the evening and immediately repairing the elevators in all four Ping Yuen buildings. The tenants also asked to amend their CDBG request to emphasize security improvements. In September, Williams requested that SFPD include Ping Yuen North on their walking beats and asked the Housing Authority Commission to declare a state of emergency to expedite security improvements. The Housing Authority appointed a committee to prepare designs and cost estimates for new gates and fences but couldn't get approval to hire new security guards. Meanwhile, the tenants were incensed by comments made by Housing Authority Commissioners that new gates and fences would present a negative image to tourists coming to Chinatown.

MRS. CHANG JOK LEE

Everyone knows Mrs. Chang Jok Lee as "Mrs. Lee." She has been a stalwart tenant leader from the 1960s, longer than most of us activists, and she is still doing it as a leader of the Ping Yuen Residents Improvement Association. Mrs. Lee had a difficult upbringing as a Chinese woman in Japan; married George Lee, a G.I. she met toward the end of WWII; emigrated with her husband to San Francisco in 1950; and raised eight children in the Ping Yuen public housing project.

Mrs. Lee, George Lee, and two of their children were at the I Hotel the night of that fateful eviction, August 4, 1977, and the pain of the eviction changed her life, making her a determined organizer and advocate. Her skills served her well, leading the Ping Yuen tenants in the aftermath of the rape and murder of Julia Wong in 1978 and the resulting successful rent strike. A solid, progressive tenant activist, Mrs. Lee has been a great inspiration to me.

Security had been a major concern of the Ping Yuen tenants long before the Wong murder. For example, the Ping Yuen Tenants Association voiced strong concerns about security and the lack of maintenance at a meeting in February 1977 with San Francisco Housing Authority Director Walter Scott at the Housing Authority Commission and before the Mayor's Criminal Justice Council. The Chinatown CDC helped the tenants to follow up on their appeals for help. In November of 1977, the CRC and Asian Law Caucus helped the tenants produce a newsletter to all tenants outlining their complaints and requests to the Housing Authority, which led to a tenants association meeting with the San Francisco Police Department and San Francisco Supervisor John Molinari. At the meeting, tenants requested CDBG funding for security improvements in all four Ping Yuen projects— including new gates, screens, and fences. The tenants were grateful for Molinari's support but were frustrated with the Housing Authority, which said it had no budget.

On September 27, 1978, the Ping Yuen Tenants Association informed the Housing Authority that the tenants would start a rent strike on October 1, 1978, which would last until security measures were implemented. The tenants were formally represented by a legal team headed by Edwin Lee and including Jack Lee of the Asian Law Caucus and Jill Nelson of the San Francisco Neighborhood Legal Assistance Foundation. The Asian Law Caucus helped establish an escrow account at the Chinatown Federal Savings bank for tenants to deposit their rents. The Housing Authority warned the tenants that going on strike was ill-advised and on October 15th issued 14-day notices to the 200 residents who had withheld rent.

On November 18, 1978, a negotiating team was set up with representatives of the Housing Authority and the Ping Yuen Tenants Association. Supervisors John Molinari and Gordon Lau acted as mediators. The first issue raised by the tenants and Ed Lee was the 14-day eviction orders, which the Housing Authority agreed to withdraw as a matter of good faith. The negotiating team met four times in November and December. At the third meeting, Molinari suggested a two-phase approach, with an immediate, temporary security program until more permanent measures could be evaluated over a five-month period. On December 22, three days before Christmas, a tentative agreement was reached to end the three-month strike:

1. Four full-time security guards stationed at night in each of the four Ping Yuen buildings for a one-year period ending September 30, 1979;

2. Full-time bilingual personnel to be hired by January 1979;

3. Repairs to all elevators with weekly checks for operation;

4. A new maintenance station established by September 30, 1979;

5. New gates and fences for all areas of access, and new window bars for all units.

The Ping Yuen rent strike, the largest and longest rent strike in the history of the San Francisco Housing Authority, was over.

The historical importance of the rent strike, then and now, is the courage shown by the tenants in taking what was an unheard of action against their landlord and against the government. It was not only the most successful rent strike in San Francisco public housing, it was one of the largest rent strikes in any type of housing, with more than 200 tenants risking their housing to demand safety for their families and neighbors.

There were other important lessons from the rent strike, notably the importance of strong community-wide support for the tenants, as exemplified by groups such as Cameron House and Self-Help for the Elderly. Also key was a strong legal team, which was a collaboration of the Asian Law Caucus and SF Neighborhood Legal Assistance. Of further importance was citywide support from the San Francisco Public Housing Tenants Association and many other neighborhood associations, as well as political leadership from Supervisors Molinari and Lau. Since 1978, the Ping Yuen Tenants

Association has continued to be a strong advocate for their neighbors and actively supports affordable housing and community issues in San Francisco.

At a press conference in 1978 during the Ping Yuen rent strike, I stood next to a 25-year-old, fiery, and long-haired Ed Lee, who promised "We will use whatever avenues we have to make the Housing Authority responsible to the tenants." At the time, I don't think either of us had any idea what the future would bring for us 33 years later when he would become mayor in charge of that responsibility. *What goes around, comes around.*

CHAPTER 10

Saving Residential Hotels

CAROL CHEUNG IS a resident at the Tower Hotel on upper Grant Avenue, a 33-room single-room occupancy hotel that Chinatown CDC acquired and renovated in 1984. In a meeting at the Chinatown CDC in 2000, she said:

> Five years ago, I found out I had nasal cancer. I went through the agonizing treatment of chemotherapy and radiation. I lost weight. I could not eat. I had no energy. I was disfigured and alone. I thought I was going to die. I could only pray for God's mercy. Because I have a clean, well-lighted, and comfortable home at the Tower Hotel, I gradually recovered. Now I am gaining my weight back slowly. The two things I am most thankful for are my housing at the Tower and my cancer support group.

I will never forget what Carol said then, and every time I see her in Chinatown it lifts my spirit to know the strength of people like Carol and to know that we had a little to do with her recovery. There are thousands of people like Carol all over San Francisco. They live in single-room occupancy (SRO) residential hotels in San Francisco's Tenderloin, Mission, South of Market, and in Chinatown. When people hear the term "SRO," they may think it means "standing room only," which may not be that far off, as many of our overcrowded low-income neighborhoods like Chinatown do feel like that.

Residential hotels have been an important resource for housing poor and working-class Americans for over a century. They were built in most major U.S. cities at the end of the 19th century to house a blue collar workforce that worked in our factories making shoes and appliances, tools and garments. In coastal cities or rural areas, the hotels also provided seasonal housing for cannery workers, merchant marine, and migrant agricultural workers. They were called tenements, dormitories, and flophouses. In San Francisco Chinatown, residential hotels housed Chinese and Filipino male workers who built American railroads, panned for gold, or worked the fields of the Central Valley. Because of America's discriminatory immigration policy, their wives and daughters in China were not allowed to immigrate. So, Chinatown and many other Asian American communities resembled male-dominated company towns where workers lived in dormitory conditions—the cheapest housing available.

But by the 1960s and 1970s, residential hotels became less valued, as American manufacturing declined. SROs became housing of last resort and experienced new problems as other populations became dependent on them, including people with mental illness after the deinstitutionalization of mental hospitals. The absence of new affordable housing due to cuts in federal support for low-income housing put added pressure on residential hotels to house the poorest of the poor. Many American cities saw their residential hotels become substandard housing and dangerous places. But, they also occupied valuable central city real estate that realtors and developers thought could be put to better use.

A Movement to Preserve Residential Hotels

The attitude toward single-room hotels started to shift in the early 1980s. Neighborhoods started to fight back. The battles in San Francisco's South of Market (once home to over 40,000 SRO rooms) against the Yerba Buena Redevelopment Plan led to the demolition of more than 3,200 residential hotel units, just as the International Hotel struggle highlighted the threat to residential hotel housing on the fringe of the Financial District. Similar uprisings in West Coast cities started a new movement to preserve residential hotels.

San Francisco groups organized. The North of Market Planning Coalition in the Tenderloin, led by Brad Paul, worked with activist groups in the Mission District, the Chinatown Coalition for Better Housing, and Chinatown CDC to mobilize for major changes in public policy to save residential hotel housing. We were assisted by outstanding attorneys, including the San Francisco Neighborhood Assistance Foundation, the Asian Law Caucus (represented by Ed Lee), and the Tenderloin Housing Clinic (represented by Randy Shaw). Brad Paul and Randy Shaw championed the preservation of SRO hotels in the Tenderloin and developed much of the policy and legal strategies needed to accomplish this goal. They also led concerted efforts to push nonprofit ownership and management of the SRO housing stock in San Francisco.

Under the leadership of Leroy Looper and Kathy Looper, Reality House West developed the first successful nonprofit SRO project in the Western

LEROY LOOPER

A former street addict in Harlem and an ex con, Leroy was known as the Mayor of San Francisco's Tenderloin. He and his wife, Kathy, founded Reality House West in 1969, one of the first mental health agencies in the Tenderloin. They developed the Cadillac Hotel in 1977, one of the first "supportive housing" projects in the nation. The hotel was the model that Chinatown CDC and many other community developers emulated in preserving and designing residential hotels as affordable housing.

Leroy was a national leader for many causes. He founded the Tenderloin Aids Network and was one of the founders of the nationally renowned YouthBuild USA program. In their "private lives," Leroy and Kathy somehow found time to purchase and operate Chateau Agape, a board-and-care facility for the mentally ill, and to raise a wonderful family including a son, Malik, who worked for Chinatown CDC for many years. Leroy Looper passed away at the age of 86 on that fateful date of September 11, 2001. Leroy was a champion and a hero to me, one of the most impressive people I have ever met, and I miss him dearly.

United States. The Cadillac Hotel was a wonderful building at 380 Eddy Street, built after the 1906 San Francisco Earthquake. Once home to a wealthy clientele, the hotel fell on rough times until Reality House West purchased it in 1977 to house former convicts and Tenderloin seniors. The Cadillac had a colorful San Francisco history, and its ballroom was once home to Newman's Gym, one of the main boxing establishments in post-War San Francisco where both Muhammad Ali and Mayor Willie Brown had worked out. The Cadillac provided a vision for other San Francisco neighborhoods, including Chinatown, of what was possible in older SRO buildings given community nonprofit leadership, supportive services, and sufficient resources. And Leroy Looper taught many young leaders like myself, Brad Paul, and Randy Shaw that our larger vision must be about both changing neighborhoods and changing lives.

While the International Hotel was the most high-profile of all residential hotel battles in Chinatown, the problem of residential hotel displacement was widespread. We started to see a new wave of displacement in the 1970s. From 1970 to 1980, Chinatown lost over 1,700 units of housing; of these, 731 were residential hotel units. The problem took on different dimensions in various San Francisco neighborhoods. In the Tenderloin, home to over 15,000 residential hotel units, the major problem was SROs being converted to tourist hotels to serve the adjacent Union Square shopping district. The Mission District experienced a wave of fires, many of them deemed arson by the San Francisco Fire Department. In Chinatown, SROs were being converted to office and commercial uses.

The SRO campaign, which lasted more than two years, culminated in the passage in 1980 of the Residential Hotel Demolition and Conversion Ordinance, the first such residential hotel preservation measure in the country. The "SRO Ordinance" banned the demolition or conversion of residential hotels, and included a buy-out provision for conversions to pay for replacement housing or a fee assessment to convert. Private residential hotel owners devised many devious ways to avoid or delay compliance. In Chinatown, some owners first converted residential hotel units into apartments and later converted these apartment units into offices. Other owners diminished critical services, such as heat and hot water, in order to force tenants out. In Chinatown and the Tenderloin, the game of musical chairs became widespread—owners would move tenants around within their buildings every 28 days in order to prevent tenants from gaining legal protections under the City's rent stabilization ordinance.

Such problems led to the strengthening of the SRO Ordinance twice in the mid 1980s. One important amendment gave community organizations the right to sue under the ordinance. Originally, only residents had such standing, and many hotels were converted before community organizations even knew about it. While the SRO Ordinance was strengthened over time, we believed stronger action was needed to address the egregious violations.

In April 1984, with the support of Supervisor John Molinari, we at Chinatown Resource Center and CCBH achieved passage at the San Francisco Board of Supervisors of the Chinatown–North Beach Residential Hotel Conversion Moratorium, a one-year outright ban of any conversion or demolition, with no provision for owners to offer payments to the City to buy out their housing obligation. This was a critical interim measure in our efforts to preserve Chinatown housing in advance of the Chinatown Rezoning in 1986.

If the experiences of the International Hotel and Mei Lun Yuen taught us anything, it was that we needed to think about strategies directed at preserving affordable housing in the entire Chinatown neighborhood. Mei Lun Yuen took more than a decade to build, and it was clear to us that it was not enough to only focus on new construction projects while hundreds more units were being lost due to private action and evictions from displacement and conversions of existing housing. We needed to build coalitions to affect public policy towards housing preservation, while also creating positive models to show that residential hotels could be improved to be clean, decent, permanently affordable housing. In our first decade, CCHC did just that in a number of our first residential hotel projects, and we learned a great deal from those projects about how to renovate and manage SRO housing.

After experiencing the process of renovating a small SRO at 523 Grant Avenue, the first residential hotel we acquired was Clayton Hotel, an 82-room SRO at 656 Clay Street between Kearny and Montgomery Streets, located on a key transition block between Chinatown and the Financial District. As such, the acquisition of the Clayton in 1981 was significant in preserving an SRO and in protecting Chinatown from Financial District expansion. At the time, Chinatown zoning did not provide policy or zoning protections from such encroachment fears.

The rehabilitation of the Clayton Hotel was modest by today's standards, with a budget of less than $400,000 to replace major electrical and plumbing systems, create common community space, and add two new community kitchens to the existing one that served its 82 residents. We learned a great deal from the planning and rehabilitation process about City building and housing codes for SROs. For instance, we learned that community bathroom requirements are different for single-sex residents versus co-ed, so the Clayton has one floor dedicated to women residents. The completed Clayton Hotel was dedicated by CCHC, Mayor Dianne Feinstein, and Supervisor Nancy Walker in 1982.

Since Chinatown CDC was the first nonprofit development corporation in the northeast area of San Francisco, it was important that we not only focus on Chinatown. We were a place-based organization, which meant that our mission was to serve all residents in the neighborhood, not only Chinese. In 1983, Chinatown CDC branched out to acquire and renovate residential hotels in North Beach and the Tenderloin. The first in this expansion outside of Chinatown was the Tower Hotel, a 33-unit SRO on upper Grant Avenue that had housed the historic Mooney's Irish Pub. When we acquired the building, Mooney's had just gone out of business and the two upper levels of SRO housing were largely vacant. We purchased the building when it fell into receivership. The court-appointed receiver was Dante Bennedetti, the owner of the New Pisa Restaurant and a local sports legend for his volunteer work at the University of San Francisco. We completed renovations in 1984 with the assistance of the City and a partnership with developer Mel Lee. The Tower Hotel became the Chinatown CDC's third SRO.

The SROs in North Beach had a very colorful history, and the Swiss American Hotel was no different. In 1984, we acquired the 65-unit Swiss on Broadway and Kearny Streets. Beat comedian Lenny Bruce once lived at the Swiss, and North Beach old-timers tell the story of Lenny, after one long night of partying, jumping out of a second-story window and surviving without a scratch. Our renovation process was completed in 1985, receiving an award for excellence in rehabilitation and design from HUD.

The St. Claire Hotel on Geary Street was our first foray into San Francisco's Tenderloin. The Tenderloin was experiencing so many conversions of residential hotels to tourist use that the North of Market Planning Coalition felt it needed a countervailing strategy in order to get as many buildings under nonprofit ownership as possible. The St. Claire Hotel, which we acquired in 1987, was one such project. It was developed with an innovative hybrid renovation. The SRO Ordinance required that the three SRO floors continue to serve the single population they had served historically. But, we were able to convert the other three floors into apartments to house couples and small families.

In 1987, we acquired the Cambridge Hotel, a 60-room residential hotel at 473 Ellis Street. We had originally envisioned the project as similar to the St. Claire Residence we did on Geary, serving a general population. But, in 1988 we were approached by the Coalition on Homelessness about making the Cambridge one of the first projects under the new mayor, Art Agnos, to serve as a model of combining affordable housing with health and mental health services. This would be a new type of housing for Chinatown CDC, which we had little experience with. Even though homelessness was not a major problem in Chinatown, we felt compelled to be a part of the citywide solution to it.

The Cambridge became a great organizational learning experience for us, which was greatly enhanced by the leadership and dedication of Property Supervisor James Brady. Chinatown CDC would acquire two more Tenderloin residential hotels in 1991, the 60-room Hamlin Hotel at 385 Eddy and the 94-room William Penn Hotel at 160 Eddy. The construction planning for all of the organization's SRO rehabilitation projects in this period were led by construction managers Mike Neumann, Michael Weintraub, and Heather Heppner and Tenderloin Property Manager James Brady.

Lessons Learned about Residential Hotels

Residential hotels in Chinatown, North Beach, and the Tenderloin could be very different from one another due to the unique history of how they evolved in each neighborhood. Many Tenderloin hotels were Class B Hotels (just a cut below the high-end hotels like the Fairmont) when they were built, with large lobbies and ballrooms or gymnasiums like the Cadillac Hotel. Chinatown residential hotel rooms were much smaller, some only 70–80 square feet. They were very much worker dormitory housing. North Beach hotel rooms on upper Grant and Broadway were larger than Chinatown hotels, and some had lobby areas. They were often upstairs from lively entertainment uses. The Swiss American Hotel on Broadway was renovated with a large community kitchen and social space on each of its two floors. We sacrificed a few residential rooms to achieve this. These spaces became the social hub of the Swiss.

The economics of how to make these SRO projects work was challenging. The income and financial sustainability of residential hotels can vary greatly. Some may have commercial ground floor income, while others may not. Some may have more kitchens and bathrooms, while others may not. The Clayton Hotel, prior to CCHC's acquisition, had one small community kitchen for 82 residents. We learned that unlike new construction projects, particularly those with federal subsidies, residential hotels had tight operating budgets and could rarely provide for resident services.

We learned that federal government programs have, until recently, not recognized residential hotels as eligible for government subsidy programs such as Section 8 or the McKinney Homeless Program. It took innovation by nonprofit developers and supportive cities such as San Francisco to show that residential hotels could be essential parts of local housing strategies, utilizing CDBG funding, Housing Tax Credits, and private bank financing.

My late Uncle Henry lived the last two decades of his life in Chinatown residential hotels. He was quite a free spirit, traveling around the country as a cook in the 1950s and 1960s. He returned to San Francisco where he worked at the Hong Kong Noodle Factory for many years. In the late 1960s, he lived at the Astoria Hotel on Bush Street and Grant Avenue before this hotel was converted to tourist occupancy prior to the SRO Ordinance. He then moved to the Royal Hotel on Clay Street where I used to visit him as often as I could. I really enjoyed those times with Uncle Henry and was always fascinated by his hotel room, overlooking Clay Street. (SRO rooms with windows cost more). He had his whole life's valued possessions in that 10-by-10-foot room: photos of his family on the dresser, packaged noodles, lots of reminders of his Army days, and boxing mementos. He knew where everything was. His room was not unlike the rooms of older manongs at the International Hotel.

Residential hotels are not just housing. They are people's homes, as modest as they may be. It is important that we understand how lifestyles are affected by living in a single room, and how people adapt to those environments. In 1980, the Chinatown CDC sponsored an important study called San Francisco Chinatown Residential Hotels, undertaken by architect John Liu, Professor in the UC Berkeley School of Architecture. In Professor Liu's words, "The single room occupancy hotel is perhaps the most controversial, most neglected, and the least understood of all housing types."

The study conducted dozens of interviews with a cross section of Chinatown residential hotel residents—single women and men, couples, young students, recent immigrants and American-born—and documented differences between them. The men were more independent, much more private, had fewer possessions, and usually ate out. The women were more sociable, cooked and ate their meals in, and looked at residential hotels as the center of their social lives. The women often had children visit them. The study concluded with detailed recommendations that were valuable in our planning for hotel renovations and management in later years, including common spaces, improved lighting, systems for intercoms and mailboxes, safety measures for stairways and hallways, techniques for improving community kitchens and baths, innovative storage and furniture systems.

I had a great appreciation for such measures, because they are so important to how residential hotel residents live their lives. I think of residents like my uncle Henry and Carol Cheung. They don't have much in their hotel rooms, and residential hotels may not be their ideal form of living. But it is important that they feel safe and comfortable and that they have input into how their homes are managed.

CHAPTER 11

Chinatown Alleyways

CHINATOWN RESIDENTS HAD the least amount of parks and playground space per capita of any San Francisco neighborhood, and the Chinatown Park Rec Committee continued to advocate for a new park for Chinatown, renovation of the few existing facilities, and promotion of easier access to outlying open space areas. The Chinatown Park Rec Committee also considered the streets and 43 alleyways as important potential places that could serve as recreational resources or just places for residents or workers to sit and rest.

Berkeley architect Mui Ho, who undertook the first comprehensive study of Chinatown alleyways, explained their origins in villages in Guandong Province of China from which most early Chinese emigrated:

> Neighborhoods in Guandong grew within networks of tiny pedestrian alleys that used bigger roads as their borders. You didn't enter houses from the street. In Chinatown, simple prefabricated wood-frame dwellings, shipped from Guandong, were set down facing alleyways instead of main streets, distinguishing these passages from other American alleyways.

Chinatown's 43 alleyways were such places. The future vision for Chinatown alleyways was greatly advanced by an important report by UC Berkeley architect Mui Ho entitled "Chinatown Alleyways... Their Potential, Their Future," completed in December 1980. The study, which guided planning of Chinatown alleyway improvements, was co-sponsored by Chinatown CDC and the Chinatown Park Rec Committee, and supported by a grant from the National Endowment for the Arts. It chronicled the historical development of Chinatown alleys (from China to Chinatown), and researched design guidelines for three Chinatown alleyway prototypes: alleys that are primarily residential thoroughfares, mixed residential/commercial thoroughfares, and dead-end alleyways.

Ross Alley

While Mui Ho's study was underway, the organization got started on its first alleyway project, Ross Alley, where my mother and her family grew up, and where I spent the first three years of my life. Ross Alley is between Jackson and Washington Streets and between Grant Avenue and Stockton Streets. As a new organization, we at the Chinatown Resource Center knew that building positive relationships with Ross Alley residents and property owners, workers, and business owners was critical to its success. We established a relationship with the Chinese Chamber of Commerce's Rose Pak and with Stephen Fong, then the President of the group. Stephen owned Sang Wo, a produce and deli store on Grant Avenue. My partner, Dorothy Yee, and her family lived upstairs from the store before the family moved into Ping Yuen in 1953. Sue Lee remembers Stephen as one of the teachers at her Chinese School. Mr. Fong was a recognized community leader, serving as President of the Sue Hing Association and also as President of the Chinese Six Companies at various times.

Stephen helped Sue Lee and me develop relationships in Ross Alley, particularly with the merchants and family associations, which was essential to gain trust and participation in the planning. Both Sue and I had some family relationships in the alley that were helpful. My mother knew Mr. James Jew, who owned the Canton Flower Shop, a long-established Ross Alley florist. Mr. Jew's daughter, Sarah, and son-in-law, the late John Chiu, both became actively involved in Ross Alley meetings. Eventually John chaired the Ross Alley Improvement Association. It was important to build not only trust, but also consensus of Ross Alley stakeholders before any new plans were finalized. We needed support from property owners, business owners, and residents who might not all agree on the improvements needed: Should there be new planting and landscaping and if so, what type? Should the walls of privately owned buildings have murals? Should we restrict commercial loading vehicles? How much new lighting should there be? Consensus on these and other questions meant the ultimate alleyway design would be more modest than our landscape architects recommended. But our goal was not just improving a physical space, but building a sense of community. After much hard work and consensus building, Phase One of the project, repaving the alleyway, was completed in 1980, with Phase Two—beautification, lighting, and landscaping—later completed in 1982.

Advocating for City Acceptance of Chinatown Alleyways

Amazingly, most Chinatown alleyways were not historically recognized by the City as parts of its street grid, and therefore are not maintained at all by the City. Ever since Chinatown was rebuilt after the 1906 San Francisco Earthquake and Fire, our alleyways were either too narrow or lacked sidewalks to qualify as official City streets. Old-timers can remember when many Chinatown alleyways were dirt. As far as the City was concerned, "It was Chinatown's problem."

While the Ross Alley project was underway, Chinatown organizations, owners, and businesses also started to work together to address this unfair City policy. The Chinatown CDC, Chinatown Park Rec Committee, and the Chinese Chamber of Commerce launched a campaign to get all the alleyways recognized and made official, and began dialogue with City agencies such as the Department of Public Works (DPW) in 1978.

Supervisor Quentin Kopp, who represented San Francisco's Forest Hill area, had put forth a resolution in 1978 for the City to accept some six miles of Forest Hill streets (which had been property owner responsibility) for City maintenance and repair. This was passed by the San Francisco Board of Supervisors, but not before Supervisors Gordon Lau and John Molinari both raised the issue of equity between neighborhoods. Supervisor Lau said he would support the resolution if other supervisors supported similar measures for the entire city, especially in lower-income districts. DPW heard this message loud and clear and recommended that 26 Chinatown alleyways be officially accepted by the City in two phases. The first phase would immediately accept for City maintenance ten alleyways that were primarily used by pedestrians. The remaining 16 alleyways, which DPW determined needed repair, would be further evaluated.

Getting the City to finally accept some Chinatown alleyways in 1978 as official City streets was an important yet partial victory. In 1993, Jasmine Kaw, a UC Berkeley Landscape Architecture graduate student, did her thesis on Chinatown alleyways with the wonderful title, "Alleyways: Turning Fish Heads into Fillets." Jasmine would join us at the Chinatown CDC staff as a community planner in 1994, overseeing the Chinatown alleyway program and other programs. It would take until 1998 for the City to finally accept Chinatown alleyways, with the adoption of the Chinatown Alleyway Master Plan, which provided a dedicated source of funding for renovation. The victory again showed us the value of building a strong community coalition backed by political support.

The Chinatown CDC and the San Francisco Department of Public Works had collaborated on the Chinatown Alleyway Master Plan, led by Chinatown CDC Planner Jasmine Kaw, which became part of the City's Master Plan. $2.3 million of gas tax monies was earmarked for Chinatown Alleyways after a community campaign led by Norman Fong, with broad Chinatown community support led by the Chinatown Park Rec Committee and political support from Supervisors Sue Bierman and Louise Renne.

The Master Plan proposed scopes of work for each of Chinatown's 31 alleyways, with estimated costs of $2.8 million (in 1998 dollars) and the understanding that the funding would need to be supplemented in the future. The Plan identified potential new funding sources: CDBG, NEA, transportation-related pedestrian improvement funds, hotel tax funds, and private and community donations. Ten alleyways were recommended for Phase One planning and implementation: Beckett, Commercial, Cordelia, Hang Ah, Ross, Spofford, Waverly (1) and Waverly (2), and Wentworth Alleys. By 2014, all of these priority alleyways had been renovated. However, those funds are depleted. While identifying a new permanent source of alleyway funding remains a challenge, Chinatown CDC and Department of Public Works have earmarked funding for individual alleyway improvements.

Jack Kerouac Alleyway

Jack Kerouac Alley is one of the best alleyway projects that Chinatown CDC has undertaken. In fact, it's one of my favorite places in San Francisco. Jack Kerouac, located between Grant Avenue and Columbus Avenue, right off Broadway, used to be called Adler Alley. It was dirty, dark, and somewhat intimidating in the late-night hours. The North Beach arts community campaigned in the 1990s to get many alleyways renamed for famous writers, poets, and artists. And Kerouac was an obvious choice, as an icon of the San Francisco Beat Movement. The Jack Kerouac Alleyway project, while not part of the Chinatown Alleyway Master Plan, was the first North Beach alleyway improved in the City and also the first alley closed to vehicular traffic. Chinatown CDC worked with wonderful local owners to plan the project, particularly Lawrence Ferlinghetti, the former San Francisco Poet Laureate and City Lights Bookstore founder, and Janet Clyde, owner of Vesuvio Cafe.

The dedication of the new Jack Kerouac Alleyway on March 31, 2007, was truly a San Francisco event. It was a beautiful day, and there must have been 300 people enjoying this wonderful new place—the beautiful planter boxes, the antique light fixtures, the murals, the inlaid poetry on the street. Mayor

Gavin Newsom gave a great speech. Reverend Norman Fong gave a prayer as did Catholic priests. Jazz singer Kim Nalley, owner of Pearl's Jazz club, sang. And before the blessings, songs, and poems, we kicked it off in a real multicultural way with Chinese lion dancers and drummers prancing into the alley from Grant Avenue (the Chinatown side if you will) and an Italian accordion band coming in from Columbus (the Italian side). In the words of Lawrence Ferlinghetti, "We tried for years to get that street fixed, but the Chinatown Alleyway Master Plan did it. All power to Chinatown CDC!"

The alleyways in Chinatown and North Beach are important places in our neighborhoods where families have raised their children and grandchildren. They are the back porches where everyone knew each other and community happens every single day. And they are important elements of the shared history of generations of Chinatown families who have called a Chinatown alleyway their home, just as my family and I can call Ross Alley.

CHAPTER 12

Chinatown Land Use Wars

I CALL THE first five years of the 1980s the "Chinatown Land Use Wars" because it was a time when the Chinatown community was confronted with more threats from private development than it had experienced in the prior three decades. San Francisco was in the midst of economic growth. The redevelopment of the Western Addition and South of Market areas had led to the demolition of thousands of housing units and small businesses. Hundreds of acres of prime San Francisco real estate were either under construction or slated for development. New high-rise office and commercial buildings were proposed for the Financial District and the newly expanded financial district South of Market anchored by the new Yerba Buena Convention Center. Investment capital was flowing in from Asia, particularly Hong Kong. This unprecedented period of growth was supported by San Francisco's elected officials, from Mayor Joseph Alioto to Mayor Dianne Feinstein, the Planning Commissioners they appointed, and most of the Board of Supervisors.

In this economic and political environment, we started to see new private sector development in and around Chinatown. These projects would displace housing, small businesses and jobs, shadow our parks, and exacerbate traffic congestion. They could also change the character of the community, which could turn Chinatown into an extension of the Financial District. Frankly, we were not prepared for this private development, either as an organization or as a community. The International Hotel and Mei Lun Yuen battles and getting a new Chinatown park were still on the front burner as critical organizing issues. We were dealing with the aftermath of the Ping Yuen rent strike and many other issues as a three-year-old organization as we entered the 1980s.

Chinatown's high-density commercial zoning, in existence since WWII, did not protect or preserve existing housing, neighborhood uses, or neighborhood. Small neighborhood businesses were getting displaced by banks and other higher-paying uses. Tenants who lived in Chinatown residential hotels found that enforcement of the Residential Hotel Conversion Ordinance was lacking. And tenants who lived in apartments had no protections at all.

The permissive zoning in Chinatown permitted displacement of residents and neighborhood businesses and allowed major new private development projects with the cover of city planning policy. Three of these projects were particularly representative of Chinatown's Land Use Wars: 1000 Montgomery Street, the Ning Yung project, and the Orangeland project. They were all high-profile issues that captured citywide attention, challenged longstanding relationships, and influenced citywide policy and political dynamics for decades thereafter.

1000 Montgomery

> My friends, my church, my doctor are all close to my home. I hope and pray to spend the rest of my days there.

Those were the words of 95-year-old Mary Ghirardini, who had lived at 1000 Montgomery Street for 35 years, when she heard in 1981 that a group of attorneys wanted to convert her building and evict her and sixteen other families from their homes. 1000 Montgomery was home to Mrs. Ghirardini and many other wonderful San Franciscan women—among them, Mary Stemburger, Frances Brandolino, and Christina Luna—who for four years led a valiant battle to save their 17-unit apartment building on the corner of Montgomery and Broadway, where tenants paid $180 to $300 per month for 1- and 2-bedroom apartments. The history of 1000 Montgomery is the history of San Francisco, a place where the Beat poet Alan Ginsberg lived when he wrote *Howl*. It's a place where Christina Luna raised her four children, including Cruz Luna, an internationally known flamenco dancer.

Anyone who grew up in the '50s and '60s will remember Jack LaLanne, the famous exercise guru and television personality. Tom LaLanne, Jack's son, led the development company that wanted to convert 1000–1010 Montgomery into law offices. 1000 Montgomery Associates submitted its proposal to the San Francisco Planning Department in April 1981, highlighting the unique location, ideal for office space, given San Francisco's booming office economy. "Broadway is a commercial corridor which is better suited because of its noise and traffic pattern, for commercial than residential use." About the Broadway area itself, he said, "The neighborhood is one that is regularly

ENID LIM

avoided by a large segment of San Francisco Society."

Broadway can be a rough street, especially late at night, but many San Franciscans who grew up on or around Broadway wouldn't agree that it is a place where people should not live. For decades, people who worked in San Francisco's Produce Market industry lived here. Employees of North Beach businesses and entertainment industry workers, as well as families whose children attended Washington Irving Elementary School also lived there. And the 17 families who lived at 1000 Montgomery were proud to call Broadway their home too.

When folks in the neighborhood first heard about 1000 Montgomery, they did what every strong and passionate neighborhood would do: they organized. The "Save North Beach" coalition was formed, led by neighborhood activists Anne Halsted, Jerry Petrozzelli, and Stephen Goldstein. They were assisted by a young planning activist Brad Paul, who had been active in the International Hotel fight and happened to live across from 1000 Montgomery. The coalition also included Chinatown CDC. Even though only 1 of the 17 families was Chinese, we got heavily involved, believing that 1000 Montgomery was a watershed issue for housing and land use in the larger Chinatown/North Beach area. Chinatown CDC community liaison Enid Lim became a primary organizer of the 1000 Montgomery Tenants Association. We were ready to fight.

The 1000 Montgomery project was very difficult for the Planning Department. Without the legal zoning or legislation to stop the project and protect housing, the department's Planning Director Dean Macris was left to artful persuasion to get developers to change their projects. In an August 25, 1981, letter to 1000 Montgomery Associates, Macris said:

> In general, we prefer that existing housing not be converted. If the conversion appears to be appropriate, it has been our position that the developer... provide replacement housing with comparably priced, comparably sized units. We prefer that the location of the replacement units be within the general area of the displaced units.

Macris tried the best he could, but to the tenants and their supporters, words such as "prefer" were not reassuring. That left it up to the developer to address those concerns. 1000 Montgomery Associates responded by offering the tenants $2,000 per household to move out and promised to provide replacement housing at a site on 17th Street and Mission, two and a half miles away. That was obviously unacceptable to the residents. The 1000 Montgomery battle would continue to rage for the rest of 1981 and the first half of 1982. The Planning Commission held an unprecedented four hearings under their "discretionary review" authority in October and December 1981 and January and February 1982. At the February hearing, the Planning Commission granted the project a Negative Declaration, a ruling that meant that no Environmental Impact Report would be required and that we opposed.

It was clear that the tenants (Enid called them "The Ladies of 1000 Montgomery") had garnered public sympathy. A *San Francisco Examiner* article by Gerald Adams featured a wonderful quarter-page photo of Mary Stemburger, Cruz Luna, and Mary Ghirardini and generated support from all over the City. In the October 12, 1981, *San Francisco Chronicle*, columnist Herb Caen wrote:

> It may be time to declare North Beach an endangered species. This delicate area, where the sun always shines and spring is around the corner... is now feeling the whiplash of progress.

I was present at the only meeting in Mayor Feinstein's office with both the developers and the 1000 Montgomery Tenants Association. Mayor Feinstein, like Dean Macris, knew that the developer had the planning code on his side, but at one point she looked at Tom LaLanne and appealed to him not to go ahead with the project. Her request, however, was ignored, and the stage was set for the final scene: the February 25th Planning Commission meeting.

San Francisco Examiner reporter Gerald Adams described the meeting scene as "A furious crowd and people weeping ... One of the most emotional

Commission hearings in recent memory." It certainly was that for me, Enid Lim, and the tenants and supporters of 1000 Montgomery. Save North Beach was out in force to support the tenants, and the list of speakers was dominated by tenant supporters, including poet laureate and City Lights Bookstore owner Lawrence Ferlinghetti. On August 12, 1982, at the end of the fifth long Planning Commission meeting on the issue over a five-month period, the Commission voted 6–1 to approve the conversion, with only Commissioner Sue Bierman voting against. We vowed never to let something like this happen again.

The tenants had lost their building and their home, but they didn't give up their fight. Over the next year, they refused to be evicted while their attorneys continued to negotiate for the best possible relocation terms. From the initial developer offer of a $2,000 payment to each household, the attorneys were able to craft a settlement calling for $20,000 for each household (a total of $250,000) to be paid over a three-year period. In exchange, the tenants agreed to voluntarily relocate and drop all lawsuits. The final settlement was reached on April 16, 1984, three years after Tom LaLanne started the project.

I am not sure where all the 1000 Montgomery families moved to in 1982, or how many of them might still be around. I do know that the development of 1000 Montgomery Associates was never completed. They started the process of renovating the building and the redesign of apartments into law offices, but they were not able to complete the construction. We had heard that they might have gone bankrupt.

In 1985 we found out that 1000 Montgomery was foreclosed on by its financial lender, American Savings in Stockton, California. This started a dialogue with Marie Louise Ansak, executive director of On Lok, the respected nonprofit serving the elderly in the Chinatown/North Beach area. On Lok, which had developed a senior care facility on Powell Street, was looking for another facility and was interested in the 1000 Montgomery site. We told Marie to go for it. And we were amazed that she carried it off, driving down to Stockton, meeting with bank CEO Bill Popejoy, and getting an option to buy 1000 Montgomery for $2.5 million.

On Lok announced the purchase on May 26, 1987. Their plans included 36 housing units (450–600 sq. ft. studios) and a day center for the elderly. They later added a Kai Ming Head Start child care center for their employees, an innovative idea at the time. On Lok hired Chinatown CDC to manage the reconstruction. Chinatown CDC staffers Daryl Higashi and Mike Neumann enjoyed it very much, as they were essentially converting the converted offices back into housing. The ribbon cutting for On Lok's 1000 Montgomery center was held on March 10, 1989. And I thought, *What goes around, comes around.*

Years later, when Enid Lim suffered a series of strokes, she moved into On Lok's 1000 Montgomery center. I can still hear her singing during one of the group activities there, Enid's voice was usually the loudest of the group. And I thought how appropriate this was. Enid who organized and became good friends with the ladies in the place they called home, now calling this place her home too in her final days.

Ning Yung and Shadows on Our Parks

The Ning Yung condominium project did not have the same citywide drama as 1000 Montgomery. Most of the action occurred behind the scenes within Chinatown, at least initially. The Ning Yuen Benevolent Association, Chinatown's largest and most powerful district association, made the building proposal. Although never built, the Ning Yung project was a crucible of development issues that polarized Chinatown and put the Planning Department in the unenviable position of evaluating a project with competing Chinatown interests and significant policy implications.

Late in 1981, the Ning Yuen Association proposed to demolish a 19-foot-high building on Stockton between Sacramento and Clay Streets. The existing building had contained three garment shops, two newspaper offices, a real estate office, and three social clubs. The rear portion of the building faced Pagoda Alley, overlooking the Chinese Playground. In place of the existing structure, the Association proposed a $6 million 12-story building with 28 condominium units ranging in cost from $160,000 to $250,000, 3,417 square feet of office space, and 3,260 square feet of retail space. Seven parking spaces would enter and exit on Pagoda Alley. The architect was Dick Wong, a member of the Association.

Ning Yung lined up impressive support for the project from other Chinatown associations, professional associations, and business leaders. Their arguments for support centered on Chinatown's need for housing and the self determination of Chinatown owners to build as they saw fit on their property.

Groups initially opposed to the project were Chinatown CDC, the Committee for Better Parks and Recreation in Chinatown, and Chinatown TRIP. "Opposition" may be an overstatement, as all three groups tried to avoid a confrontational stance, preferring to oppose features of the project or to withhold support pending possible changes. Our concerns included the overall project scale in comparison to most Chinatown buildings; the displacement of three garment shops, which employed 50–75 workers (represented by Ed Lee of the Asian Law Caucus); traffic congestion; and pedestrian safety for the hundreds of children who frequented Chinese Playground daily.

But the primary community concern was about the new shadow impact of the ten-story project on Chinese Playground. UC Berkeley Professor of Architecture Peter Bosselman did a shadow analysis, one of the first conducted in San Francisco, and determined that any new building over 50 feet high on the site would create significant shadows on Chinese Playground. Debate continued within Chinatown for much of 1982. Within the community, there were some family association leaders who felt that rental housing was a better way to serve more of their members and building rental apartments would not involve the association having to sell their building, which Chinatown associations were historically reluctant to do.

We participated in a number of meetings with Ning Yung representatives, including project architect Dick Wong. In one meeting at the Planning Department offices, former San Francisco Postmaster Lim P. Lee pointedly asked, "So what do you people really want?" Within our coalition, we didn't always agree on strategy and prioritization of issues. Some tenant members of the Chinatown Coalition for Better Housing wanted to push for a portion of the project to be dedicated for affordable senior housing. We needed to evaluate whether the displacement of the garment shops was a make or break issue, or to support them to get the best relocation deal they could. Ning Yung was the first major private development project in Chinatown where such a multiplicity of issues (housing, business, traffic, shadows) had to be weighed and prioritized. We decided that in this case, with no direct housing displacement, the most direct negative impact was the shadow issue, and that the environmental and safety issue of children outweighed the housing issue.

Mayor Feinstein continually expressed strong support for the Ning Yung project, and made no secret of her support with the Planning Commission, which at the time was chaired by Toby Rosenblatt. Other members of the Commission did not shy away from expressing concerns over the shadow issue, which was attracting more attention citywide. The *San Francisco Examiner* wrote an editorial on June 22, 1983, entitled "Don't Block Chinatown Sun." A showdown seemed imminent before the Planning Commission, which was to hear the project in July of 1983.

In the weeks prior to the July hearing, Redevelopment Commissioner Mel Lee helped broker a compromise with the coalition of Chinatown groups involved. The compromise came in the form of "conditions" under which the project would be approved. These included

- Ning Yung's full dedication, assistance, and active involvement toward site acquisition for a new Chinatown park;

- Leasing Commodore Stockton schoolyard for after-school play;

- Paying for solar fan studies;

- Paying $150 per month towards Portsmouth Square maintenance; and

- Temporarily relocating the garment shops, giving them the right of first refusal to return to the new project.

These conditions, approved by the Planning Commission on July 21, 1983, gave Ning Yung one year to perform. The City Planning Department, while supportive of the compromise reached by the Chinatown groups, also knew the issue of shadows on City parks was becoming a serious policy issue. It imposed an interim 60-foot height limit on blocks surrounding the Ning Yung site, also making it clear that a more permanent height reduction would be considered. After almost two years to gain approval, the community heard little about the Ning Yung project for months after it was approved. Then word came in 1984 that all work on the project had stopped.

The approval of the Ning Yung project was a major catalyst not only for City Planning to act to protect the quality of San Francisco's open space, but for environmental groups to mobilize on the emerging issue of "Shadows on our parks." Proposition K, the Sunlight Ordinance, was placed on the June 1984 San Francisco ballot to forbid new projects higher than 40 feet that would cast "significant" shadows on any public park. Proposition K passed with 61% of the vote, the first "sunlight ordinance" of its kind in the nation.

Orangeland

The two buildings at 1019–1055 Stockton Streets were commonly known as "Orangeland," after the produce market located on the corner of Stockton and Jackson. Everyone knew the orange sign bearing the market's name protruding out diagonally from the corner. Orangeland would become known as one of the most embattled development issues in Chinatown for many decades. Orangeland would span almost half a decade, pitting Chinatown organizations (who had worked together for many years) against each other, with our respective citywide allies on each side. The issue garnered much citywide press coverage and political drama.

Georo Development Company proposed the project, officially named Jackson Court, on two land parcels at 1019–1055 Stockton, between Jackson and Washington Streets in the heart of Chinatown. Georo proposed demolishing two buildings that housed 70 units of housing for a total of 196 people, including 40 elderly residents and 51 children and youth under 18 years old. The buildings also had 13 small retail businesses employing 40 workers.

Georo proposed to demolish these two buildings in order to construct a nine-story, mixed-use project of 105 feet with 60 units of market-rate housing, 82,900 square feet of new retail space and community service space. Jackson Court had established a development partnership with Self-Help for the Elderly, a long-established Chinatown social service agency. Georo would assist in the construction of a new senior housing project of 70 units of affordable senior housing on an adjoining site, which Georo would lease from the San Francisco Unified School District for 75 years at a cost of $150,000, and then donate for the Pineview senior housing project. Pineview would be financed by a HUD Section 202 senior housing grant of $3.5 million for construction, in addition to more than $22 million in rental subsidies over the life of the project. Georo would also replace the 20 parking spaces for the School District and provide office space for Self-Help for the Elderly and the Chinese Historical Society.

After the project was submitted to the San Francisco Planning Department for environmental review in the fall of 1983, Georo started a series of informational meetings with groups including Chinatown CDC, Asian Law Caucus, Asian Neighborhood Design, Chinatown TRIP, Chinatown Coalition for Better Housing, CBPR, as well as neighboring institutions such as Commodore Stockton Elementary School.

Georo was headed by attorney and developer Richard Lim, who brought on Stan Yee, a longtime friend and an active member of the Committee for Better Parks and Recreation in Chinatown, as Project Manager, and attorney Tim Tosta to advise on negotiations for displaced tenant mitigation. The Pineview project was represented by Self-Help for the Elderly Executive Director Anni Chung and Pineview Board Chair Rosalyn Koo. While most of the meetings with Georo involved Stan Yee and later Tim Tosta, I always believed that Lim and perhaps other silent investors made the final financial decisions about Jackson Court, including what mitigations were offered.

Throughout the next year, Orangeland became a shifting target in the public eye. To some, the project meant 70 units of much-needed senior housing. To others, it meant the displacement of many more existing Chinatown

ROSE PAK

Rose Pak worked as a reporter for the *San Francisco Chronicle* in the early 1970s and recalls that her first assignment was a piece on Hopalong Cassidy. "Hopalong what?" she thought, not recognizing the cultural reference, having been born and raised in China. *Chronicle* reporter Carl Nolte remembers her as "Feisty, funny, and wouldn't back down to anyone." This is a pretty accurate description, and Rose herself took pride in telling me about how much she enjoyed driving all those Catholic nuns crazy in her schoolgirl days in Macao.

After leaving the *Chronicle* years later, Rose, along with Stephen Fong of the Chinese Chamber of Commerce, helped a young Chinatown CDC make connections to the Chinatown business community for some of our earliest programs and projects—renovating Chinatown alleyways, advocating for improvements in street lighting and paving, and securing better trash collection. Rose and I continued to develop a strong working relationship and friendship through many challenging Chinatown issues to come in the years following—Orangeland, the Embarcadero Freeway, and the Central Subway, to name a few—each one strengthening a friendship that continues to this day.

Rose is all about Chinatown. Politics and power are only means to an end to help her community, though Rose often does enjoy the thrill of the competition and the challenge of crafting strategy, the drama and excitement.

seniors, families, and small businesses. Many issues were raised, but the primary ones involved the existing residents. Would the seniors be guaranteed units in the new senior housing? Would the new senior housing be built first, so the existing seniors can move in, instead of an interim period of relocation? For the other existing tenants, what would be the relocation plan, and would there be replacement housing for them elsewhere? These and other questions were raised at the informational meetings, and we did not feel that all the facts about the project were known or conveyed, particularly about the existing tenants in the two buildings that were being managed by Self-Help for the Elderly.

One of the early issues in the Orangeland fight was the argument raised by Georo that the building did not comply with current building and housing codes. A complaint was filed with the City's Building Department alleging that the building should not be preserved because the units lacked individual bathrooms, hence should not be defined as apartments. This led to what the tenants still refer to as the "Toilet Issue." The tenants and sup-porters went to City Hall to protest the enforcement action, and brought new toilets to the hearing as a graphic symbol of the issue.

Beyond the specific issues with the project, it was dealing with our Chinatown organizational relationships that was most challenging. China-town CDC, Asian Neighborhood Design, and the Asian Law Caucus had all worked closely with Self-Help for the Elderly for many years on issues rang-ing from Mei Lun Yuen to Chinese Playground, but in this case we were on opposite sides of the issue. It was a very difficult and emotionally charged period as we questioned and eventually opposed the project.

Chinatown CDC, the Asian Law Caucus, and the Chinatown Coalition for Better Housing believed that an independent survey of who lived in the buildings was needed and that the existing tenants needed separate legal representation. Ed Lee continued to participate, representing the Asian Law Caucus, and the San Francisco Neighborhood Legal Assistance Foundation attorney, Paul Wartelle, and private attorneys Alan Yee and Laura Schwartz were brought in to represent the residents. The survey of building residents confirmed what we had believed—the buildings housed many more resi-dents and families with children and youth than at first thought. We were stunned at the number, 176 people. It became clear that the issue was pitting the needs of Chinatown seniors against Chinatown families, a conflict that would come to dominate much of the ensuing debate about Orangeland.

The attorneys from SNLAF and the Asian Law Caucus continued dis-cussions with the developer about many different relocation options, and I remember many talks with Ed Lee and the other attorneys about different scenarios, but the complexity of the situation soon became clear. The senior tenants at Orangeland were not sure they would be assured units in the new Pineview project, nor how long they may be relocated in the interim. Some residents in each of the two existing buildings, 1019 Stockton and 1055 Stockton, wanted to stay together. Intergenerational families in both buildings wanted to stay together. In the words of Mr. Koon Wun Kwong, the President of the Orangeland Tenants Association, "Even if they find me another place when they make me leave Orangeland, I am scared that I will be forced to move out of Chinatown."

Ultimately, despite much back and forth, and many ideas explored in good faith by both the developer and the tenants' representatives, the magni-tude of relocating 176 people was simply too complex and difficult. None of the relocation proposals were acceptable to the residents who wanted either permanent replacement housing, or to stay where they were.

The first major public airing of the community split over Orangeland came in November 1984 at the City Planning Commission on the project's Draft EIR. We at Chinatown CDC, the newly-formed Orangeland Tenants Association and Orangeland Merchants Association, the CCBH, and other community organizations raised objections and questions about the development. Orangeland became a hot button issue not only in Chinatown, but in the City as well. The "linkage" of Jackson Court with the Pineview Senior Housing project became a major subject of community debate, contrasting legal opinions and planning policy discussions. Georo and Pineview maintained that the two projects were inseparable and that there was a risk of losing the HUD Section 202 funding reservation if Jackson Court did not go ahead. However, HUD spokesman Dirk Murphy, in an interview with the *San Francisco Chronicle* on May 2nd, said that HUD approval of the grant for the elderly housing was not contingent on the commercial project.

While the City Planning process moved forward, the legal teams continued to deliberate on relocation and replacement housing options in the early months of 1985. City Planning Director Dean Macris engaged in these discussions, advocating for more substantive mitigation for the tenants. Macris wanted a more comprehensive mitigation plan given the likely approval of the project and the strong support for it from Mayor Feinstein and Board of Supervisors President John Molinari. In April 1985, Macris proposed a draft relocation plan with lifetime leases for the existing senior tenants and 20-year leases for other tenants at relocation sites to be identified. He also proposed developer assistance to secure new five-year leases for existing retail businesses. Macris said these would be "Conditions of Approval" that he would bring to the Planning Commission at its May 2nd meeting. Both the tenants and the developer rejected the proposed relocation plan from City Planning. The developer said it went beyond what they were required to do, and the tenants said they wanted permanently affordable replacement housing, not relocation. At a meeting later in April with both sides, Mayor Feinstein reiterated her support for Jackson Court and Pineview, and Georo agreed to Macris's proposal for 20-year leases for relocation housing.

On May 9, 1985, close to 200 Orangeland tenants and their supporters, as well as all 12 Orangeland businesses, went to City Hall for a Planning Commission meeting for the third time, lasting several hours before packed audiences and media attention. At this final Planning Commission meeting, the Commission voted to approve the Pineview project. While many Planning Commissioners expressed strong reservations about the "linkage" of Pineview with Jackson Court, the final vote was 5–2 in favor of the project with Commissioners Sue Bierman and Vice President Yosh Nakashima dissenting. In the words of Commissioner Nakashima:

> I don't like to be put in a position where you are pitting senior citizen housing, which is needed, against family housing, which is just as greatly needed. I don't like to be put in a position of having to make a choice between the two. It's not fair to us and not fair to the community... I urge us to seriously consider separating the two projects, so we can move the senior citizen project and redo the other project in a way that the impacts can be totally mitigated.

The tenants were devastated by the final vote. The tenant's attorneys threatened legal action against HUD for allowing the linkage of the senior housing project with a commercial development.

Soon after the hearing, the fate of Orangeland would take a dramatic turn. Rose Pak of the Chinese Chamber of Commerce led a campaign to defeat the project at the Board of Supervisors. Initially not involved, Rose became interested after realizing that the residents would be displaced and that the stores would not be replaced. Rose and the Chamber had certainly been involved in the months prior to the Planning Commission vote, monitoring the negotiations and supporting the tenants, particularly the retail tenants. But the Planning Commission vote galvanized a more concerted effort with the final arbiters of land use matters in San Francisco, the Board of Supervisors. Rose had encouraged Assemblyman Art Agnos to get involved, which he did by speaking at the Supervisors hearing. Agnos was elected to the California State Assembly in 1976 in a San Francisco district that included Chinatown. He would go on to run for Mayor of San Francisco in 1987 against Supervisor Molinari, and the Orangeland issue was in some respects the first salvo in the campaign to come.

Rose Pak was not someone to shy away from a fight, despite the odds. She led the campaign to convince the Board of Supervisors to support the Orangeland tenants and merchants, going against the Mayor in the process. And in the months leading up to the Board's vote, every member of the Board was certainly besieged by folks on both sides of the issue. But Rose was most effective, and it was an amazing sight to behold. Orangeland was the start of a close relationship with Rose that she and I have maintained to this day. Rose recalls that she went to speak to each supervisor individually to make her case, and she thinks that she convinced each person on the merits of the case. She also believes that some of the personal attacks that she received during the case helped her cause. Some on the other side threatened to help get her deported—not truly knowing her immigration status—if she opposed the Orangeland project. Rose recalls, "At the end of the evening, I was able to add seven votes, and I literally sat in my apartment and laughed out loud and cried because it was so intense and emotional."

On August 12, 1985, the Board of Supervisors voted 8–2 to reject the project. The vote no doubt shocked most observers. Everyone was surprised, except Rose. She knew she had the votes. She had voiced her confidence to me in the weeks leading up to the hearing, but I didn't know the exact number of votes she had. As Rose recalls:

> The day before the vote, Gordon and I and a few principals met at attorney Paul Wartelle's office. That's when I told them that I had the votes. Everyone started crying. Then I said, "Promise me one thing, that when the Board votes it down, the community will need to heal and we will pledge to help Self-Help (for the Elderly) find a new location for the senior housing."

In San Francisco politics, anything can happen up until the last minute. Supervisors who voted to reject the project all expressed their support for Pineview Senior Housing as an independent project. Supervisor Louise Renne scolded the Planning Department for approving the linking of Pineview with Jackson Court, saying, "The money for Pineview was in no way connected to the commercial project."

Supervisor Nancy Walker, in introducing legislation to prohibit any demolition of Chinatown housing unless full replacement housing is constructed, added, "We are not going to play families and children off against senior citizens."

Supervisor Bill Maher said, "We should not approve any major development in Chinatown until we have a master plan for the area." Maher's words rang true to the San Francisco Planning Department, which realized that unless the City created a comprehensive plan and land use and development guidelines for Chinatown, they would likely have many more Orangelands to deal with in the future.

In the months after the Board of Supervisors decision, the Pineview project and its board of directors preserved the HUD Section 202 funding, subject to securing a new site. In August 1985, Supervisor Molinari identified the site as an "open air" section of the Broadway Tunnel near Mason Street and suggested that the air space be decked over for the 70 units of senior housing. The Pineview board succeeded in securing the site and raising the funding for the decking, but not before enduring another battle, this time with Russian Hill residents who pushed for the site being built as a park. This new Pineview site had unified support from Chinatown and most San Francisco neighborhood associations. The issue ended up on the San Francisco election ballot in 1988, which Pineview won by a 70% favorable vote, and the senior housing project was finally constructed and opened in 1990.

Lessons Learned

We learned valuable lessons from the Orangeland, Ning Yung, and 1000 Montgomery projects, from decisions and actions that were successful and those that were not. The lessons were about both our community dealing with private development and how development is done in San Francisco, and the land use policies and politics that influence those developments.

From Orangeland, we learned the importance of getting all the facts needed in order to make informed decisions and to be more forthright in stating our positions early on in the process, even when all the facts were not yet known. After Orangeland, all the principal organizations involved in this very emotional experience—Chinatown CDC, Self-Help for the Elderly, Asian Law Caucus, Asian Neighborhood Design, Chinese Chamber of Commerce—worked hard, over time, to keep positive working relationships for the sake of our community. We needed to maintain respect for each other even in the midst of conflict and controversy, because we all shared a love and commitment to Chinatown, and our community could not afford to have prolonged internal division.

We learned that leadership from our Chinatown CDC Board of Directors was crucial. In these cases and many other sensitive land use issues in the 1970s, I sought counsel often from my Board Chairs—George Woo, Buddy Choy, Cynthia Joe, Sam Yee. The Board made the final decision on all land uses that might generate controversy or involve community relationships. While boards can provide staff a degree of "cover" in taking on tough issues, organizations cannot expect board leadership if they are not fully involved. It is not enough to just inform a board, one must engage them throughout the evolution of an issue. And it is important not only to depend on strong board chairs, but also to fully engage other board members, as we did with a very active board Land Use Committee.

From Orangeland and 1000 Montgomery, we learned that tenants who were affected needed independent legal representation, and community organizations had to respect their independence even if we did not agree on a particular course of action. From Orangeland and Ning Yung, we learned that when a development has a multiplicity of impacts, we needed to prioritize these impacts so that community interests could not be played off against one another. And from all three issues, we learned the importance of both internal Chinatown coalition building and garnering citywide support.

In land use policy and politics, we learned that developments satisfying the needs of existing tenants did not obviate the policy need for replacing the housing stock lost to the community as a whole and to future residents. We learned that the linkage of a private, commercial development with a community-oriented project raised complex issues of which project was driving the process, and that the utilization of public resources as part of the overall mitigation package needed to clearly quantify exactly what the private developer contribution was.

We learned how to gauge the policy and political contexts at the time, and what our chances were at both the City Planning Commission and the Board of Supervisors. In poker terms, "When to hold 'em, and when to fold 'em." The mayor's position on a project was obviously a critical factor in a strong mayoral town such as San Francisco. If one were to evaluate our success rate in terms of how the Planning Commission and Board of Supervisors voted, then we won one (Orangeland) and lost two (1000 Montgomery and Ning Yung). However, none of these issues had clear winners and losers. All three issues would later result in something positive happening, even if years later. On Lok would buy 1000 Montgomery and convert it back to housing. The Pineview project retained its HUD subsidies and built on Mason Street. And the Ning Yung project catalyzed a citywide movement to reduce shadow impacts for all San Francisco parks and playgrounds.

The final lesson we learned was not a new one. But if these three battles taught us anything, it was that it was absolutely essential that we get a rezoning plan for Chinatown. Such a plan was needed to guide future Chinatown development, giving developers clear parameters as to what could or could not be built, and giving protections for existing affordable housing and neighborhood serving businesses, address transportation and environmental concerns, and chart a collective vision for Chinatown's future.

CHAPTER 13

Rezoning Chinatown

THE REZONING OF Chinatown in 1986 was the single most important achievement of Chinatown CDC in its first 35 years. While we are very proud of the many individual neighborhood improvements and affordable housing projects we have worked on, the rezoning affected the entire community, influencing what could and could not be built. Equally important, the rezoning helped define the very character and identity of Chinatown. What was this place we call Chinatown? The City Planning Department, in its April 1986 study identified three major roles of Chinatown:

1. A residential village primarily serving its residents;

2. A Capital City serving the broader Bay Area Chinese American population; and

3. An important tourist attraction for San Francisco's economy.

Of course, Chinatown plays all of these important roles. But as the Land Use Wars showed, these roles are often in conflict. They're most pronounced in the worlds of land use and development. The challenge was finding an appropriate balance between these three identities. And achieving a consensus on that balance through zoning policies was no easy task. It first meant that we needed to challenge some basic assumptions about Chinatown. For old student activists who participated in the 1968 Chinatown Demonstration and who hated the tourists gawking at our community, it meant accepting the fact that tourism is important to Chinatown. For those businesses that cater to tourists, it meant understanding that preserving housing was important because tourists did not come only to see pagoda-style buildings, but to see Chinese people living in them in a real-life neighborhood.

The story of Chinatown rezoning is about how leadership and power play out in a neighborhood. It's about how internal community power dynamics can influence City Hall, and how citywide relationships and politics can influence community politics. And, it is about the evolution of events spanning a decade. We developed our internal Land Use Strategy in 1979 and made a proposal to the Chinese Six Companies in 1981. Then in 1985, the production of three different Chinatown zoning plans—one by us, one by the Chinese Six Companies, and one by City Planning—together led to the passage of the Chinatown Rezoning in 1986 by a unanimous vote of the San Francisco Board of Supervisors. As they say in sports and in politics, *Timing is everything*.

From virtually the beginning of Chinatown CDC in 1977, we had been thinking about land use and the goal of rezoning Chinatown. However, as a new organization we knew that something as politically hot as downzoning, essentially reducing allowable height and density of new development, and lowering property values, could not be done overnight. A great deal of research, relationship-building, community education, and political strategy was needed first. The 1970s was still a period when the established business and fraternal associations in Chinatown distrusted new community organizations. The Chinatown establishment perceived the drama of the I Hotel and other Chinatown activism as "trouble making" at best and "communist-inspired revolution" at worst. A fair amount of red baiting was still prevalent, and our young Chinatown CDC was not immune to such stereotyping. So we needed to do our homework and research, not just the technical mechanics of land use and zoning, but on Chinatown itself—its history, community, physical interface with adjoining areas of the City, and perhaps most importantly, its leadership and power structure.

Our early land use and zoning started with a review of past studies, particularly the Community Design Center's 1969 study, "Chinatown Analysis of Population and Housing," and City Planning's 1972 "#701 Chinatown Housing and Recreation Study." In December of 1979, we at Chinatown CDC developed our "Land Use Strategy for San Francisco Chinatown," prepared by planning coordinator Jennie Lew. It outlined overall land use objectives for Chinatown:

1. Preserve the community's housing stock of apartments and residential hotel units.

2. Balance commercial uses...with priority to the preservation and enhancement of retail and services for residential and community needs.

3. Restrict and limit the scale and location of light industrial and business services uses.

SUE HESTOR

Sue Hestor is probably at the top of the list of people developers fear in San Francisco. Since Sue came to San Francisco in 1969, she has led more campaigns to limit high-rise commercial development, protect our parks from shadows, preserve blue collar industrial uses, and save affordable housing than any other San Franciscan. She represented Chinatown CDC in most of the hot land use issues the organization has dealt with, particularly in the 1980s prior to the Chinatown Rezoning. And she did much of this representation on a pro bono basis.

Sue is known for speaking her mind, whether you want to hear it or not. She is also known for her many hats and for the knitting she brings to every meeting she attends, sitting through hundreds of seven-hour Planning Commission meetings in her time. She has taught me and Chinatown CDC staff much of what we know about land use and zoning, and she remains a great mentor and teacher for many San Francisco neighborhood activists.

4. Maintain and improve community educational, social, cultural, recreational, and health facility uses.

5. Protect and enhance the pedestrian environment of the community.

6. Plan and control traffic, parking, and transit systems to maximize resident convenience and accessibility to the retail core, and minimize congestion.

7. Preserve structures having architectural, historical, and/or environmental merit.

The Land Use Strategy proposed specific strategies for each area, many of which were quite prophetic and included in rezoning proposals five years later. For instance, while the Strategy did not address height limits, it did propose changing Chinatown's C-3-G zoning (allowing height and densities of new projects at levels similar to the Financial District) to a C-2 zoning classification, which was the norm for most mixed-use neighborhoods in San Francisco, to reflect the current scale of the community. It proposed a ban on any housing conversion and a requirement for housing above the second floor in any new development. And to address the small business character of Chinatown, it recommended that any new fast food restaurant, bar, or financial institution could be approved only with a "Conditional Use" approval requiring a Planning Commission hearing.

The Land Use Strategy was less of a formal proposal and more an internal document to guide our input into the City Planning Department's impending Neighborhood Commercial Conservation and Development Study of 10 San Francisco neighborhoods. Chinatown was slated to be included in Phase II of this study starting in February 1980. It was our hope that the City's study would be an opportunity to push interim development controls for Chinatown. And we believed a more organized effort to involve many parts of the community was necessary to create an equitable community plan. As our Land Use Strategy concluded:

> Although everyone in Chinatown can see the rapid turnover of small businesses, traffic congestion, poor housing, etc., Chinatown is still a long, long way from any consensus on what to do about these problems ... Thus, an enormous community organizing effort is in store before any permanent system of controls can be enacted. It remains to be seen how property owners, businesses, and residents will react when presented with specific control proposals. Can the community be educated, organized, and united on land use issues before Chinatown, as it has existed historically, disappears altogether? That is our challenge in the 1980s.

A Proposal to the Chinese Six Companies

In October 1981, we made a proposal to and for the Chinese Six Companies. We did not have a close relationship with the Six Companies, which was considered the Chinatown establishment by young activists. However, we had developed a working relationship with Stephen Fong, then President of the Chinese Chamber of Commerce, on Chinatown improvement issues such as street cleaning and repairs. Stephen suggested we talk to Jack Lee, President of the Chinese Six Companies, about Chinatown zoning. We had taken to heart what George Woo taught us—the importance of "giving face" to our elders. George wasn't espousing a strict Confucian code of subservience to the older generation (we were far from that). Rather he was talking about a sense of respect and inclusion of all major community stakeholders that younger activists did not always embrace. So, through the invitation of Stephen Fong and Jack Lee, we offered to volunteer as advisors to develop a plan for them. (I am sure they regarded us more as students than advisors.) The proposal, by Chinatown CDC Planning Coordinator Marilyn Chu, was entitled "Land Use Abstract for Chinatown" and given to the Six Companies in October 1981, before a formal presentation to the Six Companies board on December 30, 1981.

The abstract, translated into Chinese, included many policies we had developed in our earlier Land Use Strategy. It also included a specific recommendation to lower Chinatown height limits down to a base of 65 feet, while allowing for height and density bonuses for new buildings up to the current 160 feet height if proposed new developments included affordable housing.

We emphasized a sense of urgency, given the rapid pace of change occurring in Chinatown for residents and small businesses. The late 1970s to early 1980s was rife with many examples of longtime Chinatown family businesses being displaced by exorbitant rent increases. These included Tin Bow Tong, a 50-year-old herb store, which saw its rent quadruple in 1978; Sang Wo, Chinatown's oldest grocery store; and Wing Duck Market on Grant Avenue. Many other historic family-run businesses had similar stories to tell. Cheng Jeng Book Store, Chinatown's only comic book store; Baskin Robbins, Chinatown's only ice cream parlor; and the Ping Yuen Bakery—all were displaced by new banks from 1979 to 1981. We knew that zoning itself could not solve the problem of escalating commercial rents, but some control over the proliferation of high-income businesses could help decrease incentives for property owners to force out longtime retail tenants. Our proposal and presentation appealed to the Chinese Six Companies for leadership:

> The associations in Chinatown can take the lead... the end result will be a revitalized Chinatown, accomplished by Chinese associations... and a long range protection against the Financial District coming into Chinatown.

Early in 1982, the Chinese Six Companies thanked us but declined to proceed with our recommendations. Frankly, we were not surprised by the outcome, but saw the opportunity as an important phase of relationship building. We had given our elders "face" and tried to put our ideas into a context that respected the historic role that Chinatown family associations had played. The experience helped to tone down the debate about Chinatown zoning, lessening some of the hysteria about downzoning that had characterized much of the previous decade. This greater civility in community dialogue would be important over the next three years when new private development both in and around Chinatown would intensify the call for rezoning.

City Planning Responds

As San Francisco in the late 1970s and early 1980s underwent a prolific period of growth, much of it from redevelopment, Chinatown also faced more new development than it had since WWII. We saw more small businesses displaced. The International Hotel block alone saw 400 housing units lost (the International Hotel was only one of four buildings demolished on the block, with the Bell, Victory, and Dante Hotels also demolished). And Chinatown lost more than 600 more housing units, most of them residential hotel rooms, due to conversions to other uses.

In February 1982 there were 16 development proposals containing over 2.5 million square feet either under construction or approved in and around Chinatown. These included five projects of 4 to 10 stories in the Chinatown core, and seven high-rise office buildings of up to 38 stories on the downtown edges of Chinatown. In addition, there were 12 pending applications (three in the Chinatown core) that were filed but not yet approved. The cases of Ning Yung, Orangeland, and 1000 Montgomery may have been dramatic examples, but they were certainly not the only new projects affecting Chinatown and surrounding neighborhoods.

With such rapid growth in a short period of time, Planning Director Dean Macris and his planning staff knew that they needed to act proactively. Otherwise, they would continue to see egregious development proposals. In 1983, the department began its "Chinatown Planning and Rezoning Study," the most comprehensive Chinatown community plan since the 1972 #701 Chinatown Study. The Department had also been deeply involved for two years in the 1983 San Francisco Downtown Plan. And while Chinatown (with its C-2 and C-3 high density zoning) could have been incorporated into the Downtown Plan, the department decided to do a separate Chinatown study. This was important symbolically as a statement that "Chinatown is not downtown." The Chinatown study process had five Issue papers—each followed by a community meeting:

I.   Environmental Setting: History, People, Land Use Regulations, Development Trends

II. Housing in Chinatown

III. Commerce and Employment in Chinatown

IV. Transportation in Chinatown

V.   Urban Design, Preservation, Open Space, Social Services in Chinatown

The department published the issue papers over two years between February 1984 and April 1986 and stimulated much interest at the meetings. It was by design a lengthy process, and it was no accident that while the first four issue papers were all issued in 1984, the final paper on urban design, which would include recommendations on the more provocative issues of height limit changes and an historic district, was not completed until 1986. The two-year study period stimulated not only interest on the part of many Chinatown organizations, but also provided a framework for the development of formal Chinatown zoning plans by both Chinatown CDC and the Chinese Six Companies for consideration in the eventual City plan.

The Chinatown Community Plan

Early in 1984, we at Chinatown CDC (led by planners David Prowler and Alton Chinn), along with Asian Neighborhood Design and the Chinese Chamber of Commerce, collaboratively developed a "Chinatown Community Plan." The Chinese Chamber was helpful in our previous efforts to produce a plan for the Chinese Six Companies, but with the City Planning process starting, it became incumbent upon each of the three organizations to develop formal policy recommendations for the City. The collaboration was a good partnership of roles. The Chinese Chamber, led by Rose Pak and the Chamber board, actively addressed issues related to small businesses, and Asian Neighborhood, led by architects Tom Jones and Harry Wong, took the lead on urban design. Chinatown CDC coordinated input from other community groups on issues of housing, open space, and transportation.

The plan, published in December 1985, drew on our experiences with the many recent Chinatown developments that impacted the quality of playgrounds, the viability of small businesses, and the preservation of housing. Among the plan's recommendations were:

- Acquiring a new park for Chinatown;

- Setting special guidelines to limit new financial institutions and fast food establishments;

- Prohibiting the conversion of upper story housing;

- Setting strict conditions before any demolition of housing, including a one-for-one requirement for replacement housing.

The recommendations were not new, but our new urban design recommendations were more assertive and provocative than in the past:

- Establishing a Chinatown Historic District including most of the Chinatown core area;

- Lowering height limits in the Chinatown Historic District to 50 feet;

- Lowering height limits in the outlying areas of Chinatown to 65 feet, with a provision to go up to 80 feet for the development of affordable housing;

- Prohibiting new commercial development in the Chinatown core area, but allowing higher densities along the major corridors of Broadway, Columbus, and Kearny.

The Chinese Six Companies Plan

The Chinese Six Companies published its own plan entitled "A Plan for Chinatown" on September 25, 1985, a few months before our "Chinatown Community Plan" was released. The planning firm of Blayney-Dyett and the law firm Tosta & Browning assisted with the plan, which was very similar to ours in seeking a balance between Chinatown's competing needs for space and land. Both plans included a Chinatown Historic District, although the Six Companies's plan limited the district to Grant Avenue. Nonetheless, we each viewed Chinatown's priorities differently. The Six Companies plan, in our view, was too permissive of new development. It recommended maintaining a high-density, C-3 zoning for Grant Avenue and a continuation of most existing height limits. The only major changes the Six Companies recommended were adherence to the Proposition K Sunlight Ordinance (passed by 80% of San Francisco voters in June 1984) in new development around Chinatown parks and the lowering of heights to 105 feet in the former C-3-G area bordering the Financial District west of Kearny Street.

One surprising part of the Six Companies plan was its recommendation that a parking garage on the Chinese Playground be reconsidered. We had thought that the significant community opposition when it was first raised in 1968 had killed this idea. But the plan recommended the Chinese Playground site as one of three potential new garage sites.

"A Plan for Chinatown" allowed development of all commercial buildings up to five stories, which in our view was a clear disincentive for building new housing. The plan also did not prevent housing demolition or go far enough to require replacement housing. (It required the replacement housing to be in place for only 20 years.) The Six Companies plan, if it became official policy, would enable a maximum "build out" of 1.3 million square feet of commercial space and up to 2,600 units of new housing. In contrast, our plan, which prioritized preserving housing, allowed a build out of 470,000 square feet of new commercial space and up to 2,358 new housing units.

The CIA

When the citywide reaction to the Ning Yung project in 1983 led to the City Planning Commission's interim downzoning (to 60 feet) of the blocks surrounding the Chinese Playground, a new group formed calling itself the Chinatown Improvement Association, but it would come to be known as "The CIA." It began meeting earlier in 1983, while the Ning Yung project was still being deliberated. The CIA was headed by architect Tom Hsieh, a Public Utilities Commissioner, and included some original supporters of the Ning Yung project. It also included Redevelopment Commissioner Mel Lee and Civil Service Commissioner Louis Hop Lee. I received a letter in May 1983 inviting me to join the new CIA board—which I declined. The CIA invited other community nonprofit leaders to join this effort to "unify" Chinatown in zoning matters, land use, and development. SF State Professor George Woo, who always taught younger activists to be wary of any group that claimed to speak for all of Chinatown, said, "The CIA only represents the self-interest of its Executive Committee."

It was odd that community nonprofit leaders like me were asked to join a group ($25 dues) that had already staked out an aggressive public stance on the Chinese Playground and Ning Yung issues. At the March 17, 1983, CIA meeting, speaker after speaker berated Planning Director Macris for downzoning blocks surrounding the Chinese Playground and asked that it be rescinded. Macris did not agree and instead referred to the larger Chinatown Rezoning Study just underway as the forum to debate specific zoning and land use policies.

During much of 1983, the official membership of the CIA became a matter of contention. The CIA listed many names on its literature but grouped them into two columns, board members and invited members. My name and many others continued to be listed in the "Invited" column until I made it clear that I was not a member. Other community leaders (including Sue Lee and Anni Chung) reacted similarly to being listed as a member or board member without their knowledge. The CIA dissolved by 1984. Focus and Chinatown participation then became directed into either the Chinatown Community Plan or the Six Companies planning processes.

The City's Final Plan

The City Planning Department completed its Chinatown rezoning plan in April 1986. "Chinatown: An Area Plan of the Master Plan of San Francisco" called for reducing Chinatown height limits and building density, preserving existing housing and incentivizing new housing, creating new use districts for retail and a Chinatown Historic District. The plan was supported by the groups who had been most active in the process: Chinatown CDC, Chinese Chamber of Commerce, Asian Neighborhood Design, and the Chinese Six Companies.

The plan limited new building heights in Chinatown to 50 feet on Grant Avenue, 65 feet in the remaining blocks of the Chinatown core area, and 85 feet on the Broadway and Kearny corridors for projects with affordable housing. For housing, the plan recommended the preservation of residential hotels be extended to include Chinatown apartment housing stock. It strongly discouraged any housing demolition and required one-for-one replacement housing for any demolished housing. The plan's revised height limits were proposed to incentivize new housing and recommended that residential housing be included in new commercial development.

The plan created three "use districts" to guide appropriate retail uses based on predominant commercial uses in each district:

- Chinatown Visitor Retail on Grant Avenue allowing more retail and tourist uses;
- Chinatown Community Business allowing a mix of retail uses along the Southern and Western edges of Chinatown; and
- Chinatown Residential Neighborhood Commercial for most of Chinatown, allowing primarily neighborhood-serving businesses.

The City recommended the establishment of a new Chinatown Historic District to protect the neighborhood's more than 250 historically or architecturally important buildings.

The long-awaited City Planning recommendations amplified many of the visions and policies outlined by the department at the outset of their planning process in 1984. The vision was a Chinatown that continued to play three roles—as a residential village, as the capital of the Bay Area Chinese American community, and as an important San Francisco tourist attraction. But the plan prioritized the residential village role, due to the needs of low-income residents and small neighborhood businesses that served them. The housing preservation policies were an important milestone that has preserved thousands of affordable housing units. And the reduced height and density limits have been essential to the maintenance of appropriate neighborhood scale.

The one area of the plan that did not proceed was the recommendation for a new Chinatown Historic District. While it was supported by the Chinese

Six Companies plan, it became evident that the idea needed a great deal more education and dialogue in the community because of the hundreds of property owners affected. While property owners did not necessarily embrace the housing preservation controls, they understood them. And while many thought the lowering of height limits affected the value of their buildings, it did not infringe on how they could use their building. An historic district, however, would require strict historic preservation guidelines and restrict any renovation to their buildings. So, we decided that the historic district would be a flashpoint that would inhibit support for the overall plan.

Chinatown Rezoning Lessons Learned

Many important lessons came out of the decade-long challenge of rezoning Chinatown. We learned the importance of community relationships built on mutual self-interest and coalitions with other San Francisco neighborhoods. We learned that we needed to prioritize what was most important to achieve in rezoning and what could be addressed at another time. We learned that our neighborhood strategy would be impacted by larger citywide zoning and land use policy initiatives, in our case the Downtown Plan.

Our Chinatown Community Plan partnership with Asian Neighborhood Design and the Chinese Chamber of Commerce was a collaboration based on a strong working relationship established since the beginning of Chinatown CDC. AND shared our values for participatory design involving a broad spectrum of community stakeholders, and their architectural expertise complemented our planning capacity very well.

Our relationship with the Chinese Chamber of Commerce was built through many collaborative projects, including the Ross Alley Improvement project where Stephen Fong was incredibly helpful. The emerging focus, with Chinatown TRIP on transportation issues, proved critical to future work on public transit, a new garage to serve Chinatown/North Beach, and advocacy for the Central Subway.

Strong community relationships must be based not only on shared values, but also on mutual self-interest. The Chinese Chamber's constituency was Chinatown small businesses. We needed to establish credibility with them to get them to see that preserving Chinatown and rezoning were in their economic self-interest. Since they were predominantly small, family-owned businesses, they understood that large new development in Chinatown could impact or displace them. Protections could only come from the government zoning process. The Orangeland experience was not lost on them.

One of the best community outreach projects with Chinatown TRIP in

1981 was a "Chinatown Shopper Survey." It asked Chinatown shoppers two simple questions. 1) "Where do you live?" and 2) "How did you travel to Chinatown to shop?" With community volunteers, we went door to door to every Chinatown retail shop. Our initial perceptions about these questions were reinforced. The response to the first question showed overwhelmingly that the primary customer base of Chinatown retail stores was Chinatown residents or residents who lived in the larger northeast sector of San Francisco. This was particularly the case on Stockton Street, which comprised food, produce, and meat markets and dry goods (in contrast to the more tourist and visitor shoppers on Grant Avenue). The responses to the second question confirmed that over two-thirds of shoppers in Chinatown (again, other than Grant Avenue) arrived by walking. The second most common mode of travel to Chinatown was by public transit, and a distant third were customers who drove to Chinatown.

The survey provided concrete information to show Chinatown merchants that it was in their economic self-interest that Chinatown housing be preserved, since their primary customer base was residents in and near Chinatown. Having this support and that of the Chinese Chamber of Commerce was important in showing that the stakes of rezoning were high not only for low-income residents, but also for the business community as well.

As for the CIA, we learned that in a community as diverse as Chinatown with a broad spectrum of class and ideological differences, no one organization can speak for the entire community. Nor can one coalition of groups claim to represent every interest. On very specific issues where there is unanimity of agreement, such as opposing anti-Asian violence or supporting family reunification in immigration policy, short-term coalitions can be effective. But on more complex and contentious issues such as land use and zoning policy, sometimes we must agree to disagree, hopefully with mutual respect.

Chinatown Is Not Downtown

Chinatown residents and small businesses knew that Chinatown's residential role, cultural character, and neighborhood-based economy would not be served by turning the community into an extension of the San Francisco Financial District. They learned from the experiences of the Western Addition and South of Market and knew that the vision espoused by big real estate and development interests to turn Chinatown into a major investment center ("Hong Kong of the West" as one local realtor put it) was not the Chinatown they knew and wanted.

Understanding the planning efforts of other San Francisco neighborhoods and the Downtown Plan cannot be overstated for its impact on the rezoning of Chinatown. John Elberling of TODCO first coined the phrase "The Ring around Downtown," referring to all the neighborhoods contiguous to San Francisco's Downtown and Financial Districts—South of Market, Tenderloin, North Beach, and Chinatown. Each of these "ring neighborhoods" had started aggressive efforts at rezoning. These neighborhoods had long relationships with each other and aligned with citywide groups.

The Downtown Plan calls for heights in the Downtown and Financial Districts to be coordinated with the "scale of surrounding districts." The Downtown Plan stated:

> The Downtown area should be the most intensive and largest scale retail and office area in San Francisco. Surrounding commercial districts, including Chinatown, therefore should be developed less intensively and complement the functions and scale of Downtown.

After the experiences of Orangeland, Ning Yung, and 1000 Montgomery, the City Planning Department knew that comprehensive planning guidelines and protections were needed in order to prevent the "Chinatown Land Use Wars" from continuing.

Since the Downtown Plan lowered height limits for the downtown retail district south of Chinatown to 80 to 130 feet, it was clear that the Chinatown height limit of 160 feet on the southern part of Stockton Street simply had to change. A similar inconsistency was the western edge of Chinatown, the two blocks west of Kearny Street that abut the Financial District. Since the Downtown Plan's lower height limits went into effect before the Chinatown Rezoning Plan was finalized, there was a period of many months in 1985–86 when a portion of Chinatown had higher heights than portions of the Financial District!

The issue of Chinatown height limits, which was synonymous with the downzoning rhetoric debate at the beginning of the decade, had become almost anticlimactic when the City's Chinatown Plan was completed. The Downtown Plan lowered heights downtown, and the height limits in the ring neighborhoods, including Chinatown, had to be lowered too. There was no choice, and this was becoming evident to community opponents of the Chinatown Rezoning, who still expressed opposition at the final hearings before the San Francisco Board of Supervisors but were resigned to its passage. At the final hearing in 1987, the Board of Supervisors passed the rezoning of Chinatown unanimously, and our 10-year effort was successful. *Timing was everything.*

Planning for Chinatown and Its Place in San Francisco, 1988–1999

Section Three: Revitalization

Chinatown CDC celebrated our 10th anniversary on April 1, 1987. The "Chinatown Land Use Wars" had challenged the organization to build comprehensive strategies and strong community relationships. The 1986 Chinatown Rezoning meant that we would not have to fight endless land use battles. The election of Mayor Art Agnos in 1987 brought renewed neighborhood sensitivity to the City, and Mayor Agnos's newly appointed Planning Commission was very mindful of the impacts of development on neighborhoods, as were Agnos deputy staff appointments of Brad Paul to oversee neighborhoods and James Ho to oversee business development.

The San Francisco of the late 1980s and early 1990s was a big change from the Alioto and Feinstein eras. The influence of Downtown declined somewhat, and the City had more neighborhood leaders occupying positions of authority on commissions and leading City departments. The reinstatement of district-based Supervisorial elections in 1996 shifted the political balance of power more to neighborhoods. It was in this new planning and political environment in the 1990s that Chinatown CDC embraced one of its central values, "Community Building," shepherding an expansion and greater integration of our roles in community organizing, neighborhood planning, and housing development.

Program Director Norman Fong joined the organization on April 1, 1990. It was just fitting that Norman and I share April Fools' Day as our anniversary date. His leadership enabled me to become more engaged in external roles. Norman led a skilled group of community planners Wai Ching Kwan, Jasmine Kaw, Helen Kwan, Ilene Dick, Melanie Young, David Prowler, and Brad Paul and organizers Anna Chang, Angela Chu, David Ho, and Tan Chow. These planners and organizers would lead the organization's program for the organization's second and much of its third decades dealing with ever-challenging community issues, particularly those involving land use, housing policy, and zoning.

I joined the board of the Chinese Chamber of Commerce and started helping on the Chinese New Year Parade. In 1987, Mayor Agnos appointed me to the City's Public Utilities Commission, and at end of the decade

Norman Fong

Norman Fong is like a brother to me (he still calls me "Bro"), and in some ways I feel that I have known him all my life. Maybe it's because our families knew each other. Norman's mom, Helen, worked her whole life alongside my Auntie Bee at the Canton Bazaar gift shop on Grant Avenue, and my aunt and my mom both knew Norman before I did.

Norman personifies the best of what community development is all about: a passion and commitment to a place and the people who live in it. Norman is a real Chinatown kid, hanging out in the streets with his old gang, "The 880 Boys," and starting his soul band Jest Jammin', which is still going strong after four decades. Norman became a youth leader and ultimately Youth Director of Cameron House, a base from which he served as a fierce advocate and organizer for racial and social justice throughout the 1980s and 1990s. Norman became one of the most recognized and effective voices in the

Asian American community, not only in San Francisco, but nationwide.

Norman's social justice values were greatly affected by two early experiences: in the early 1960s when he saw his family's pain when they were evicted from their apartment and then in the early 1970s when he was inspired by the courage and commitment of his Presbyterian Church leaders in their fight for Mei Lun Yuen. These affordable housing experiences were probably more influential than my recruitment (and begging) of Norman to join Chinatown CDC as Program Director in 1990. He became Deputy Director in 2007 and then Executive Director on April 1, 2011. It was Norman's leadership and vision that led to Chinatown CDC's growth and strength in community organizing, tenant organizing, and youth organizing, all core activities that have contributed to the organization's successes and reputation.

Mayor Willie Brown appointed me to the San Francisco Recreation and Park Commission. These Commissions gave me a great education on the inner workings of City Hall, even if it meant I had to wear a suit every couple of weeks.

I also became more active in state and national boards as Northern California Co-Chair of the California Community Economic Development Association, and the national boards of the Local Initiatives Support Corporation (LISC) and the Center for Community Change (CCC), which gave me two very different perspectives on the Community Development Movement. LISC was the preeminent national intermediary serving community developers, and CCC was a progressive think tank leading national policy and advocacy.

A key resource supporting Chinatown CDC's community planning strategy in the 1990s was the Neighborhood Preservation Initiative (NPI), started in 1985 by the Pew Charitable Trusts to identify strategies to stabilize working-class neighborhoods across the country. San Francisco Foundation asked Chinatown CDC to be its community partner for their Chinatown NPI Initiative, which provided a total of $700,000 to the organization over a three-year period, But the Chinatown NPI Initiative almost didn't happen. NPI's premise that working-class neighborhoods in America had been ignored in American urban policy, as places that were neither inner-city slums nor middle-class suburbs, was based on University of Pennsylvania research on working-class neighborhoods.

When our proposal was submitted, it was not rejected outright, but it faced questions from Pew about whether San Francisco Chinatown really qualified for NPI given the Penn research that American working-class neighborhoods could be defined by key characteristics, including 1) a high proportion of home ownership and 2) a high level of voluntary neighborhood associations. We made the case to Pew that even though Chinatown was 96% renter, it was still a working-class neighborhood. (San Francisco as a city was over 68% renter) And we challenged the premise that neighborhoods of homeowners were inherently more stable and committed to those places than neighborhoods of renters. We described the hundreds of Chinatown civic, fraternal, business, and religious associations in this place that Saul Alinsky praised for its abundance of "social capital," unseen by most Americans. The San Francisco Foundation strongly supported our case, and Chinatown was accepted into the NPI Initiative. Two additional awards would raise the organization's national profile.

In 1992, I accepted the National Alliance to End Homelessness Award in Washington, D.C., on behalf of Chinatown CDC, which was presented by HUD Secretary Jack Kemp and First Lady Barbara Bush. I gave the framed original photo of myself and Mrs. Bush to my parents, but I made sure to bring along a copy every time I had an important meeting with Republicans. And in 1994, we were very honored when the Fannie Mae Foundation chose the Chinatown CDC for its Sustained Excellence Award as one of the 10 best community development organizations in the nation. And in 1998, I was honored with a Silver SPUR award by the San Francisco Planning and Urban Research Association.

Chinatown was opposed to the demolition of the Embarcadero Freeway after the 1989 Loma Prieta Earthquake, sparking a concerted effort to improve transportation services to the community. *(Photo by Dave Glass.)*

The 1989 Loma Prieta Earthquake would come to have a profound impact on Chinatown's housing stock and transportation system. *(Photo courtesy of Chinatown CDC.)*

In 1994, Chinatown CDC in partnership with the A.F. Evans Company developed the Tenderloin Family Apartments at Turk and Jones Streets in the Tenderloin, making available 175 apartments serving seniors and working families, and including a large interior courtyard and child care center. *(Photo courtesy of Chinatown CDC.)*

Chinatown tenants and youth rally in support of Proposition B, "Homes for the City," an affordable housing bond campaign in 2002. *(Photo courtesy of Chinatown CDC.)*

In 1991, Chinatown CDC started the Chinatown Adopt-An-Alleyway Youth Empowerment Project (AAA), an important leadership program engaging youth in neighborhood improvement, home visits to seniors, and advocacy campaigns for affordable housing, pedestrian safety, and civil rights. *(Photo courtesy of Chinatown CDC.)*

In 2000, Chinatown CDC acquired the 200-unit Notre Dame senior housing project at Broadway and Van Ness Streets, with assistance from the San Francisco Redevelopment Agency and resident leadership from Mrs. Bao Yan Chan, saving this affordable housing from conversion to market rate rentals. *(Photo courtesy of Chinatown CDC.)*

The Broadway Family Apartments on Broadway and Battery Streets was built by Chinatown CDC in 2005 on land that was formerly the off-ramp to the Embarcadero Freeway, providing 80 units of affordable housing for working families. *(Photo courtesy of Chinatown CDC.)*

The Broadway Family Apartments ribbon-cutting ceremony in 2005. L to R: Enid Lim, Gordon Chin, Mayor Willie Brown, Daryl Higashi, and Rose Pak.

On October 7, 1999, Chinatown CDC and the Committee for Better Parks and Recreation in Chinatown dedicated the first new park in Chinatown in over half a century, Wo Hei Yuen Park ("Garden of Peace and Joy") on the corner of Powell Street and John Alley. *(Photo courtesy of Chinatown CDC.)*

Since the mid 1980s, Ellis Act evictions have became one of the more severe threats to low-income tenants in Chinatown and other San Francisco neighborhoods. Pictured at this press conference protesting the Ellis Act eviction of tenants at 663 Clay Street were (L to R) Supervisor Aaron Peskin, Tenderloin Housing Clinic Executive Director Randy Shaw, State Senator Mark Leno, and tenant union activist Sister Bernie Galvin. *(Photo courtesy of Chinatown CDC.)*

Speaker Nancy Pelosi has been a champion for many important projects benefiting Chinatown, including the International Hotel and the Central Subway. Pictured here with Chinatown CDC staff and board (L to R): Jane Kim, Joanne Lee, David Ho, Norman Fong, Kwong Chack Choy, Gordon Chin, Pui Yee Law, Anna Chang, Thai An Ngo, and Susie Wong.

Formed in 1968 and still going strong, Jest Jammin' is the last of many local Chinatown bands who embraced soul and Motown music in the 1960s. Jest Jammin' has been an important community cultural resource for Chinatown. L to R: (standing) Haley Wong, Victor Ng, Jo Ellen Chew, Brad Lum, Norman Fong, Phil Wong, Jan Yonemoto, and Bill Keast; (kneeling) Ed Toy and Gordie Jeong *(Photo courtesy of Jest Jammin'.)*

The Chinese Recreation Center on Mason and Washington Streets was rebuilt by the San Francisco Recreation and Park Department in 2012 and renamed the Betty Ann Ong Chinese Recreation Center. *(Photo courtesy of Sing Tao Daily.)*

Betty Ann Ong was the American Airlines flight attendant who was the first American to alert the nation of the terrorist attacks on September 11, 2001. Betty Ann and her siblings grew up playing at the Chinese Recreation Center. *(Photo courtesy of Tim Ho.)*

CHAPTER 14

The Loma Prieta Earthquake

MOST EVERYONE IN the Bay Area remembers where they were at 5:04 p.m.on October 17, 1989, when the Loma Prieta Earthquake struck. I was at Game 3 of the World Series at Candlestick Park with my brother-in-law Al sitting in the upper deck watching the light standards sway back and forth. That event itself was historic as the first Bay Bridge Series between the San Francisco Giants and the Oakland A's. The entire nation, expecting to see a ballgame, was riveted with the devastation and seemingly surreal scenes of a broken Bay Bridge, the collapse of the Cypress Freeway in Oakland, and the fires in San Francisco's Marina District.

Loma Prieta would affect Chinatown and San Francisco for many years thereafter. Concerns over disaster preparedness and seismic safety would have a profound impact on the issues of affordable housing, transportation, and infrastructure planning, and on community and political relationships in San Francisco throughout the decade following.

The resilience of San Francisco has been part of our City identity since the 1906 Earthquake and Fire. The courage of San Franciscans recovering from one of the worst natural disasters in American history has been well chronicled, and the miraculous rebuilding of the City within a single decade has exemplified the "can do" image of the City. That courage and resilience was a hallmark of how the Bay Area responded to Loma Prieta in 1989, with the heroism of countless "regular people" rescuing people trapped in the Cypress Freeway and burning buildings in the Marina District, helping their neighbors with food and shelter, and directing traffic at intersections. Our civic courage was met with a calm patience, which to me was symbolized by that sight of Joe DiMaggio waiting patiently in line for help at Marina Junior High alongside his Marina neighbors. He was the Yankee Clipper (and "Mr. Coffee"), but that day he was a San Franciscan.

I think we learn a lot from our experiences with major disasters. We learn about our neighborhoods and our cities. We learn a lot about ourselves, and we are forced to think beyond ourselves. San Francisco writer Rebecca Solnit in her book, *A Paradise Built in Hell,* wrote about the shared sense of community from her memories of both Loma Prieta and 9/11:

> We don't even have a language for this emotion, in which the wonderful comes wrapped in the terrible, joy in sorrow, courage in fear. We cannot welcome disaster, but we can value the responses, both practical and psychological.

In Chinatown, many nonprofit community organizations were on the street immediately after Loma Prieta. The Chinatown NICOS+ Health Coalition of health and social service agencies coordinated Chinatown's immediate recovery efforts and used its collective learning to later develop the first comprehensive Chinatown Disaster Plan. Chinatown CDC implemented our own disaster plan for all of our affordable housing developments, evaluating building damage and checking on our residents.

In the aftermath of the earthquake, many Chinatown tenants were fearful of the safety of their buildings, particularly with the many aftershocks. Chinatown seniors didn't know if there would be another big quake, perhaps in the weeks following Loma Prieta. Being monolingual, they could not read the City Building Inspection postings (identifying which buildings were safe and which were not). As a result, Chinatown agencies found elderly men and women staying in nearby parks and playgrounds, unsure if their buildings were safe. In other cases, some residents of posted unsafe buildings were afraid to leave because they were concerned with the security of their possessions. Others feared that landlords would use the crisis as an excuse not to allow them to return. The issues of disaster preparedness and disaster response, building safety, and affordable housing preservation were becoming interrelated, and it became clear to us that major new strategies in each area would be needed for Chinatown and other low-income San Francisco neighborhoods.

Local police and fire personnel are the first public responders who displayed heroic efforts after Loma Prieta. But, local public safety leaders also tell us that we should be prepared to make it on our own for the first 72 hours after a disaster with adequate supplies, home security, and communication plans. San Francisco's Neighborhood Emergency Response Team (NERT) program, operated by the San Francisco Fire Department, has trained hundreds of residents to help themselves after a natural disaster, and Chinatown organizations have actively participated in many NERT classes.

But there must be resources to support such volunteer programs. After Loma Prieta, Chinatown CDC and many other nonprofits were heartened to receive emergency grants from local foundations, including the Hewlett and James Irvine Foundations. Their grants were made not to help us in our response efforts, but to help our organizations do our normal work, which would be stretched and impacted because of our disaster emergency work. More recently, the San Francisco Foundation created a program offering many Bay Area nonprofit organizations advance emergency grants to be used after a future natural disaster. These are innovative, philanthropic-led programs that recognize that we can help community responders respond, and we don't have to wait for the disaster to happen before we do so.

Loma Prieta taught us the importance of having proactive and coordinated community-based response plans. In Chinatown, NICOS+, a coalition of community health agencies developed the Chinatown Emergency Response Plan, identifying key community resources, emergency facilities, and home response plans for Chinatown. The plan was bilingual and distributed widely to community agencies, churches, and fraternal organizations and residents. We learned that in emergencies the Chinese language media—print, radio, and television—can be critical resources to transmit key information, especially for seniors in residential hotels, many of whom are illiterate and need direct, hands-on help after a fire or natural disaster.

In addition to strengthening emergency response strategies, Chinatown organizations focused their attention on neighborhood recovery, particularly measures to promote and market Chinatown businesses. The Chinese Chamber of Commerce appealed to the City for help in this area from Mayor Agnos, who allocated $2 million in redevelopment funds for a four-year Chinatown Recovery Program, which supported a number of cultural fairs and events, merchant websites, neighborhood clean-up programs, and a small business loan program. However, the two most important and long-term recovery issues facing Chinatown after Loma Prieta were transportation (discussed in the next chapter) and the need to make Chinatown buildings safer.

Brick Buildings

Loma Prieta was a wake-up call for San Francisco to be prepared for the next "big one." After all, it was only 7.1 on the Richter Scale, and the world has seen many more powerful earthquakes. Preparedness meant not only knowing what to do before, during, and after a quake, but ensuring that the building you live in can withstand a major quake. Thus began the Seismic

Retrofit Era in San Francisco, a concerted effort to evaluate the safety of both public and private buildings and implement measures to strengthen them before the real big one hits.

San Francisco embarked on an ambitious plan to seismically retrofit all public buildings—City Hall, recreation and community centers, museums and cultural facilities. Schools and hospitals had long had stringent seismic safety and building codes mandated by the State. But the real challenge was the seismic safety of the existing housing stock. San Francisco's older housing stock, particularly its multi-unit apartment buildings, presented a complex problem of balancing resident and public safety needs with the financial challenge of figuring out how and who should pay for the retro-fitting. One estimate after the quake was that 6,300 units of rental and affordable housing were either destroyed or significantly damaged by Loma Prieta.

The first large-scale seismic safety initiative in San Francisco focused on the City's large inventory of unreinforced masonry buildings (UMBs). The City identified 1,987 such brick buildings that lacked wood or steel framing. (Ironically, brick was the material of choice following the 1906 Earthquake because of its fire-resistant capacity). Of the nearly 2,000 UMBs, most were concentrated in South of Market, the Mission, Tenderloin, Downtown, and Chinatown. Chinatown alone had nearly 300 such unreinforced brick build-ings, over 20% of its housing stock.

While Chinatown did not suffer any building collapse during Loma Prie-ta, a number of buildings were "red tagged" as unsafe for occupancy. Most Chinatown UMBs were cleared for continued occupancy but were listed for mandated retrofit. In 1982, the City passed its UMB Seismic Retrofit Ordi-nance, requiring the retrofit of all 1,987 UMBs over a 10-year period. These UMBs included commercial buildings, but the majority were single-room occupancy hotels housing more than 20,000 low-income residents in San Francisco's South of Market, Tenderloin, and Chinatown. As an inducement to property owners to support the seismic ordinance, the City proposed a UMB Seismic Safety Bond Issue on the 1992 ballot, which passed easily, providing $300 million in low-interest loans to UMB property owners. To date, most of the 1,987 UMB buildings in San Francisco have been retrofit-ted, including most of the Chinatown UMBs.

As this is written, San Francisco is deliberating another seismic-related ordinance, this one covering the City's so-called "soft story" buildings. These are commercial or residential buildings with large ground floors, most commonly garage levels, lacking sufficient load-bearing interior walls, which are susceptible to collapse in a major quake. During Loma Prieta, San Francisco's Marina District had many collapses in soft story buildings, and the City estimates nearly 3,000 such soft story buildings exist, housing over 58,000 people.

Chinatown Planning

Many management consultants have cited the story that the Chinese phrase for "crisis" combines the Chinese characters for the words "danger" and "opportunity." Loma Prieta resulted in a number of Chinatown projects that would not have happened were it not for the events of October 17, 1989.

A number of Chinatown community centers were also affected by the quake. The Jean Parker Elementary School on Broadway was the only public school in San Francisco red tagged as unsafe for occupancy after Loma Prieta. It went through a planning process with the San Francisco Unified School District, and this was an opportunity for the community to propose a new idea, a Chinatown Beacon School. The Beacon School concept, conceived in New York City, created community services centers at school facilities for gatherings and public events in the evenings and weekends, thereby becoming more integrated with local communities. The seismic retrofit of Jean Parker was an opportunity to bring the concept to Chinatown, led by a coalition of Chinatown youth and child care agencies. The Chinatown Beacon Center was officially opened in 1996.

Loma Prieta was indirectly responsible for the International Hotel project as well. St. Mary's Elementary School on Stockton Street, while not red tagged, suffered interior damage from the earthquake. This was impetus for the school to talk with the San Francisco Archdiocese to explore an idea that the school had long desired—a new and larger Chinatown facility to house a rapidly growing student demand. The Archdiocese and St. Mary's then made connections with Supasit Mahaguna, owner of the Four Seas Corporation, which owned the International Hotel site. They eventually secured an option to purchase the site for a new St. Mary's School, and as we covered earlier, a new International Hotel Senior Housing project.

Other Chinatown community institutions affected by Loma Prieta were the United Presbyterian Church on Stockton Street and the Methodist Gum Moon building on Washington Street. The Presbyterian Church was totally renovated after a long deliberation over whether to rebuild anew or renovate the existing church building. Gum Moon's renovation was managed by Chinatown CDC, and a ribbon cutting celebrating its completion was held in June 2013.

We Won't Move

Comparisons with the Great Earthquake of 1906 were constant themes in San Francisco after Loma Prieta. San Franciscans who know the full history of the 1906 disaster know that Chinatown was not only destroyed in 1906, but also was the target of a concerted movement by some San Francisco leaders to "move Chinatown" to the undeveloped Hunters Point area in the City's southeast sector. In the words of author Rebecca Solnit, "The plan was nothing but a real estate grab, fueled by racism."

"Let Us Have No More Chinatowns in Our Cities," was a headline in the *Oakland Enquirer* on April 23, 1906, one week after the 1906 Earthquake and Fire, and calling for San Francisco to not rebuild its Chinatown. For me, Loma Prieta was a reminder about racism and the courage of Chinatown leaders to save their community in 1906.

After the 1906 quake, Mayor Eugene Schmitz appointed two committees to deal with Chinatown as part of his Committee of 50 recovery team. The first committee was the Chinese Relief Committee aimed to ensure that the Chinese, homeless after the fire, were served in segregated camps (the Chinese camp was eventually moved four times). The second committee was The Committee for the Permanent Relocation of Chinatown. Its leaders included former Mayor Abe Reuf, nicknamed "Boss Reuf" for the cronyism that characterized his mayorship, and James Phelan, who had been a leading advocate for the 1882 Chinese Exclusion Act. Among the committee's strongest allies was the San Francisco Merchants Association, which was controlled by business and real estate interests, who issued a special newspaper headlined "San Francisco May Be Freed from the Standing Menace of Chinatown." The real agenda was about the valuable land on which Chinatown sat, which was adjacent to the San Francisco downtown and financial center.

But the Chinese fought back. A coalition of interests formed with Chinatown's major *Chung Sai Yat Po* newspaper, religious leaders, and a group of 25 white landowners in Chinatown who were worried that the big San Francisco real estate interests would take them over if Chinatown moved out. The *Chung Sai Yat Po* published an editorial entitled "On How the Chinese Should Rebuild Chinatown As Soon as Possible," calling for the immediate hiring of attorneys, negotiations with white owners of Chinatown buildings, and for Chinese owners to rebuild without notifying the City officials. "The present city officials are with the anti-Chinese faction," they wrote. Powerful leadership also came from the Chinese Consul General Chung Pao His, who told California Governor George Pardee that "Chinatown must stay" given its key role in facilitating China trade with the state. Within three months of forming, the Permanent Relocation of Chinatown committee had dissolved. Chinatown would remain in place.

I often tell young Chinatown housing activists that the mantra of "We Won't Move" was heard in Chinatown long before contemporary housing battles such as the I Hotel. Chinatown was saved after the 1906 Earthquake and Fire by courageous community leadership and smart coalition building.

CHAPTER 15

Transportation Aftershocks

THE AFTERSHOCKS FROM Loma Prieta that may have the most long-term impact on San Francisco might be in the area of transportation, particularly the Embarcadero Roadway (constructed after the demolition of the Embarcadero Freeway) and the Central Subway (currently under construction). These major projects, and others such as the Central Freeway/Octavia Boulevard Plan, are among the largest public transportation infrastructure projects in San Francisco since the completion of the MUNI metro system in 1982. And each project would impact both Chinatown and the larger Chinese American community in important and at times dramatic ways.

The Fight over the Embarcadero Freeway

After San Francisco's initial response to Loma Prieta, a fight began over the Embarcadero Freeway and whether to repair it or tear it down. It was a typical San Francisco Battle Royal. With images of the double-deck Cypress Freeway that had pancaked in Oakland indelibly etched in our minds, the Embarcadero Freeway raised many issues—public safety, transportation access to San Francisco neighborhoods, and the future of the San Francisco waterfront. And the Embarcadero Freeway fight would have lasting impact on Chinatown power dynamics and relationships both within the community and with City Hall.

The Embarcadero Freeway, built in 1958, was a double deck viaduct that was one of the final vestiges of the San Francisco Freeway Revolt in the 1960s, when San Francisco's emerging environmental and neighborhood movements stopped the original master plan for the state and federal freeway system to crisscross the City and link the Bay Bridge and Golden Gate Bridge. The debate over whether to dismantle the Embarcadero Freeway actually started before Loma Prieta. In 1986, a proposition to tear down the freeway, backed by Supervisor John Molinari, was defeated by San Francisco voters after a hard-fought campaign. The defeat of the measure sparked Supervisor Dianne Feinstein, who supported the measure, to say that the future of the two-decade campaign to demolish the Embarcadero Freeway would be over. Dianne was probably right in her prediction. But everything changed on October 17, 1989.

Mayor Art Agnos took advantage of the public support he received from his leadership during Loma Prieta to unveil his plan to tear down the freeway and replace it with a new submerged roadway. His vision was centered on opening up public access to the San Francisco waterfront. Other advocates for tearing down the Embarcadero Freeway felt that the submerged roadway would be too difficult and expensive, and instead favored a surface-level roadway. But others such as the business community in Chinatown, North Beach, and Fisherman's Wharf wanted the Embarcadero Freeway repaired as a transportation link to their communities. It was a key artery to Chinatown from other areas of the City and Bay Area. The battle was on and would dominate San Francisco politics through much of 1990.

Rose Pak and the Chinese Chamber of Commerce led Chinatown's opposition to the Embarcadero Freeway demolition. We at Chinatown CDC along with Chinatown TRIP joined with most Chinatown organizations to urge the repair of the freeway, an essential transportation lifeline to business, which was down 30% to 40% after the earthquake. On April 9, 1990, the Chinese Chamber with Chinatown CDC and Chinatown TRIP issued a detailed statement, "The Embarcadero Freeway Should Be Repaired!" It raised concerns and criticisms of the Agnos plan and concluded:

> The Mayor's recommendation of a new submerged freeway is an ill-conceived plan, if it can be called a plan at all, having been developed in three weeks, with no broad-based citizen input, with no substantive professional analysis, with no solid information on costs or timeframe.

Among the major points in the Chamber statement were:

- The State of California Transportation Department (CAL-TRANS) stated that the freeway could be repaired by September of 1990, at a cost of $32 million.

- No studies had been conducted on a submerged roadway in terms of soil conditions, seismic impact, or traffic circulation.

- The submerged roadway would reduce the capacity of the previous freeway, which carried 80,000 cars daily, with another 40,000 on the surface road below the freeway.

- It was unlikely that the new submerged roadway would obtain federal Earthquake Recovery funds targeted for earthquake-related repairs.

- The estimate of completion in five years was totally unrealistic, with the environmental review period itself likely to last two to three years.

- The estimated $120 million cost was not based on any cost analysis and would surely escalate.

The Chinese Chamber and other Chinatown organizations felt betrayed by Mayor Agnos, who did not consult with anyone in Chinatown before announcing his plan. We felt that while differences of opinion on policy issues could be expected, the Mayor was not respecting a community that had strongly supported his election. Leaders from Chinatown, North Beach, and Fisherman's Wharf were not alone in opposing the Agnos plan. In the words of a *San Francisco Business Times* editorial:

> Our position is grounded in the unglamorous practicalities of the issue—why spend an extra $60 million to $90 million in funds we may or may not get to have Downtown traffic disrupted for another five years? That is, we believe, the true alternative to shoring up the Embarcadero Freeway.

On April, 16, 1990, Chinatown leaders went to City Hall for a Board of Supervisors hearing on the Embarcadero Freeway. That morning, I walked around a Chinatown that I had never seen before. On this day, everything was closed. Chinatown was shut down. Many businesses had signs in their windows supporting the Embarcadero Freeway and urging people to protest. With more than 1,000 Chinatown residents, businesses, and workers showing up, City Hall was packed. The Board of Supervisors' chamber was filled to capacity, as were the overflow rooms. Hundreds of people were in the corridors and stairway of City Hall to register their strong opposition to the demolition of the freeway. Rose Pak observed that "Chinatown has never been this organized in two hundred years!"

At the end of a four-hour hearing, the Board of Supervisors voted to continue their position for demolition of the freeway, urging further study of both Mayor Agnos's plan for a new submerged roadway and a new surface roadway. We were greatly disappointed, but the vote did not come as a surprise on April 16th, given the public opinions that supervisors had announced before the hearing. The real surprises would come in the two months following.

PHIL CHIN

I first met Phil during the 1968 San Francisco State Third World Student Strike, and later we both lived at 641 Balboa. Phil was driving a U.S Postal truck at that time. He loved to drive and really knew the City—knowledge that would come in handy when he applied to be one of San Francisco's first Chinese bus drivers. Phil and I shared a love of soul music and were just getting into jazz at the time when Keystone Korner was in its heyday.

Phil was a founding member of Chinatown TRIP and Chinatown CDC, becoming our first Board Chair in 1977 (he recently rejoined the board), and was the first Chinese American district staffer for newly elected Assemblyman Art Agnos in 1979. Phil went on to work as City Parking Director in 1989 and as Deputy General Manager for the San Francisco Municipal Railway in 1992.

In the six months since Loma Prieta, the State Department of Transportation (CalTRANS) had analyzed retrofitting the Embarcadero Freeway, assessing engineering, cost, and seismic safety issues. CalTRANS cost estimates had been increasing from an original estimate of $15 million to $46 million as of May of 1990, with a presumption that it would escalate further once the State's review was completed. In July 1990, CalTRANS announced that the Embarcadero Retrofit plan and cost estimates were not only inadequate, but would have to be totally redone, with the repairs delayed to April of 1991 or beyond.

Most critically, CalTRANS announced on July 26 that the Terminal Separator—the network of ramps connecting the Embarcadero Freeway to the Bay Bridge—would have to be demolished. The cost of repairing it was so high that a total rebuild was preferred. And state engineering experts had determined that new construction of both the Terminal Separator and the Embarcadero Freeway would be safer seismically. This made retrofitting the Embarcadero Freeway moot. The Embarcadero was coming down. On July 30, 1990, the Chinese Chamber of Commerce issued a new position statement, abandoning the retrofit and supporting the Agnos plan. The Chamber's statement noted:

> It has become evident that CalTRANS can no longer state with assurance that the retrofit alternative can guarantee the safety of the Embarcadero Freeway... The Chinese Chamber believes that it would be irresponsible on our part to maintain a position not

supported by a sound factual basis or merely to maintain "face..."
However, we need to call it as we see it, and act as a responsible
civic organization, not afraid to take on powerful interests (even
our friends), not reluctant to adopt unpopular positions, and mature
enough to change our position when the facts so dictate.

While the Chinese Chamber's change in position was widely praised outside of Chinatown for its honesty and maturity, this was not necessarily the
case in Chinatown. Three weeks after the Chamber's new position was pub-
licized, a group of Chinatown businesses formed the Chinatown Merchants
Association, led by gift store owners May and Sinclair Louie, Grand Palace
(and *Asian Week*) owner Florence Fang, realtor Pius Lee, and others. They
held firm for retrofitting the Embarcadero Freeway, criticized the Chinese
Chamber for not consulting with the community before changing its position, and claimed that Rose Pak was selling out Chinatown to curry favor
with Mayor Agnos. Rose denied that the Chamber had misled the community: "We disseminated information throughout the press. We made it clear
that it was (only) the Chinese Chamber taking a stand." The Embarcadero
Freeway fight, which initially united all of Chinatown, had later exposed
some old divisions between the various Chinatown business organizations.
While policy disagreements are expected in any diverse community, sometimes clashes in personality or politics also enter in. In Chinatown, it is
sometimes hard for an outsider (or even an insider) to decipher whether any
given conflict is about policy, personality, or politics.

The Central Freeway and the "Westside Chinese"

By San Francisco standards, the profile of the Sunset District over recent
decades has been much lower than other Supervisorial districts. But in the
early 1990s, a new organization sought to change that. The San Francisco
Neighborhood Association (SFNA) was started in the early 1990s by Julie
Lee and Rose Tsai. SFNA claimed to represent the "silent majority" of Chinese homeowners in the Richmond and Sunset districts, San Francisco's
"Westside," raising the banner of homeowners who wanted to expand their
homes to accommodate extended families. These projects, which did not
meet existing zoning, became known as "Richmond Specials." For a period
of time, Julie and Rose became media darlings, as just two "Chinese house-
wives" who were speaking for the silent majority of middle-class Chinese
homeowners whose interests were supposedly being ignored by both City
Hall and Chinatown leaders such as Rose Pak and Gordon Chin.

But the issue that put the SFNA in the headlines was the fight to retain the old Central Freeway. Like the Embarcadero Freeway, the Central Freeway was also a double-deck freeway near Civic Center that the City sought to demolish after Loma Prieta. But there was significant debate as to how far into the city a new freeway off-ramp would extend. Residents in the Civic Center and South of Market and environmental groups advocated for the freeway to end at Market Street, thus freeing up land for housing and community uses, and creating a more human scale environment.

The SFNA led a contrary proposal to continue the freeway past Market Street, providing a more direct connection to the Westside neighborhoods. They emulated Chinatown's arguments against the tear down of the Embarcadero Freeway, claiming that the Central Freeway was essential to the lifeblood of the Westside neighborhood economies. After years of debate and three ballot initiatives, San Francisco finally decided on a new Central Freeway to end at Market, and the new Octavia Boulevard Plan has been widely praised and the recipient of many planning and urban design awards.

The San Francisco Neighbors Association had lost their battle for the Central Freeway, the start of many setbacks for the organization. Rose Tsai ran for Supervisor in 1998, losing badly. Lee maintained some public profile as a Housing Authority Commissioner appointed by Mayor Brown, but soon became front-page news. She was indicted for money laundering and federal mail fraud in connection with contributions to Secretary of State Kevin Shelley, who was not implicated in any wrongdoing, and sentenced to a one-year prison term in 2008.

Chinatown Transportation Innovation

Chinatown CDC's transportation planning program has been unique in the Community Development Movement, as most CDCs founded in the 1960s and '70s centered their strategies on affordable housing, employment, business creation, community centers, and social services. I credit Chinatown TRIP for the foresight in recognizing early on the importance of transportation—adequate transit service, affordable parking, effective traffic circulation, pedestrian safety—as the lifeblood of our community.

Since Chinatown TRIP first proposed the Chinatown Traffic Circulation Study in 1978, three decades of major transportation projects have been implemented, benefiting not only Chinatown, but also many San Francisco neighborhoods, including the #83 Pacific Avenue bus, electrification of the #1 California line, and improvements to the Stockton Tunnel.

The Embarcadero Freeway demolition gave added urgency to transportation issues, and Chinatown organizations believed we needed a comprehensive set of transportation strategies. The City's top transportation priority was the Embarcadero Roadway, not Chinatown, but there was a sense of obligation from City transportation agencies and elected officials that they must do more for Chinatown's transportation needs. There was a time when most Chinatown businesses would have cited parking as the most important transportation need. But the Chinatown business community, led by the Chinese Chamber of Commerce, also embraced public transit, pedestrian safety, traffic improvements, and other non-parking measures as essential elements of an overall transportation agenda.

In 1990, Chinatown TRIP and Chinatown CDC developed an innovative transportation project called "Chinatown Park and Ride" as one of the mitigation measures for the tear down of the Embarcadero Freeway. Transportation planners called it an "intercept garage" concept. The idea was to take advantage of underutilized parking garages in one area to serve another more congested, parking-poor area. Chinatown overflows on weekends with shoppers and churchgoers coming into the community, joining San Francisco residents and tourists and making transportation and parking a nightmare. In contrast, the nearby Financial District and its parking garages are underutilized on weekends. We worked with the City's Parking Authority, then headed by Phil Chin, to dedicate its public Golden Gateway Garage (located five blocks from Chinatown/North Beach) as an intercept garage. Any driver could park there on weekends at a reduced rate with validation at a local business. The Chinese Chamber helped us to reach out to over 200 Chinatown businesses to participate. The program also features a free shuttle bus service to take drivers from the garage to Chinatown and back. The Chinatown Park and Ride program has been a great success and a model that many communities in San Francisco and across the country have sought to emulate.

To enhance transit service between Chinatown and the Visitation Valley and Bayview areas, TRIP successfully advocated for the expansion of the #8x line from weekdays only to a line running seven days and evenings. In 2002, Mayor Brown helped dedicate two important transportation improvements in Chinatown. In February 2002, the new Vallejo/Churchill Public Parking Garage was completed. It was a project that Chinatown TRIP and the Chinese Chamber of Commerce had worked on for over a decade. And in June of 2002, the new Chinatown Pedestrian Crossing System was started on four Chinatown intersections on Stockton Street. The idea, known as the "Chinatown Scramble System," replicated the diagonal crossing that existed in many Financial District intersections. We thought "Hey, if they can do it for investment bankers, they can do it for Chinatown!" It took some time for residents to get used to the new system. I remember how much fun it was watching Mayor Brown escort groups of Chinatown children back and forth across the intersection to show people how to do it.

Throughout the 1990s Chinatown organizations and the City also worked together on new sidewalk "bulb outs" to help ease congestion on Stockton Street bus loading platforms, pedestrian safety improvements on Broadway, and new traffic signals at the key intersections of Powell/Pacific and Broadway/Grant. These and other proposals were part of Chinatown CDC's Chinatown Pedestrian Safety Plan.

All of these new transportation projects have been important to Chinatown over the two decades since Loma Prieta. A more recent and very important transportation project, the new Central Subway, will be discussed in the section covering the third decade of the CDC.

CHAPTER 16

Preserving Housing, Preserving Neighborhoods

IT WAS IN the second decade that Chinatown CDC's affordable housing development role really took off—"Going to Scale" as it is known in the community development field—expanding beyond Chinatown to develop a number of large-signature affordable housing projects. We did not embark on this expansion without a great deal of internal assessment about organizational capacity and an analysis of how expansion would impact our core neighborhood, Chinatown. Ever since the 1971 HUD #701 Chinatown Housing and Recreation Study recommended both Chinatown preservation measures and new housing construction strategies in the larger northeast sector, we knew that new housing opportunities would be limited within the core area of 23 blocks and that preserving Chinatown's existing housing stock would depend on strategies of rezoning and SRO preservation. We also knew that the demographic growth of the Chinese American population in the 1980s into the northeast sector and in other districts of the City would require a broader strategy of expansion of our development role into other neighborhoods involving more diverse constituencies.

Diminishing federal government support for affordable housing in the 1990s created a crisis for thousands of residents of HUD assisted housing built in the 1960s and 1970s. With expiring federal subsidies, over 100,000 affordable units were lost nationwide. In San Francisco, more than 8,000 residents in 35 properties, primarily in the Western Addition area, were "at risk." But, thanks to the Redevelopment Agency's Housing Preservation Program established in 1997 to assist community developers in acquiring these buildings, San Francisco has yet to lose a single affordable unit. Chinatown CDC worked with the Redevelopment Agency and bank partners in our second decade on three such projects—Golden Gate Apartments, Namiki Apartments, and the Notre Dame senior housing project.

Chinatown CDC's first two acquisitions under the Housing Preservation

Program were the 72-unit Golden Gate Apartments (in 1999), financed by Bank of America, and the 33-unit Namiki Apartments (in 2001), financed by Merritt Capital and Citibank. Both projects were located in the Western Addition/Japantown area and reflected the wonderful diversity of San Francisco. In the case of the Golden Gate Apartments, here was a Chinatown-based organization acquiring a building across the street from the Kabuki Theater in Japantown, an apartment building whose occupants were half African American and half Korean American.

Our third Housing Preservation Program acquisition was the 200-unit Notre Dame Apartments located in a highly visible area on Van Ness and Broadway. Notre Dame was a former hospital converted into senior housing in the 1970s, and when word spread that the building was at risk of conversion to market rate, the senior residents—half Chinese American and half recent émigrés from the former Soviet Union—were devastated. But, they organized with the help of Chinatown CDC. The Notre Dame Resident Association made sure that every tenant knew what was at stake. They met, wrote letters, held press conferences, and formed alliances with other tenant organizations throughout the City. They made it clear that they would do anything to save their homes. One of their main leaders was Mrs. Bao Yan Chan, who was also a leader of the Community Tenants Association. It was through such sustained tenant leadership and the persistence of the Redevelopment Agency that Notre Dame was ultimately acquired by Chinatown CDC in 2000, with financing from the City, Merritt Capital, and Citibank.

Preserving Residential Hotels

Despite the passage of the SRO Ordinance in 1980, serious challenges continued for residential hotel housing into the 1990s with spotty enforcement of the ordinances and disreputable owners harassing low-income residents in an "indirect" way to force them to move. Fire and arson were constant concerns. Further, the Ellis Act led to the displacement of hundreds of residential hotel residents in Chinatown, North Beach, the Mission, the Tenderloin, and South of Market.

To address ongoing concerns about the SRO Ordinance and other issues important to the health and safety of SRO residents, including security, earthquake safety, and fire safety, "SRO Consortiums" were organized in Chinatown, the Mission, and the Tenderloin. In 2003, the Consortiums were successful in the City's passage of an SRO Sprinkler Ordinance requiring sprinklers to be installed in all residential hotels, and on the state level, legislation banning residential hotel conversions using the Ellis Act.

The Chinatown and Central City SRO Consortiums have also been active

RANDY SHAW

In the 1970s, Randy Shaw became a champion for the Tenderloin and for tenants living in residential hotels. With fellow law students from Hastings College of the Law in San Francisco, Randy founded the Tenderloin Housing Clinic in 1980. I met him during the organizing for the San Francisco Residential Hotel Preservation Ordinance, one of the first housing policy issues for Chinatown CDC. Randy has continued to be a key advocate since then, and he drafted San Francisco's first successful rent control measure, passed in November 1992. He has also written five books, including the acclaimed *Beyond the Fields*, telling the story of the United Farm Workers, *The Activist's Handbook,* an essential manual for progressive organizing, and *The Tenderloin,* his most recent. Randy is well known for his commentary on San Francisco policy and political issues, and he writes a daily blog, "Beyond Chron."

The Tenderloin Housing Clinic has been a critical resource in supporting hundreds of low-income tenants throughout San Francisco, including many high-profile Ellis Act eviction cases in Chinatown and North Beach. Randy relates to low-income tenants as more of an organizer than an attorney, a rare ability that a young Ed Lee had as well. Randy has been a wonderful friend and advisor for me and Chinatown CDC for four decades.

in a protracted fight for adequate mail delivery services for residential hotel residents. Lacking lobbies, common space, or individual mailboxes, SRO residents are at the mercy of building managers who often leave mail undistributed and unsecured on a table or shelf, putting residents at risk of not receiving their SSI or Social Security checks, Medicare information, and other important correspondence. In 2008, the San Francisco Post Office, seeking to reduce costs, started to transfer SRO resident mail to a bulk delivery center instead of delivery to individual mailboxes, a policy affecting two-thirds of San Francisco's 30,000 SRO residents. The Chinatown SRO Consortium and the Central City SRO Consortium (also known as Tenderloin SRO Consortium) joined with other tenant organizations and the San Francisco City Attorney's Office in a lawsuit alleging that the U.S. Postal Service policy was discriminating against low-income residents. While the court dismissed the case under summary judgment in 2011, the City Attorney and Central City SRO Consortium are exploring other possible solutions on either local or federal levels.

One of the most dramatic SRO problems surfacing in the late 1990s was the growing trend of entire families residing in a single hotel room. In 2001, the Citywide Families in SROs Collaborative issued a "census" of families with children living in San Francisco SROs. The census found more than 450 families living in SRO housing, including 760 children. The majority of these families lived in Chinatown residential hotels.

Having received media coverage, the census findings were presented to the San Francisco Department of Public Health and a special SRO Health and Safety Task Force was established by the San Francisco Board of Supervisors on October 23, 2001. The Board's Task Force had issued its own report in April 2001, consistent with the census findings. The problem was probably worse than either report indicated, given likely under-counting and under-reporting.

The report recommended measures including the acquisition or master leasing of apartments to house SRO families, more effective code compliance, increases in San Francisco's living wage, job training for adult family members, expanded family and children services in SROs, and peer-based outreach to all SRO families. While this growing San Francisco problem was met with great surprise and sympathy by the media and the public at large, follow-up on the report's recommendations has been lacking and challenging, both for community advocates and City departments.

Tenderloin Family Apartments

Developed on the site of a former Yellow Cab garage, the Tenderloin Family Apartments at 201 Turk Street was a partnership with the AF Evans Company for 175 new apartments to serve working-class families and seniors. Overseen by Housing Director Susie Wong, the Tenderloin Family Apartments was the single largest Housing Tax Credit project in San Francisco at the time. It was a "workforce housing project" that served many working families, the majority of whom lived within a one-mile radius of their employers, many working in the food and hotel industries. The project was another example of San Francisco's diversity—17 different languages were spoken by its residents.

Tenderloin Family Apartments was completed in 1994. The project was dedicated by Mayor Frank Jordan, our primary financial partner Wells Fargo Bank, and equity investors Pacific Gas and Electric, Phillip Morris, and Prudential. They helped to celebrate a wonderful new eight-story building fronting on two-thirds of a block on Turk Street. It includes an open space courtyard, which is still the largest open space in the Tenderloin neighborhood, and the Cross Cultural Child Care Center for project residents and the larger community. KCBS reporter Barbara Taylor called it "A jewel in the middle of the Tenderloin."

A Partnership with the Post Office

After working at the Post Office three different times in the '60s and '70s, I thought I had seen my last mail sack. But, in 1990 I was back. The Larkin/Pine Senior Housing project is the first affordable housing project ever built above a U.S. Post Office (and may still be the only one). The site at Larkin and Pine Streets was a former gas station, but shortly after the feasibility study was completed, we discovered that the site had been acquired by the U.S. Postal Service, which wanted to build a new district post office to replace an old facility that had been damaged in the 1989 earthquake.

Chinatown CDC approached the San Francisco district of the Postal Service and proposed an innovative air rights project to develop 63 affordable senior housing units over the new post office. The Postal Service had planned a two-story facility, and we proposed to build housing above it. The District Post Office initially had many questions and concerns—possible added costs and time delays, the complexities involved in an air rights development and the partnership structure, and safety issues with seniors and postal workers sharing one building. The Postal Service had never done such a mixed-use, joint venture before and would need approval from the Postal Service in Washington, D.C.

We worked to show that the project could work, describing many examples of successful air rights projects in San Francisco, negotiated an air rights lease, and worked closely with Postal Service staff to develop a construction plan and schedule. We got support from the Postal Union with the help of union leader (and former "Team 40" youth leader) Ray Fong. I flew to Washington and met with U.S. Postmaster General Anthony Frank. (I knew Mr. Frank from San Francisco when he headed First Nationwide Savings and was a banking leader who had supported affordable housing.) Our partnership with the U. S. Postal Service had been formed and the new Larkin-Pine Post Office project was completed in 1995 with financing from the Redevelopment Agency and Wells Fargo Bank.

These signature affordable housing developments together with the SRO and the housing preservation projects described earlier represented the most ambitious housing development period the Chinatown CDC had experienced to date and could not have been accomplished without a strong Chinatown CDC Executive and Housing Department staff led by Deputy Directors Margaret Gee and Joanne Lee, and Housing Directors Daryl Higashi and Susie Wong.

Property Management and Tenant Services

With a growing portfolio of affordable housing projects, the roles of property management, asset management, and resident services became critically important. By the end of our second decade, Chinatown CDC was managing 16 buildings housing more than 1,800 residents. Our Property Management Department had become the largest department in the organization. It started with the leadership of our first Property Management Director Gordie Lam and was sustained for 35 years by Angela Robinson Spencer, Tyrone Moore, Aleta Dwyer Carpenter, and Gordon Leung.

Asset management was also becoming important for all affordable housing developers. Distinct from the property managers, who are responsible for the physical condition of our buildings, the organization's asset managers are accountable to a project's financial partners, lenders, and investors, overseeing the long-term financial health of each property. The organization's asset management role since its second decade has been led capably by Asset Managers Glen Kellerer and Marc Slutzkin, overseen over the years by executives Margaret Gee, Joanne Lee, and Anna Yee.

Chinatown CDC's Tenant Services department supports the overall health, economic self-sufficiency, and success of our seniors, families, children, and youth. Tenant Services deal with family households undergoing lost employment, escalating health care and education costs for their children, and the shortage of affordable child care. For larger community development organizations, resident services departments have become essential in-house social service agencies. The department was capably led initially by Tenant Services Director Wyland Chu and in recent years by Director Grace Gin. These important roles—property management, asset management, and resident services—have been underappreciated in the community development field. Being a landlord and providing for the needs of both buildings and people can be thankless jobs, but the Chinatown CDC decided early on to take on these roles after developing housing. While the organization had always been known for our tenant organizing work, we wanted to challenge ourselves to be good landlords as well. At times, internal conflicts arose between the landlord role and the tenant organizer role, but we learned that we had to work conflicts out, and I believe we became a stronger organization for having to do so.

Our housing developments and housing development departments deserve all the credit they receive. But after new projects are completed, the work of taking care of our buildings, our assets, and our residents is just beginning. One way I've looked at the mutual importance of all our housing roles is an analogy with love and marriage. Housing developers fall in love with their new projects, thinking about nothing else until their projects get financing and approvals. Then they turn the project over to construction management, who takes the project through a period of engagement, bearing unforeseen change orders. But after all the parties and the big ceremony, the builders turn their attention to their next project, their next love. In contrast, property managers, asset managers, and tenant service providers have roles that are like marriage—forever.

Serving San Francisco

At the end of the century, Chinatown CDC had established itself as a capable and innovative affordable-housing developer. While many nonprofit housing developers specialized in particular housing occupancies or housing types (either for seniors, families, or the homeless, either rehabilitation or new construction) our housing projects spanned quite a spectrum. Our portfolio included projects that served seniors, families, single individuals, or formerly homeless. We had acquired residential hotels for rehabilitation, and we built new single-room occupancy housing. We did new construction projects serving seniors and working families. We did some projects with one financing source and others with multiple sources and private investors. We did a little bit of everything because we wanted to learn how to do new types of housing. But, we also learned that doing so many different types of projects, each with its unique financial reporting structure, challenged the organization to create administrative and reporting systems that could accommodate a variety of accountability requirements.

We had expanded our housing strategy beyond Chinatown to North Beach and the Broadway Strip, the Tenderloin, and the Western Addition/ Japantown. This geographic expansion resulted in much greater racial and ethnic diversity in our housing, which by the end of our second decade had grown to 23 developments with over 2,300 housing units serving more than 5,000 San Francisco residents. Of this constituency, 42% were Chinese American, 20% were émigrés from the former Soviet Union, 16% were African American, 9% Filipino, 6% Latino and Native American, and 7% were other Caucasian. While we continued to serve Chinatown as our primary community, Chinatown CDC had grown to serve many neighborhoods of need in San Francisco.

CHAPTER 17

The Broadway Corridor

BROADWAY IS ONE of San Francisco's great streets, stretching from the Waterfront through Chinatown to the mansions of Pacific Heights. The street was home to the Beat Movement, jazz, art, theater, and food in the '50s but became a depressed, edgier commercial strip after the "topless craze" of the 1960s. Broadway remained in this depressed state throughout the '70s, '80s, and '90s.

Broadway has been important to the work of Chinatown CDC. We were community organizers for tenants at 1000 Montgomery who waged a valiant fight to save their homes, and for the tenants in the Ping Yuen North public housing project, where Julia Wong was murdered, sparking the Ping Yuen rent strike.

Chinatown CDC was at the forefront of planning for the Broadway Corridor revitalization, particularly new affordable housing, developing the Swiss American Hotel in 1985 (later to house the Beat Museum) and the 31-unit Bayside Senior Housing project, on the site of a Ping Yuen parking lot, in 1991. On the Polk Gulch side of the Broadway Tunnel is Chinatown CDC's Notre Dame senior housing, on Broadway at Van Ness Avenue.

The Loma Prieta Earthquake and subsequent demolition of the Embarcadero Freeway in 1991 brought new challenges as well as opportunities to the Broadway Corridor. The Jean Parker Elementary School was closed for seismic repairs, the only San Francisco school closed after the earthquake. Retail businesses on Broadway were suffering from the lack of transportation access, which the Embarcadero Freeway provided from both the East Bay and South Bay. Restaurants and nighttime entertainment establishments felt a severe drop in foot traffic and patronage.

In 1993, we started a two-year Broadway Envisioning Project led by Chinatown CDC Planner Jasmine Kaw. The project brought together key stakeholder groups in Chinatown, North Beach, and Telegraph Hill to improve the streetscape environment on Lower Broadway. The Hewlett Foundation funded the planning. It was one of the best foundation grants we have ever received, because it supported an inter-neighborhood collaboration. That led to our partnership with the City's Department of Public Works to secure two rounds of Livable Communities funding from the Metropolitan Transportation Commission. The first phase was completed in spring, 2005 with new street benches and bus stop "bulb outs" on Broadway from Montgomery to the Embarcadero. Phase two, now underway, will include pedestrian improvements and pedestrian safety for upper Broadway—west of Columbus to the Broadway Tunnel.

The second phase also funded the "Language of the Birds" art exhibit jazz mural on Broadway and Columbus, in front of the Sun Hong Kong Restaurant building, along with the new Jack Kerouac Alleyway bridging City Lights Bookstore and Vesuvio Cafe in that historic intersection of Broadway, Grant, and Columbus. And most recently, Broadway merchants led a community effort to create a new Broadway Improvement District, which will be a great opportunity to develop new ideas in the future.

Connecting Chinatown to the Waterfront

After the final decision to demolish the Embarcadero Freeway, I wrote to Mayor Agnos in July 1990, sharing with him my thoughts about the Broadway Corridor and advocating a planning vision that would connect the new Embarcadero Roadway to Chinatown and North Beach, with Broadway being a major link. In 1992, the San Francisco Planning Department initiated a planning process to evaluate new uses of three sites on Broadway that had formerly been Embarcadero Freeway on-ramps and off-ramps. Both Mayor Brown and District Three Supervisor Aaron Peskin helped initiate this. With the demolition of the freeway, these sites were transferred from the state to the City of San Francisco.

The City Planning report evaluated potential uses for each site, and the City eventually designated one site for affordable family housing, a second site for the relocation and expansion of the Central Police Station, and the third site for a hotel to be developed by the Port Department. The housing site on Broadway and Battery was transferred to the Mayor's Office of Housing, which conducted an RFP for interested developers and selected Chinatown CDC as developer for the 80-unit Broadway Family Apartments. The SF Police Department could not secure financing to develop a new police station, so the City designated this site for family housing as well.

Chinatown CDC was selected as the developer for this site and 75 new family apartments. The hotel planned for the third site was never developed.

The Broadway Family Apartments on Broadway and Battery Streets, on the site of the former off-ramp to the demolished Embarcadero Freeway, is a project serving working adults with incomes up to 60% of median San Francisco income. Construction began in September of 2005 with financing from the Mayor's Office of Housing, housing tax credits, and Wells Fargo Bank and was completed in fall 2008. An award-winning design by architect Daniel Solomon features two wonderful courtyards (dedicated to Rose Pak and Aaron Peskin for their support), a child care center operated by Kai Ming Head Start, and a large community room dedicated to Mayor Willie Brown for his leadership on the project.

Located one block from the Golden Gateway market-rate housing development, there was some initial concern from neighboring residents about the low-income project. But Chinatown CDC took special efforts to seek community input about the design and project operation, including arranging a tour of other similar affordable developments in San Francisco. The Broadway Family Apartments has fit seamlessly into the surrounding neighborhood.

The Broadway/Sansome Apartments will soon join the Broadway Family Apartments as another project contributing to the revitalization of the Broadway Corridor. The site is the former on-ramp to the old Embarcadero Freeway. The Broadway/Sansome Apartments will provide 75 affordable apartments for low-income and working families, including 25 formerly homeless families. The project began construction in the summer of 2013 and is slated for completion in 2015. Financing came from the Mayor's Office of Housing and the San Francisco Municipal Transportation Authority (MTA). The funding partnership is an innovative precedent with the MTA financing the portion of the project that will house 14 Chinatown households who were displaced by the Chinatown station of the Central Subway. That fulfills the project's obligation to provide replacement housing for any displacement from the Central Subway.

The two Broadway family developments will help to serve as anchors for the lower Broadway area. Together they will bring 156 new affordable family housing units to a neighborhood and a City desperately trying to find ways to keep families from being forced out. The sensitive development of the lower Broadway area intersects the rapidly developing Embarcadero Boulevard, which has seen new developments such as the San Francisco Exploratorium and proposed new Cruise Terminal.

Also along the Broadway Corridor is the Chinatown Wells Fargo bank branch at 1150 Grant Avenue, a well-known building at one of San Francisco's most photographed intersections, Grant and Broadway. It has pagoda-style architecture and a location adjacent to both Chinatown and City Lights Bookstore on Columbus Avenue. This picturesque building houses 12 apartments on the second floor. Wells Fargo initially approached Chinatown CDC in 2009 about providing some technical assistance to help the bank with its seismic retrofitting and taking over management of the housing. Later, as the project evolved, we were stunned when the bank decided that it would just donate the building to Chinatown CDC!

In 1992, I wrote a letter to Mayor Agnos stressing the importance of visionary planning for the Broadway Corridor. In it, I said:

> My vision is one of two grand urban corridors—The Embarcadero and Broadway—together forming a critical nexus between the Waterfront, Chinatown, North Beach, Fisherman's Wharf, Downtown, and Mission Bay. Corridors linked North-South by your Embarcadero and the new F Line [trolley], and linked East-West by a complementary system of the #83 Pacific bus line, the Park and Ride Shuttle, and a new transit service on Broadway.

Looking back today, much of what we had conceived in the years after Loma Prieta has been completed or put underway. Broadway still has a ways to go, and the street is still pretty rough on weekend nights. But there is great momentum, reflected in the new Broadway Business Improvement District. After I retired in 2011, I thought it would be cool to start a new career driving a jitney van up and down Broadway. I would call it the Broadway Shuttle, with a super sound system blaring out the Drifters' 1962 hit "On Broadway."

CHAPTER 18

Building Community, Chinatown Style

COMMUNITY BUILDING HAS become a common theme in the community development field, one which is so broad in concept as to mean different things in different communities. At its core, Community Building is about looking at an entire community in a holistic manner, engaging all community stakeholders in solving problems today and planning for the future. It is about nurturing indigenous community resident leadership and building the capacity of low-income seniors, families and youth, businesses and institutions to advocate and plan for their community.

It is not only about building new physical improvements in a community. As important as these new places are, Community Building is also about the community leadership and processes that led to the creation of our new housing, parks and playgrounds, community centers, and engaging in participatory design principles to involve seniors, families, and youth in planning. Community Building is about strong inter-neighborhood collaboration, which for Chinatown CDC has meant with North Beach and Nob Hill, Union Square and the Tenderloin.

Chinatown CDC's mission of Community Building would be defined by the programs and strategies created by Program Director Norman Fong. Participation in the Neighborhood Preservation Initiative also helped us develop more intentional and explicit strategies for empowering resident leadership and youth leadership, and the organization's vision of community development broadened to incorporate community facilities, the arts, and culture as important strategic elements to complement organizing and housing.

Chinatown CDC has built community through the nurturing of indigenous leadership of Chinatown's seniors, youth, and families, and through the important gathering places of our community, our parks and playgrounds, our cultural and community centers.

Community Organizing

In my time at Chinatown CDC, I was asked many times, "What is the most important thing you do?" I always replied, "If we only had one role to play it would be as community organizers." We started out in 1977 as organizers, working with the grass roots coalition of five volunteer activist groups and later helping to form new volunteer, resident, or youth-led associations. I consider myself more of a community organizer. And let me be clear, I am of course very proud of the many roles Chinatown CDC has played—community planning, housing development, property management, resident services, and public policy advocacy. But without community organizing, we would not be able to plan for Chinatown with the active vision of all community stakeholders. Without community organizing, our housing development projects would not have the resources needed to build housing that have come from successful housing revenue campaigns. Without community organizing, our advocacy would be lacking the legitimacy of resident leadership.

After Norman Fong came on as Program Director in 1990, our Chinatown CDC community organizing program expanded in size, scope, creativity, and vision. Norman's vision created many community organizing programs that were imbued with his own values of active resident and youth engagement, and leadership.

Chinatown CDC has never subscribed to any one model of community organizing. There are many styles—the traditional confrontational Alinsky style, issue-based organizing, and the more contemporary community building organizing, which emphasizes consensus building. In 1998, Norman attended an organizing training with Alinsky-trained organizer Mike Miller. Miller said the challenge for the future of community organizing is the need to create and sustain permanent community-based associations for the long term. This was something Norman already understood, embraced, and enacted by creating two resident-led associations: the Community Tenants Association and the Chinatown Adopt-An-Alleyway Youth Empowerment Project.

Community Tenants Association

The Community Tenants Association (CTA) is the single largest tenants association in San Francisco, with a dues-paying membership of over 900 residents, primarily monolingual Chinese American seniors. Chinatown tenant leaders active in Orangeland started CTA in 1987, both for the

MRS. BAO YAN CHAN

Mrs. Bao Yan Chan was born in Shanghai, China, on August 4, 1918. When she was 12, her family moved back to their hometown of Shun Duk in Canton Province, where she became a teacher and eventually the dean of an elementary school for 25 years. She emigrated to the United States in 1984 and was elected President of the Community Tenants Association in 1989. "I joined the Community Tenants Association in 1988 to help give voice to the Chinatown CDC and CTA's efforts to improve housing and living conditions in San Francisco. As a teacher and dean for 25 years, I believe in the power of the people, if folks are educated on the issues and given the opportunity to speak out."

Mrs. Bao Yan Chan passed away in 2006 at the age of 88.

residents who lived in that building and others who supported them. Mr. Koon Kwong, who had been the President of the Orangeland Tenants Association, became CTA's first President. They recruited other Chinatown tenants who had experienced evictions, unsafe and unsanitary housing conditions, and excessive rent increases to join them. They asked Chinatown CDC to provide them with organizational support and organizing help.

The strength of CTA has been their ability to turn "Self-Interest" into "Community Interest" as Mrs. Bao Yan Chan did with her neighbors to save their housing at Notre Dame and the SSI benefits of thousands of immigrant seniors in America. When tenants in a particular building are facing a crisis that might result in mass evictions and displacement, they have a natural self-interest to organize, protest, and mobilize support. This is not always easy as tenants in such situations are very vulnerable and may fear owner retaliation for speaking out. Throughout the last three decades, Chinatown CDC and other organizations have supported many building crises faced with Ellis Act evictions and demolitions from private development.

After these battles are fought, win or lose, the greater challenge remains in keeping these tenants active in the larger affordable housing and tenants movements, sharing their leadership and strength with other tenants in a coalition framework for the larger community interest, in Chinatown or other neighborhoods. CTA has done this very well, and as Chinatown senior tenants often have a long tenure in their building and in Chinatown, they have succeeded in keeping residents engaged on behalf of their community.

CTA is perhaps the most consistent volunteer tenant association in San Francisco and statewide in bringing out their members and showing their presence at public hearings, rallies, and campaign events for affordable housing. CTA members never leave home without their huge red Community Tenants Association banners, which have been prominent in hundreds of affordable housing events at City Hall and in the state Capitol. Since its founding, CTA has been a leading grass roots association in every major affordable housing and tenants' rights campaign in San Francisco, including the successful San Francisco Affordable Housing Bond campaign in 1996 and the creation of a San Francisco Housing Trust Fund in 2012 (see chapter 22).

Chinatown CDC's commitment to community organizing, from day one, is evidenced by three decades of outstanding organizers who have worked with CTA. We have counseled thousands of tenants in need and organized numerous buildings in Chinatown and North Beach. Chinatown CDC has had a three-decade history of dedicated community organizers. Community and tenant organizing is hard work, at times underappreciated and often misunderstood. It is not only about the high-profile roles of bringing the troops out to a hearing or managing an issue campaign (which are certainly hard work, too). It is about managing and nurturing democratic associations that, like CTA, have a large number of people, each with their own needs and their own ideas. Tammy Hung, like other organizers at Chinatown CDC, is often considered a "daughter" by CTA members, a member of their family. This closeness is what inspires great trust in organizers like Tammy, but it can also be quite challenging whenever tenants are at odds with each other. Managing large associations with a large senior membership can present its own set of challenges, including dealing with leadership transitions.

In the nonprofit sector, there has been an increasing emphasis on the importance of planning for leadership transition, most often directed at the thousands of "Boomer Generation" executive directors in America who are nearing retirement. Thousands of nonprofits have planned at some level for executive succession, as I did with the Chinatown CDC.

But those of us who work in community organizing, building indigenous leadership of our seniors, families, and youth, also need to deal with leadership transition. Leadership transition in a volunteer resident-led association is just as important as dealing with staff transitions in nonprofit organizations that are serving those associations. Organizations of senior leaders, such as the Community Tenants Association, must deal with transitions of people in leadership who are in the latter years of their lives. And when a senior leader passes on, the association and their community organizer must not only deal with organizational matters, but also deal with loss, as any family does. The work of organizing is personal.

Leaders of associations of low-income families, such as the SRO Families United, may have transitions in their lives—the loss of a job, family illness, lack of child care, or even moving away because they are becoming first-time homeowners. The organizer or tenant services staff must deal with such transitions all the time, because life does happen. It means that any association cannot be overly dependent on that one charismatic leader, and for voluntary associations and organizers the work of identifying, training, and nurturing new leaders is never ending—you can never have enough organizing leadership.

Youth Leadership

One of best things Chinatown CDC ever did was to embrace youth leadership as a core value of the organization. It started in 1990 with Norman Fong, who brought with him a great vision for what youth can do for themselves and for Chinatown. Chinatown youth giving "grades" for Chinatown alleyways in the *San Francisco Progress* was the beginning of many great programs that not only inspire our youth, but inspire all of us.

While it has been a while since I was a youth organizer in Chinatown, I remember many of those experiences working with the Chinatown Youth Council, Chinatown Police Activities League, or Chinatown Youth Center like they were yesterday. We all tend to remember times from our youth that were most exciting and fun, most challenging and new. When I hear our Chinatown youth leaders talk about their experiences, I can relate to their enthusiasm and emotions about all the new stuff they are learning and the new people they are meeting, because I experienced that same type of wonder in discovering Chinatown in the late 1960s.

Chinatown has been well served by many great youth agencies and community centers, including Cameron House, Chinatown YMCA, Chinatown Youth Center, and Chinese Progressive Association.

Integrating youth leadership development into the work of Chinatown CDC has likewise been extremely valuable in looking with some intentionality on our program strategy. The question has never been "How can we serve youth?" It is "How can youth serve Chinatown?" And the answer to this question is not something an organization determines for youth, but one that the youth must discuss and answer for themselves. That is why all Chinatown CDC youth programs have embraced the philosophy of "Youth Run, Youth Led." It is a philosophy that has been nurtured by Norman and embraced by all of the organization's Youth Program Coordinators over the past two decades—Joni Tam, Jane Kim, Rosa Wong-Chie and Angelina Yu.

I learned the hard way what "youth run, youth led" means when I was asked to meet with the Adopt-An-Alleyway (AAA) Cabinet one year. Jane Kim was our Youth Program Coordinator but could not make the meeting that day. Just before I walked into the meeting, Angelina Yu, who was on the cabinet at that time, pulled me aside and told me that I was not supposed to speak, just listen. I was somewhat taken aback since I had my rap ready, which I had done many times. But it was cool, and I learned a lot just listening and observing.

Another thing I learned is to be very careful about using the word "kids." I am sure Norman and thousands of others who work in youth serving organizations have encountered the same retort quite often, being told "Don't call us kids!" Just when does a kid become a youth? When does a youth become a young adult? When does a young adult become an adult? Is there an age threshold? I have no idea, but I do know that when in doubt, just say "youth."

Chinatown Adopt-An-Alleyway Youth Empowerment Project (AAA)

Started by Norman Fong in 1991, the Chinatown Adopt-An-Alleyway Youth Empowerment Project has been the foundation from which all of Chinatown CDC's youth programs have emerged. Norman started it with a handful of youth from Galileo High School, cleaning up Chinatown and later sharing their "grades" for Chinatown alleyways in the *San Francisco Progress*. Everyone calls it "AAA." AAA has always led Chinatown clean-up campaigns, recruiting over 200 youth from many high schools and junior highs. AAA leaders know that neighborhood clean-up activities have been a great starting point for youth to experience a sense of community service.

AAA expanded to deepen Chinatown youth engagement with two great programs to help Chinatown seniors and families. AAA youth make regular home visits to seniors living in Chinatown CDC buildings, leading activities and games, sharing food, and sometimes just listening to what the seniors want to talk about. In our monthly "Super Sundays" at the Gordon J. Lau Elementary School, while SRO family members are inside discussing new issues or meeting with City officials, AAA youth have a program of games for their kids in the playground or auditorium. In their own words:

> This is why I come and volunteer with AAA on Saturdays for alleyway clean-ups and graffiti removal. This is why I enjoy spending

time with the children during Super Sunday. It is why I chill with the seniors in Chinatown on Wednesdays, creating a bond between grandparents and grandchildren. —Nelly Liang

I grew up in Chinatown, and finally moved away from this community when I was five years old. Currently, I live in the Outer Mission district. Although I no longer live in Chinatown, I still see Chinatown as my community. Chinatown continues to feel at home for me. By joining AAA, I have found a purpose and motive to improve this community. —Wendy Chan

AAA has been a great training ground for youth to teach each other about how to run meetings, how to make consensus decisions, how to work together towards common goals. I like how Helen Hui described being on the AAA Cabinet in the AAA newsletter, "Chinatown Youth Monitor":

We always leave with a feeling of great reward because we take on every item on the agenda, satisfying each person in the room by coming up with compromises. The fact that we may disagree on some ideas is progressive as well, because we can synthesize conflicting opinions and reach a compromise that may be better than the original thought.

Building upon the foundation of the Chinatown Neighborhood Clean-Ups, the Home Visits to Seniors, and Super Sunday, AAA and the Chinatown CDC have developed a comprehensive, multifaceted array of strategies to nurture youth leadership. Youth for SROs engages young people whose families are among the 350 Chinatown families living in single-room hotels. ACCESS (Advocates for Community Change, Empowerment, and Social Services) was formed by AAA as a vehicle for young adult AAA "alumni" to continue their activism.

Chinatown CDC started the Urban Institute in 2010 as a summer program for high school and university students who want to learn about urban planning and Chinatown planning. They work in teams to study issues such as affordable housing, transportation circulation, playground design, or corridor revitalization and present their findings to a large audience (which has included City Supervisors and City Planning Commissioners) at summer's end.

Campaign Academy

AAA chose the name Campaign Academy to describe the seriousness with which they approach community problems and issues. Started in 2009, the Campaign Academy has tackled issues important to themselves and other youth, as well as issues important to residents citywide. The first public policy issue they worked on was the successful Affordable Housing Trust Fund campaign in 2012. The second issue was healthier school lunches, which saw them building coalitions with San Francisco school and youth groups citywide. Their voices changed San Francisco's cafeteria menus, even before the First Lady led her campaign for healthy food. The Campaign Academy has been active in supporting the Central Subway at public hearings and in Chinatown's petition drive, which resulted in more than 15,000 signatures. And their presence has been very important in numerous housing displacement fights, such as supporting the tenants in Jasper Alley ward off eviction.

The Campaign Academy project that really elevated their game was taking on the San Francisco Unified School District to demand an ethnic studies curriculum in their schools. It was a special challenge because it came with a $200,000 cost. The Academy led the advocacy, organized petition drives and a neat postcard campaign (with photos of 500 youth leaders) and an outreach strategy reaching out to many other San Francisco youth groups and civic leaders. On February 23, 2010, the San Francisco Board of Education voted unanimously for the new program to enable ninth graders to choose ethnic studies as an elective while earning college credit. Adrienne Tran, one of the Academy leaders, says:

> Joining the Campaign Academy has had a profound impact on my life. I've learned how to facilitate group meetings, organize letter writing campaigns, create strategies to get a campaign started. I've learned a lot about historical movements in San Francisco—from SRO evictions to the gentrification of Manilatown—which has allowed me to grow more connected to my roots and culture... Campaign Academy has helped me realize that youth are capable of making change and starting new revolutions.

In 1968, some of us "won" ethnic studies at San Francisco State College, and the lesson that Adrienne learned was a lot like the lesson I learned from the SF State Strike, but she learned it much quicker. That lesson is that it wasn't so much the "prize" of ethnic studies that changed our lives. It was the struggle to get there and the lessons we learned along the way, lessons about ourselves, our community, and our city. I guess *What goes around, comes around.*

Chinatown Alleyway Tours (CATS)

CATS was another great program that Norman Fong conceived of in 2001 to engage Chinatown youth to talk about and show their Chinatown. Their audiences on the tours are other youth groups, tourists, and many San Franciscans who want a different way to see and hear about Chinatown. It is still another "youth run, youth led" program. Norman got it started, but the youth really run the tours. They research the curriculum about Chinatown history and contemporary issues, devise their alleyway routes and highlights, and develop their own scripts. CATS tour guide Wendell Lin put it best: "This is about community, by people from the community who want to show Chinatown for what it is, not just for profit."

The Chinatown Alleyway Tours program brings out the best in our young leaders. It challenges them to tell not only Chinatown's story, but also their own. Most of the tour guides grew up in Chinatown, so it is very much their personal story that tour participants remember most and a reason why the CATS program has been featured in many national publications, including the *New York Times* and *LA Times*, and television shows such as *Bay Area Backroads*.

Thoughts from a Former Youth Worker

One message that I share with youth is that they can embrace Chinatown as "their community" regardless of where they came from and that they can also serve this community in whatever way they decide for their future careers. They don't have to work in a Chinatown nonprofit organization (unless they want to, of course). They don't have to be an organizer, planner, or housing developer. They can be a teacher or nurse helping our families, children, and seniors in Chinatown, or play a role in influencing health care in the larger policy arena. They can be a banker making loans to community residents and businesses, or an accountant offering free income tax advice to our immigrant families. They can be a minister, open a restaurant, or run for elected office. It's all good. And if they choose Chinatown as their community, they will have unique skills and experiences that can help this community today or whenever they come back.

Chinatown CDC youth programs have made a difference in the lives of many of our future leaders. I am frankly amazed at the scope of their leadership and the breadth of roles they have played, roles that may help give them choices for their futures. With AAA, they have an appreciation for Chinatown's environment and the need to keep it healthy and clean. Doing home visits to seniors, they have shown their appreciation for the seniors just like their grandparents. Taking care of children at Super Sundays, they understand that they, too, are role models.

Organizing their peer youth who live in residential hotels, they can better appreciate the places where they live. Planning and carrying out issue campaigns, they educate themselves and learn that they can really effect change in public institutions. Spending their summers in the Urban Institute, they learn that community planning is about creating visions for our community, which they can contribute to. With ACCESS, they have a vehicle to stay engaged in their community, their City, after they become young adults. With the CATS program, they have learned how to tell the story of our community in a way that is very real, very personal.

When I think about CATS, I think back to that historic 1968 Chinatown Demonstration, when so many youth and students like me were protesting the living conditions in Chinatown. The signs we held shouted "Tourists out of Chinatown!" and reflected the contradiction we saw in Chinatown as both a ghetto and a tourist attraction. Some of us even spent our free time following behind and heckling Chinatown tour groups for coming to gawk at our community. Things are different today. Today's Chinatown youth leaders, as exemplified by the CATS program, have a deeper understanding, a more confident understanding, of what the Chinatown community is today than what my generation of youth knew and felt in 1968. Today's youth leaders know that Chinatown is a place with many problems, but they also have pride in the knowledge that Chinatown is a strong community with history and courage, with great culture and institutions, and a great place for nurturing leadership. And they know that "You can never have enough youth leadership."

Saving Housing for 200 Seniors

On the front door of Chinatown CDC's Program Office on Clay Street is a wonderful mosaic picture of Mrs. Bao Yan Chan. Chinatown CDC staff are reminded every day of the importance of leadership and courage as exemplified by Mrs. Chan. For over a decade, Mrs. Chan fought to stay in her home at the 200-unit Notre Dame Senior Apartments on Broadway and Van Ness Streets. Notre Dame was the single largest building in San Francisco threatened with displacement and conversion from affordable housing to a market-rate complex.

Mrs. Chan led the advocacy and organizing of the Chinese-speaking tenants in the building, which was half Chinese seniors and half émigré seniors from the former Soviet Union. They waged a decade-long campaign to oppose the conversion and were victorious. The win was sealed by the acquisition of Notre Dame in 2000 by Chinatown CDC with the assistance of the San Francisco Redevelopment Agency. Although Mrs. Chan was a monolingual Chinese speaker, she was able to relate to her non-Chinese neighbors who hailed from Russia, Latvia, Estonia, and Lithuania. They were all immigrants and shared a love of not only their home, but of San Francisco.

Mrs. Chan, elected as CTA President in 1989, expanded CTA's vision beyond Chinatown and the Chinese American community. Her values and her experiences at Notre Dame embraced not only multiracial and multi-cultural understanding, but coalition building with other communities for affordable housing and other social justice issues facing all seniors in San Francisco.

We have many leaders in our community like Bao Yan Chan who do not receive the recognition they deserve simply because they do not speak English. But, it is more than about translation. It is about the gap in our collective understanding and appreciation of the full breadth of leadership that serves our community on a day-to-day basis. They have wonderful stories that can and should be shared with a much larger audience. There are times when we are moved by the sheer passion in the voices of our Chinese-speaking tenant leaders. Even if we don't understand a word they are saying, you can *feel* what they are saying. Mrs. Bao Yan Chan had this effect on people when they heard her speak.

Saving SSI Benefits for Immigrant Seniors

One issue that Mrs. Bao Yan Chan spoke out about every day for over a year was the Welfare Reform proposal (Personal Responsibility Act) put forward by the Clinton administration in 1994. While welfare reform was largely directed at moving low-income American families off of welfare ("incentiv-izing them to work"), one provision in the Act would have been devastating to tens of thousands of low-income American seniors. The Personal Re-sponsibility Act proposed to exclude federal income assistance programs, including Supplemental Security Income (SSI), public housing, medical, and food stamps, to all legal immigrant seniors over the age of 60 (except those over 75 who have lived in the U.S. for more than five years). The act was not directed at undocumented seniors, but seniors who are here legally as Permanent Residents but had not chosen to become U.S. citizens. It was estimated that between 30–40% of Chinatown seniors would be thrown off these programs, which were their primary means of support.

Nationally, there was an outcry and mobilization from a wide range of immigrant rights groups, senior citizen groups, health care organizations, and city and state governments. The Asian American community mobilized nationally with groups such as NAKASEC (National Korean American Ser-vice and Education Consortium) leading the way. Reverend Norman Fong led coalitions in the local religious community, in particular with Jewish congregations who were serving the large émigré population from the former Soviet Union. Norman was also part of a delegation that met with Vice President Gore in the White House.

Like Norman, Bao Yan Chan spoke as loud and as often as she could on the injustice in the proposed act, and like Norman, she also built coalitions at Notre Dame with her neighbors from the former Soviet Union, most of whom would have been adversely affected. But Mrs. Chan did something more. She started the CTA Citizenship Class program. And though she received help from her fellow CTA leaders and Chinatown CDC, Mrs. Chan taught all the classes herself, four sessions of three months each, offered free of charge. And she did it from a new curriculum emphasizing verbal, rote learning since so many of the Chinese seniors were illiterate in both English and Chinese. By the end of a year and a half, Mrs. Chan and CTA had helped 550 Chinatown seniors become American citizens.

This was a great example not only of the courage and determination of our senior tenant leaders like Mrs. Chan, but her sophistication and understanding of organizing strategy. She and CTA were protesting an unjust policy, and they recognized they would need allies. With Chinatown CDC's help, they joined a national coalition effort. But at the same time, they recognized that the new policy might very well become law, and they needed to register as many new citizens as possible out of self-interest and to show that they were proud Americans.

Chinatown tenant leaders like Mrs. Bao Yan Chan are heroes to me. If and when the history of tenant leadership in San Francisco is written, her name will go alongside other San Francisco tenant heroes—Mary Helen Rogers, George Woolf and Peter Mendelsohn, Felix Ayson and Bill Sorro. They were all San Franciscans whose lives epitomized courage, who spoke truth to power, who shouted to the world, "We Won't Move!"

Intergenerational leadership

Some of you know that I love Hawaii. I'll surely be spending time there after I *really* retire. The Hawaiian word for elder is "Kapuna." The word for adult is "Makua." And the word for the younger generation is "Opee'o." I guess I am at the Kapuna stage of my life (not to be confused with "Kahuna ("boss") or "Big Kahuna," which I was in my last stage). Anyway, the relationship between the generations in Hawaii and many immigrant and indigenous communities has always fascinated me. They are not as hierarchal as some might perceive.

As adults we sometimes stereotype our elders as being valued only for their wisdom, and our young people only for their energy. If truth be told, you and I know a lot of old folks who ain't got no wisdom at all, and younger folks who are simply lazy. I have drawn great strength from many of our senior Chinatown leaders who have been energetic leaders for eight or nine decades, and who are still doing it. I have also benefited from the wisdom of our youth who have the ability to cut to the chase on what needs to be done, and our senior tenants also "speak truth to power."

When I was a student activist in 1969 involved in the first student strike in the nation at San Francisco State College, I remember the difficult and stressful time I had in talking to my parents and extended family about what I was doing. I was "embarrassing the family" by challenging authority and, worst of all, it was in the newspapers and on TV! Painful times for me and them. Not too many years later, as Executive Director of Chinatown CDC, I remember how proud my folks were to see my picture in the paper, wearing a suit and standing next to the mayor of San Francisco at one of our Chinatown events. It didn't matter that my politics hadn't changed that much. What did matter was that they understood I was an emerging leader for *their* community, and I was a proud symbol of the many generations of our family in that place we call Chinatown. Place matters and family matters. And of course, cutting my hair and wearing a suit helped, too.

When I was working at the Chinatown Youth Council in 1971, Al Miller, one of the Native American activists I had met in the SF State Third World Student Strike, asked if I wanted to take a group of Chinatown street kids out to the American Indian Occupation at Alcatraz (The Occupation lasted over a year and a half, and there was selected access to the island.) We spent an unforgettable day there in the summer of 1971.

One of my memories of that day was sitting around in a big circle right on the shore, me and a coworker and 10 Chinatown kids about 14–18 years of age. We were joined by a Native American woman, an elder probably in her 80s. She talked about the struggle of her people, about the importance of her place called Alcatraz. I'll never forget watching those kids, so quiet and rapt in attention, listening to an elder with a respect they didn't show to their own parents or grandparents. What was also cool was that the elder did not just preach, but asked the youth about the struggles they were going through in their own lives, engaging them in an intergenerational sharing of story. The youth from Chinatown also really liked what she said about the "medicinal and spiritual qualities of peyote," too.

Chinatown youth, and other youth of low-income families, are asked to do a lot more for their parents or grandparents than is expected of youth from more well-to-do families. I have seen Chinatown youth have to translate medical and other health care forms, notices from City building departments, wage and tax statements, and most any English language communications, simply because they are the only ones in the house who can speak or read English. I'm not talking about high school youth here, but sixth, seventh, or eighth graders. We have wonderful social service agencies in Chinatown, but sometimes a family may be too proud or too embarrassed to seek help, and they will ask their children for help first. As such, I think many Chinatown youth develop a sense of responsibility early on in their lives, a sense that they, too, have a contribution to make to the family, across generations.

AAA's home visits and social programs with Chinatown seniors, their Super Sunday programs with the children of SRO families and their Campaign Academy, all exemplify an intergenerational approach to community building and community organizing.

Chinatown seniors, families, and youth have also worked together on many public policy campaigns affecting their individual and collective interests. These have included three different affordable housing bond campaigns in San Francisco, protests against welfare reform and the Personal Responsibility Act and in support of the Dream Act, and hundreds of demonstrations at City Hall and the State Capitol against devastating government budget cuts. It has been heartwarming to see our youth and seniors organizing together on such issues, conducting joint voter registration drives, and sharing leadership.

It is important to integrate such intergenerational leadership into the governance of our organizations. Chinatown CDC's board of directors has four low-income senior members and three youth/young adult members who help decide the policy positions and strategic directions of the organization. Fei Tsen has served three separate terms on Chinatown CDC's board of directors, and during a period when she was not on the board, Fei's daughter, Nicole, a recent architecture graduate, was elected to serve.

One of my favorite youth programs is "In Search of Roots" started in 1991 by Albert Cheng and sponsored by the Chinese Culture Center, Chinese Historical Society, and the Overseas Chinese Office of Guangdong Province in China. Inspired by Alex Haley's *Roots*, the program trains Chinese American youth to research and explore their ancestry. It has trained over 250 youth in a year-long program to learn genealogy and create their family tree, culminating in a trip to visit their ancestral village in the Pearl River Delta region of Guangdong. The visit to the village is emotional for most of the youth. In Search of Roots is a wonderful program bringing youth closer to their families and building their connection to their family history. My niece Pam Tse was in the second Roots class in 1992, and the program brought her closer to her family, particularly her grandmother. Many young staff of Chinatown organizations have participated in Roots as well, and it has given them much more personal meaning for the work they do in Chinatown.

I have been excited to see in recent years an expanded focus on generational change and the challenge and opportunity presented by the retiring Baby Boomer Generation, including yours truly. National CAPACD's Next Gen leadership program, the Marguerite Casey Foundation's "Equal Voices Campaign," the wonderful Building Movement Project, a recent paper from Compass Point about Next Generation Organizations—all suggest a new paradigm of generational and inter-generational leadership between all of us, Kapunas, Makuas, and Opee'os.

Art and Culture

Everybody loves a parade. I have fond memories of the Chinese New Year Parade. Even though my family lived in Oakland, we never missed coming over for the parade, usually taking the "B" train, which ran on the lower deck of the Bay Bridge. We would have front row seats on Grant Avenue (the parade's main route before it moved to Kearny), sitting on teak benches that my Uncle Frank moved onto the sidewalk from his herb store on Grant and Washington. Like many other Chinese kids, my brother and sister and I were always in awe of the colors, the pageantry, the music, and most of all of the Chinese lions and the Golden Dragon.

The Chinese New Year Parade is the largest nighttime parade in the country outside of Mardi Gras in New Orleans. I don't think I have missed a Chinese New Year Parade in my 65 years. For the past 25 years, I have volunteered for the parade as a member of the board of the Chinese Chamber of Commerce, whose sponsorship of the parade and Chinese New Year events provides exposure and publicity of immeasurable economic benefit to both Chinatown and to San Francisco.

Chinese New Year Parade volunteers come from all walks of life—some very active in Chinatown, others who may only come to Chinatown once a year just to work the parade. For the old-timers, the parade is another point of connection to a community they have grown up in, a reunion of sorts with friends who they may not see but once a year at the parade. For youth from Bay Area suburban schools, the parade is a great access point to a community they may not know. For Chinatown youth who may be part of a lion dance troop, kung fu studio, marching band, or drill team, it is a chance to show off their stuff in front of half a million people.

Parades, festivals, and fairs celebrate our communities, and Chinatown has always valued such celebrations as important elements of building the "social capital" in the community—bringing families together, introducing new generations to art and culture, promoting a sense of community. Asian American communities across the country share the value of celebrating through arts, culture, and of course food.

It is important that we embrace arts and cultural events in our community development and community building work. They are integral to the value we place on volunteerism and "giving back" to a community. I have found that people who volunteer on arts events, street fairs, or free concerts may very well become more interested in other ways to stay connected with the community, to volunteer, or join organizations. Celebrations are social events, and community organizers know that any social event is also an opportunity to organize.

In the 1960s, the emerging Asian American arts community was an important force in the Asian American Movement. I met early Asian American writers such as Judy Yung, Genny Lim, Nancy Hom, and Kitty Tsui in the early 1970s. All of them hung out around the International Hotel. Genny Lim and Nancy Hom would start "Unbound Feet," the first Asian American women writers collective in 1978. The Asian American Women's Movement has inspired and been inspired by Asian American women writers and advocates in issues such as the International Hotel and Chinatown as well as global issues such as human trafficking and sweat shop working conditions, bringing these issues to the forefront of public attention.

The Asian American Movement led to the emergence of indigenous Asian American artists and arts organizations moved by a search for racial justice, cultural identity, an awakening political awareness, and a strong desire to find a place to call their own. For many, those places were the inner-city Chinatowns and other Asian American communities across the country.

Located in a storefront at the International Hotel, the Kearny Street Workshop (KSW) was founded in 1972 by local artists Jim Dong, Lara Jo Foo, and Mike Chan, and later joined by Leland Wong, Genny Lim, Nancy Hom, Dennis Tanaguchi, and many others. KSW would become the home for progressive Asian American artists—painters, sculptors, writers and poets, actors, filmmakers, photographers, muralists—and the Kearny Street Workshop was the central place for much of the Asian American Arts Movement in the 1970s. The whole environment around Kearny Street—the

International Hotel, the memories of the old Hungry i, Everybody's Bookstore, the Manilatown String Band and Filipino music at Mabuhay Gardens, City Lights Bookstore up the street—was rich with artists, poets, musicians of all races, all embracing creative arts as part of an activist San Francisco lifestyle. You might see Leland Wong performing kung fu one moment, taking photos the next moment, then working on a Chinatown mural. San Francisco Supervisor Norman Yee used to sell his handmade leather belts and purses on the street. Kearny Street was the place to be.

Jazz pianist Jon Jang and saxophonists Fred Houn and Frances Wong have inspired so many young Asian American musicians. Jon founded the Pan Asian Arkestra, one of the first Asian American jazz groups in the nation, collaborating with African American jazz artists. It was at one such collaboration with esteemed tenor sax player David Murray at Cameron House many years ago when I gave Jon a gift that I had discovered at my mom's house, but never really appreciated. It was an old recording, probably made in the 1950s, of Paul Robeson singing "Chi Lai," the Chinese National Anthem. And he sung it in Mandarin. Paul Robeson was the multitalented African American singer and civil rights leader who was persecuted by the American government during the McCarthy era for his "communist beliefs." Jon appreciated the gift, as he knew the significance of what it represented: a collaboration of an African American leader for social justice and the Chinese struggle for independence, a metaphor for the values that Jon and other Asian American artists continue to embrace in their music.

Jon Jang recently wrote a new jazz suite entitled *Central Subway,* not only to proclaim his support for this important community project, but also for the value the project will have in bringing different San Francisco neighborhoods together. I thought this was so cool, and Jon was careful not to call it his own *"Take the A Train."* Yes, Jon Jang still gets it.

The Chinatown of my mother's generation, growing up in the 1930s and 1940s saw the phenomenon of the *Forbidden City* and the *Skyroom,* with Chinese Americans doing Sinatra, chorus lines, or comedy. To me, these were part of the Chinese American Arts Movement as well, with Chinese Americans with personality and creative expression. Chinatown's many "soul bands," including The Bold Rebels, The Illusions, The Persuasions, and of course, my favorite, Jest Jammin' (which is *still* doing it), were important parts of the Asian American Arts Movement in the 1960s and '70s. They were singing Motown, African American created music, not only because the music resonated with them, but because the African American struggle for civil rights also resonated with them as Asian Americans.

Art and culture have a profound impact on the health and vitality of our neighborhoods, helping to tell the stories of our communities in verse, in images, and in song. The celebration of our communities happens through the arts, in festivals and parades, on building murals and signage, in historic storefronts and museums. The arts and culture build community, sustaining the soul of community. In recent years, there has been expanding national attention in both arts and community development fields seeking to promote this synergy and better understand the important role that artistic expression, culture, and history play in the Community Development Movement.

A few years ago, I was part of the consultant team for the Shifting Sands Initiative, led by the Partners for Livable Communities. Funded by the Ford Foundation, it explored the intersection of art and culture organizations with community development organizations. Ford selected 10 neighborhood-based organizations, some were arts organizations, others community development groups, but all had created strategies using arts and culture to impact more traditional community development program areas—affordable housing, parks and playgrounds, promoting the neighborhood economy, job creation, and youth leadership.

Community development organizations have embraced arts and culture in many development projects, and Chinatown CDC has implemented such creative planning in many of its projects. Our William Penn Hotel has housed the Tenderloin's Exit Theater for over two decades, a trailblazing theater that has been a cornerstone of the community since its inception. The Swiss American Hotel houses the San Francisco Beat Museum. After the I Hotel Eviction, the basement of the Clayton Hotel housed the Manilatown Senior Center, and the new International Hotel houses the Manilatown Center and its multicultural arts program.

In recent years, Chinatown CDC has created arts spaces in our Chinatown streets and alleyways. The "Language of the Birds" exhibit on Broadway and Grant Avenue and the Jack Kerouac Alleyway project, both at the intersection of Chinatown and North Beach, are prime examples of the arts building a sense of community, across different communities. Community murals bring life to our streets, most notably the wonderful mural of Ping Yuen tenant leaders on Stockton and Pacific, but also murals in our alleys by Chinatown artists such as Jim Dong and Leland Wong, two artists and leaders of the Chinese American Arts Movement. Alleyway mural projects have been a great vehicle for youth leadership, as had Chinatown CDC's Arts in Storefronts project, a joint project with the San Francisco Arts Commission to develop temporary art exhibits in vacant storefronts.

I don't know what Chinatown will become in the next century, but I do know that arts and culture in whatever form they take will be important elements in the envisioning of the community's future, and that the creativity, the artistic creativity, of our young leaders will be essential to that envisioning. That was true in the 1960s and 1970s at the Kearny Street Workshop, and it is true today with Chinatown Adopt-An-Alleyway youth leaders who are proud to lead tours of their community and are capable of planning for its future.

Places That Build Community

During the second decade of Chinatown CDC, Chinatown would experience a virtual renaissance of important open space and community facility projects. They provide valuable services to our residents and help build a greater sense of community by showcasing Chinatown's identity as a place that values art, culture, and history.

The decade started with a key vote of the San Francisco Board of Supervisors to acquire a site for a new Chinatown park, a longstanding goal of the Chinatown Park Rec Committee. In April 1990, the Board of Supervisors voted to acquire through eminent domain the Cathay Mortuary site on Powell and Jackson Streets. This decision had come after a previously targeted site, the Churchill Alley garage site on Vallejo Street, was stalled for years by North Beach businesses who did not want to lose parking. The acquisition of the Cathay Mortuary site was not without controversy as it was one of only two mortuaries serving the larger Chinatown community, and there was the expected concern over the City exercising its eminent domain powers to take over a private business. But, after a long advocacy and organizing effort, it became clear that this was the best site for a new park that had been promised to the community for over three decades.

At the end of the decade, on October 7, 1999, Chinatown and the City Recreation and Parks Department dedicated the new Wo Hei Yuen Park ("Garden of Peace and Joy") as a new one-third-acre park with plenty of sunshine and a new recreation center offering Kindergym programs for preschool children, and tutoring and arts programs for school age youth. The twenty-year dream of the Chinatown Park Rec Committee, then led by Terry Ow-Wing and Gary Wong, for a new Chinatown park had finally come true.

An obvious concern all along for the Cathay Mortuary site was that it had been a mortuary for many decades. Chinatown families (mine included) had attended many funeral services there, and superstition was something we knew we had to deal with—what one pundit called the *Poltergeist* factor. It was only after a thorough community outreach process, particularly involving our seniors, that we learned that putting a park on a former funeral home site wasn't the concern we had feared. The seniors said to us, "Chinese have always lived with their ancestors" and that we young folks shouldn't worry about it. Old-time San Franciscans also told us that there are former cemeteries all over San Francisco, replaced over two centuries with new homes, schools, office buildings. We were relieved. But just in case, when the dedication ceremony was held for the new Wo Hei Yuen, not only did Reverend Norman Fong preside as a Presbyterian minister, we had blessings from Catholic and Buddhist priests as well. We had to cover the bases. And Chinatown finally had its new park.

In 1993, the Chinatown CDC and Chinatown Park Rec Committee completed the Portsmouth Square Master Plan, sharing a vision for the redesign of Portsmouth Square, the central gathering place for San Francisco when it was first constructed in 1883. The master plan used $3.9 million in City open space funds for improvements. The first phase, which included new benches, elevators, trellises and planting, and two new children's playgrounds, started in 1994 and was completed in 1998. The second phase, which created a new small community center, was completed in 2001. Both the new Wo Hei Yuen Park and the redesign of Portsmouth Square exemplified participatory design principles with input from hundreds of seniors, youth, and children.

Many of Chinatown's community centers and churches are themselves living symbols of our history. Cameron House, the Chinatown YMCA, and the Gum Moon residence home are all centuries-old institutions who continue to provide invaluable services in their historically significant buildings filled with murals, artifacts, and stories of Chinatown's past. In 2012, Chinatown celebrated the completion of the new Chinatown YMCA, a terrific project that combines the preservation of its historic building with a newly constructed wing, enabling the YMCA to expand its health and fitness and youth leadership programs. Our youth centers build community

The Chinese Historical Society of America Museum (CHSA), founded in 1963, celebrated its 50th Anniversary in 2013. Located for decades in a small storefront on Adler Alley (now Jack Kerouac Alley), the CHSA could exhibit less than 10% of the Chinese American history exhibits they had curated, leaving most of the collection in storage. The long-term dream of the CHSA had been for a larger museum that would be not only a venue for its exhibits, but also a place to promote learning and education about the Chinese in America. This dream came true in 2001 when they dedicated the new Chinese Historical Society Museum at the site of the former Clay Street

Center of the Chinatown YWCA at 965 Clay Street, a wonderful building designed by Julia Morgan. Community-based museums build community.

Within a two-block area of Stockton Street, a number of important community centers have been completed or are under construction. The United Presbyterian Church in Chinatown completed the renovation of its new church building on Stockton Street, and The Asian Women's Resource Center, with the construction planning help of Chinatown CDC, celebrated the seismic retrofit and renovation of its historic Gum Moon building in 2013. The new Chinese Hospital, one of Chinatown's most historic and important institutions, is under construction on Jackson Street. And once completed, the new Central Subway Chinatown Station on Stockton and Washington Streets will serve as a community plaza and gathering place as well. Churches, community centers, hospitals, and public plazas all help to build community.

The new North Beach Library was completed in 2014 and is a wonderful place serving North Beach and Chinatown, designed to be integrated with the North Beach Playground. Along with the Chinatown Library, renamed for the late historian Him Mark Lai, the new North Beach Library underscores the critical importance of libraries not only for education and learning, but for community building as well.

The Betty Ann Ong Chinese Recreation Center

On July 14, 2012, over a thousand Chinatown residents joined with the San Francisco Recreation and Parks Department to dedicate the Betty Ann Ong Chinese Recreation Center. The Chinatown CDC facilitated active community input from Chinatown residents and organizations. It was a joyous and emotional event, celebrating the reconstruction of one of Chinatown's most important recreation facilities. Originally built in 1951, the new center was expanded to include a new basketball court, arts and crafts rooms, and outdoor play areas.

The center was renamed the Betty Ann Ong Chinese Recreation Center after Betty Ann Ong, one of the flight attendants on-board American Airlines Flight #11 that was flown into the north tower of the World Trade Center on September 11, 2001. She made the first phone call after the hijacking to tell the world that America was under attack. She stayed on the phone with American Airlines ground crew, relaying critical information that led to the closure of American airspace by the FAA for the first time in U.S history.

Betty Ann Ong and her family lived on Jackson Street near the Chinese

Rec Center, and Betty and her siblings were regular "Rec Center kids." In 1970, I lived next door for about a year and would buy bags of their famous homemade beef jerky (the best in Chinatown). Betty's family has established the Betty Ann Ong Foundation in her honor to support youth and education programs.

On November 25, 2013, President Obama chose to deliver a major address in Chinatown on Immigration Reform, and it was quite an honor that the Betty Ann Ong Chinese Recreation Center was selected as the venue for the address. The President called Betty an American hero and highlighted her strong family and the importance of Chinatown families. It was a proud day for all of us who attended.

It seems amazing that so many important new Chinatown facilities of all types have come to fruition in the span of one decade. But, we must remember that many of these projects have been years in the making, and it is a testament to leadership that Chinatown has celebrated so many ribbon cuttings in recent years.

To New Visions and New Leadership for Chinatown, 2000–2012

Section Four: Transitions

IT WAS THE beginning of the new millennium, a decade that started with great disaster, 9/11, and then had other horrendous disasters, including Katrina, Darfur, and tsunamis. It was Bush/Gore and "hanging chads," and Bush/Kerry and "swift boating," and perhaps these were disasters, too. The latter half of the decade was much better. American history was made with the elections of President Barack Obama and Speaker of the House ("Madame Speaker") Nancy Pelosi. San Francisco history was made with the election of Ed Lee as San Francisco's first Chinese American Mayor. The decade was about all of these historic events—and also about the World Champion San Francisco Giants in 2010, 2012 (and 2014)!

Chinatown CDC started the decade without me. After three decades, I was finally able to take a three-month sabbatical in 2000. (My board had promised me one only after I learned how to spell the word "sabbatical.") My sabbatical was supported generously by a grant that came with my selection for an inaugural James A. Johnson Fellowship by the Fannie Mae Foundation. I spent those three months doing a lot of different things. I traveled to China with Mayor Brown and Rose Pak and, of course, to Hawaii, my favorite place after San Francisco. I also conquered my fear of technology by taking some computer classes. And most importantly, I helped my family organize a big family reunion to celebrate my parents' 50th anniversary.

In 2004, Chinatown CDC was selected by the Bank of America Foundation for its inaugural Neighborhood Builders Program, which selected from each of the bank's major markets one community development organization and one youth organization that epitomized excellence and innovation. In 2005, I was selected as a member of the prestigious Bank of America National Advisory Council. Also in 2005, I was honored to be one of 25 lifetime achievement awardees by the National Local Initiatives Support Corporation (LISC) on their 25th anniversary. Both Chinatown CDC and I would celebrate our 30th anniversary in April of 2007.

In 2008, Chinatown CDC was chartered as the first Neighborworks

America network organization in San Francisco. As one of over 200 Neighborworks organizations in the nation, the Chinatown CDC has greatly benefited from the program's financial support, training, and technical assistance. It has been a key national relationship for the organization.

The Chinatown CDC joined with two dozen other San Francisco community organizations to form an important new citywide coalition, the Asian American and Pacific Islander Council (AAPI Council), to foster program collaboration, policy coordination, and advocacy on behalf of the growing Asian American and Pacific Islander communities in the City.

In San Francisco, the decade opened with the rise of the International Hotel, the place "where it all started" for many Asian American activists, Ed Lee and myself included. Celebrating the new I Hotel was a watershed moment not only for me and Chinatown CDC, but also for the larger Community Development Movement in San Francisco and across the nation (given the iconic symbol that the I Hotel struggle represented) and for the Asian American Movement for whom the I Hotel became a rallying cry.

In 1998, longtime tenants at 53 Columbus Avenue were shocked when City College of San Francisco announced plans to demolish their building as part of the new Chinatown City College campus. Assisted by Chinatown CDC, Asian Law Caucus, and the San Francisco Community Land Trust, the tenants waged a near-decade-long campaign to save their homes. This culminated in the formation of the Columbus United Cooperative, which purchased the building in 2009 as one of San Francisco's first affordable housing cooperatives. *(Photo courtesy of Chinatown CDC and Asian Law Caucus.)*

The Central Subway has been one of largest and most important public infrastructure projects impacting Chinatown in over half a century. Pictured here at a ribbon cutting ceremony in July 2013 are (L to R) Gordon Chin and Norman Fong, Mayor Ed Lee, Chinese Chamber of Commerce Consultant Rose Pak, Supervisor David Chiu, (person unknown), and Department of Public Works head Mohammed Nuru. *(Photo courtesy of Sing Tao Daily.)*

On August 26, 2005, community and tenant leaders celebrated with Mayor Willie Brown the opening of the new I Hotel. L to R: Alan Wong, Gordon Chin, tenant leaders Etta Moon and Bill Sorro, Pam Tau Lee, and Mayor Willie Brown. *(Photo courtesy of Chinatown CDC.)*

In 2005, the new International Hotel on Kearny and Jackson Streets was built, 28 years after the infamous I Hotel Eviction. The building includes 105 affordable housing units for low-income seniors, and houses the Manilatown Center on the ground floor. *(Photo courtesy of Chinatown CDC.)*

On January 30, 2013, Chinatown CDC, Swords to Plowshares, and House Minority Leader Nancy Pelosi dedicated Veterans Commons at 150 Otis Street, serving 75 formerly homeless Vietnam-era veterans. *(Photo courtesy of Chinatown CDC.)*

CHAPTER 19

The Rise of the I Hotel

FOR A QUARTER of a century, from the demolition of the International Hotel in 1978 until construction began on the new International Hotel in 2002, the northeast corner of Kearny and Jackson Streets was just one big gaping "Hole in the Ground," chain-link fenced and rat-infested, and occasionally homeless-encamped. I think I must have walked by it over 20,000 times (at least twice a day) during those 25 years. The rise of the International Hotel was a testament to a commitment of a lot of people to seek justice for those who were evicted on August 4, 1977, and to make sure that it never happened again.

In 1977, the cause shifted to ensure that whatever was built on the site of the International Hotel, include affordable housing. Chinatown CDC devoted much of the next two years to the Chinatown Block Study, which was completed in December 1978 and had evaluated both a rehabilitation plan to preserve the I Hotel, and a new construction plan for the block.

In October 1979, Mayor Feinstein appointed the first International Hotel Citizens Advisory Committee to advise the City on new strategies. The IHCAC was co-chaired by Linda Wang, then co-chair of CCBH, and Chinatown physician Dr. Rolland Lowe, and included many prominent activists and tenants from the Chinatown and Manilatown communities, including myself. The Committee was staffed by Lois Scott from City Planning Department and Housing Director Bill Witte.

The IHCAC set upon its goal of developing a new plan for the International Hotel site, including recommendations for the entire International Hotel block. Chinatown CDC updated the earlier Chinatown Block Study with the assistance of Asian Neighborhood Design to develop a number of planning scenarios. During the first few years of the 1980s, the Committee also continued its advocacy for more funding set-asides for the construction of a new I Hotel, securing over $4 million from a variety of City funding sources. The IHCAC was clear that it wanted affordable housing in sufficient numbers, quality, and affordability to replace what had existed before, and they made this goal clear as development proposals from the owner, the Four Seas Corporation, began to surface in 1981.

Over the next dozen years, the IHCAC experienced many frustrating fits and starts over the development plans of Four Seas Corporation and its successors. While the discussions with the IHCAC were usually cordial, there was always an undercurrent of mistrust by the community activists in the motivations or ability of the developers to deliver on promises. After all, they were responsible for the eviction in the first place. The City staff who assisted the IHCAC throughout the decade—Brad Paul (under Mayor Agnos), Ted Dientsfrey (under Mayor Jordan) and Marcia Rosen (under Mayor Brown)—also shared some of the frustration, but they were committed to a new plan, as evidenced by the City's continued funding of the International Hotel fund.

The first development plan from Four Seas in March 1981 called for a 12-story building on the I Hotel site and included 60–75 units of housing, 36,000 square feet of office space, and 12,000 square feet of retail space. The IHCAC felt that the number of proposed housing units was unacceptable given the units that had previously existed. We rejected the proposal, taking the added step of getting the I Hotel Block rezoned from its C-2 (commercial) zoning to RC-4 zoning requiring predominantly residential use.

Subsequent proposals from Four Seas in 1983 and 1984 increased the housing to 120 units, but also included commercial development of the other parcels they owned: the Columbo Building on Columbus Avenue and an adjacent site on Washington Street (this was the former Bell Hotel, which was cleared of tenants before the I Hotel).

Another major concern was the proposed rent levels of $740/month in the Four Seas's proposals, which was dramatically higher than had existed in the I Hotel. The accepted affordable senior housing rent scale was 25% of SSI income, or approximately $220/month. This was the affordability standard embraced by the IHCAC, as well as a commitment to maintain this for a 40-year period.

A 1984 Four Seas proposal was opposed by Chinatown CDC, due to its excessive office space. Four Seas withdrew the proposal, but not before a frustrated Mayor Feinstein proposed that eminent domain proceedings be started to acquire the International Hotel site, which the Board of Supervisors approved in March 1984.

LINDA WANG

In 1970, Linda was a medical social worker for the Chinese Hospital. She was very helpful and patient when I interviewed her for a paper I was writing for a class. When I got involved in the Chinatown Coalition for Better Housing, I saw a different side of her. She was passionate in her advocacy for new affordable housing for Chinatown. Her CCBH co-chair, Harry Chuck, was more laid back, and he would often play the "good cop" to Linda's "bad cop" in meetings with the City and HUD, when we were appealing for help or "scolding" them for not moving fast enough on Mei Lun Yuen.

After the International Hotel Eviction, Linda and Dr. Rolland Lowe co-chaired the International Hotel Citizens Advisory Community, a role Linda continued to play for over three decades, until "justice" for those evicted in 1977 was finally rectified with the opening of the new I Hotel. Linda's persistence and patient leadership were important examples for young activists like me. She devoted her career to the San Francisco Mental Health System but found time to be an active board member of many organizations, including board chair of Self-Help for the Elderly.

In 1985, the San Francisco Parking Authority and the Portsmouth Square Garage Corporation proposed to become the developer, assuming an eminent domain scenario. They planned to expand the existing parking garage under Portsmouth Square, excavate under Kearny Street and connect the garage to the I Hotel site, expanding Chinatown parking capacity and creating revenue to help finance the housing development. The plan was later dropped as all Portsmouth Square garage revenue had to go to the City's Recreation and Park use.

A final proposal in 1987 from 868 Associates (the successor to Four Seas) created a financing plan with new federal Housing Tax Credits to build housing on the I Hotel site in tandem with a commercial building on the Columbo site. The IHCAC accepted this proposal, starting the public process of designating the I Hotel Block as a Redevelopment Area, but in 1993 868 Associates informed the City that the project was "no longer feasible."

"Divine Intervention"

A decade of frustration reacting to proposals from Four Seas (then Pan Magna and 868 Associates) finally ended in July 1993. Father Daniel Mc-Cotter of St. Mary's Chinese School and the San Francisco Archdiocese were in serious discussion with Four Seas to purchase the I Hotel site, and St. Mary's wished to pursue a partnership to jointly develop the site. They knew that any new project on the I Hotel site must include affordable housing. The old St. Mary's School on Stockton Street was damaged during the Loma Prieta Earthquake in 1989, and their goal was to develop a new expanded facility. Father McCotter and parishioner Jerry Lee, along with Ralph Marchese of the Archdiocese, traveled to Thailand to meet the owner of Pan Magna and obtained an option to purchase the site, which was formally consummated in 1998. This was the game changer, and both the IHCAC and the City were overjoyed that the dream of a new International Hotel might finally come true.

In March 1994, the IHCAC formed a development entity, the Kearny Street Housing Corporation (KSH), and selected Chinatown CDC as developer. Ten years later in May 2005, KSH and Chinatown CDC formed a new partnership entity, the International Hotel Senior Housing Inc., with a board of directors appointed jointly by both groups. The plan developed with the Archdiocese and St. Mary's called for the Archdiocese to first develop a 150-car underground garage, above which would be built both the new International Hotel Senior Housing and the new St. Mary's School. Meanwhile, Chinatown CDC and Gordon Chong Architects devised a plan for a 12-story building of 166 feet to house a total of 104 senior housing units (88 studios, 16 one bedrooms), and two large community spaces, including a third-floor tenant and community meeting space with senior meals provided by Self-Help for the Elderly. The design plan also embraced an intergenerational concept of shared space, incorporating an open space courtyard between the I Hotel Senior Housing and the new St. Mary's School to be shared by seniors and children. The exterior of the building would feature 24 beautiful etched-glass photos of original I Hotel tenants and a mural by local artist Johanna Poethig depicting the I Hotel history.

The plan for the new International Hotel was in place. All that was left was to raise the money to build it. In September 1994, the U.S Department of Housing and Urban Development awarded the International Hotel project a $7.6 million Section #202 loan, along with Section 8 subsidies for 20 years to ensure rental affordability (a value of almost $8 million). I remember the joyful celebration at the International Hotel site when Congresswoman Nancy Pelosi announced the award. The HUD award, with the $14 million the City had set aside for the project over a 10-year period, was almost enough to complete the construction budget. The Bank of America put in additional financing through the Federal Home Loan Bank's Affordable

DR. ROLLAND LOWE

Rolland Lowe was the quintessential "community doctor," with his office on Jackson Street filled with patients waiting to see him, most of them elderly Chinese immigrants on Medi-Cal. Dr. Lowe was born in Chinatown, a prodigy who graduated from high school at age 15, college at 18, and medical school at 22. He was active in the Mun Ching (Chinese American Democratic League) youth group, which earned him an investigation by the U.S government. Dr. Lowe's distinguished career includes leadership in many Chinatown and San Francisco institutions, including the Chinese Hospital and the San Francisco Foundation and his election in 1997 as the first Chinese American to head up the California Medical Association.

Dr. Lowe, with Linda Wang, co-chaired the International Hotel Citizens Advisory Committee, which persevered through almost three decades to make the new I Hotel a reality. I first met him when I interviewed him for a college paper I was writing on the Chinese Hospital. Rolland became an early mentor to me and to many other new Chinatown nonprofit Executive Directors, with whom he would engage over lunch at his home. I will always remember and appreciate Dr. Lowe's calm and supportive counsel.

Housing Program. Finally, the City provided a bridge loan of $2.8 million to fill the remaining gap, requiring that the project make a "good faith effort" to raise funds from the community, of which Chinatown CDC raised more than $1.8 million.

Critical to the success of the overall financial feasibility plan was the strong support and guidance of staff from the Mayor's Office of Housing—Marcia Rosen, Joel Lipski, and Teresa Yanga—helping us to navigate the complex project and the dedicated project management of Chinatown CDC Housing Director Susie Wong. There were a couple of times when Mayor Brown had to step in to ensure that negotiations with the Archdiocese went smoothly in deciding how cost sharing would be split between the different entities (Man, the Archdiocese are some "tough" negotiators). In 2002, the construction of the garage and podium began. Chinatown CDC consultant Wayne Hu with Ralph Marchese worked out the complexities of an air rights development, in order to build the housing and school over a garage. The International Hotel Senior Housing was completed in August 2005. When the rentals were announced, more than 8,000 applications came in for the 104 senior units, a record for any San Francisco affordable housing development, with a lottery process with preferences given to former residents of the I Hotel, then to those living in substandard or overcrowded housing and veterans.

"Long Live the I Hotel!"

August 26, 2005, was the ribbon-cutting ceremony celebrating the "Rise of the International Hotel," more than 28 years after the eviction and 26 years of that "Hole in the Ground." It was a beautiful San Francisco day to spend with more than 700 San Franciscans, more than a few with tears in their eyes. Helping to cut the ribbon was Senator Dianne Feinstein and San Francisco Mayor Willie Brown. I will never forget being able to say, after so much pain and frustration, after so much hard work by many wonderful and dedicated people, "Long live the I Hotel!" At the ceremony, Emil de Guzman told Estella Habal, "We were getting our heads bashed in back then, and now we're going inside to drink champagne."

An important element of the new International Hotel was planning the Manilatown Center occupying the key ground floor cornerstone intersection of Kearny and Jackson Streets. The Center was established by the newly formed Manilatown Heritage Foundation, which over the next two years would complete its renovation of this new community center offering a wide range of visual and performing arts programs for the Filipino community, I Hotel residents, and the community at large.

The fight for International Hotel was a catalyst for both the Asian American Community Development Movement and the San Francisco Affordable Housing Movement, with reverberations across the country. Chinatown CDC and many other community organizations had been borne out of the International Hotel struggle. On August 26, we were not just celebrating the rise of 104 new senior housing units, we were celebrating three decades of struggle and courage, three decades of youthful and at times confused energy, three decades of maturation and commitment. "Long live the I Hotel!"

CHAPTER 20

The International
Hotel Block

THE INTERNATIONAL HOTEL has always represented much more than a single building. It was a cornerstone of much bigger things. For decades, the I Hotel had been the de facto capital of the Manilatown community, which stretched 10 blocks down Kearny Street. It had also been the anchor building on a very important block that joins Chinatown and Manilatown and is adjacent to North Beach, Jackson Square, and the Financial District. Bounded by Kearny, Jackson, Columbus, and Washington Streets, the International Hotel Block has continuously been a very important location.

When we did the Chinatown Block Study ("Sanger Study") with the IHTA and CCBH before the demolition of the I Hotel in 1978, we already knew that the International Hotel Block was different from any other block of Chinatown. It had many parcels that were "developable," including the International Hotel "hole in the ground," a vacant corner parking lot, and another small vacant lot on Washington Street (which had once been the Bell Hotel). The block had more development potential than any other block in Chinatown, in part because it had experienced historic displacement. The block also allowed higher density and higher height limits than the rest of the Chinatown core area.

In addition to the International Hotel, there were other important projects undertaken on the block—the new St. Mary's School, the Columbus United Cooperative, and the new Chinatown Community College Campus.

St. Mary's, 53 Columbus, and City College

The St. Mary's School has been an important Chinatown institution since it was founded by the Catholic Church in 1911 in order to provide a broader range of educational services for Chinese children and youth. The only public school open to Chinese families at that time was the San Francisco

Oriental School. St. Mary's graduates have included many Chinatown leaders, including Supervisor Gordon Lau and USF basketball star Willie Woo, and also my mother.

After obtaining site control in 1993, the Archdiocese and St. Mary's, under the leadership of Father Dan McCotter ("Father Dan"), developed a master plan for a new St. Mary's International Academy, a K–8 school with four floors of classrooms, a social center and gymnasium, a pre-school and child care center. At a cost of $27 million, it took St. Mary's longer than planned to fundraise for all of the building's spaces, but the new St. Mary's School opened for classes in 2011.

In 1998, City College of San Francisco purchased the building at 53 Columbus (called "The Fong Building" after the former owner Paul Fong, a respected Chinatown attorney), with plans to demolish the building to make way for a new Chinatown campus. For years, Chinatown CDC and Asian Law Caucus organized the tenants, some who had lived in the building for 40 years, to oppose the eviction and ensure that if an eviction did occur, there would be adequate relocation and replacement housing. Nearly five years later in 2003, City College informed the residents that they could not fulfill the obligation for replacement housing, which sparked a lawsuit filed on the behalf of the tenants by the Asian Law Caucus. For the next two years, negotiations and mediation sessions were held with the tenants and City College, but no acceptable settlement could be reached. Then, in 2005 the tenants received the unexpected and great news that City College was abandoning its plan to develop 53 Columbus (and the adjacent Columbo building) since they had acquired a site on Kearny and Washington Streets for the new campus.

It was then that the idea of the tenants buying the building surfaced, and the tenants approached the San Francisco Community Land Trust (CLT) to help explore the idea. The CLT, Chinatown CDC, and Asian Law Caucus negotiated the purchase from City College. Financial assistance came in the form of $6 million in loans from a variety of sources, including the City's Seismic Safety Loan Fund. Construction took 15 months, led by Chinatown CDC Construction Manager Heather Heppner and architects from AND. The CLT and Chinatown CDC developed the financial plan for the cooperative, calling for the families to invest $10,000 each to purchase shares in the cooperative, with the CLT acting as master residential tenant overseeing 99-year leases to the family tenants. Asian Law Caucus became the commercial tenant in the new cooperative, also with a 99-year lease for its new headquarters.

AL ROBLES

Al Robles was the Poet Laureate of San Francisco's Manilatown. Born in 1930 in San Francisco's Fillmore District, he helped make San Francisco the special place it is. He did this with a spirit and outlook on life that was always positive, emanating from his love of Manilatown and of a City that has not always treated manongs with the respect they deserved. Al said, "As a poet, I've followed the footprints of the manongs," and his spiritual leadership was just as important to the I Hotel struggle as the tenant and community organizers who led the fight.

In the years following the I Hotel eviction, Al, Bill Sorro, and I would usually greet each other (each of us wearing a Hawaiian shirt) with a shout out, "Hey, Brother, what's up?" Al focused his attention on the manongs at the Manilatown Senior Center (operated by Self-Help for the Elderly), which, post-eviction, had moved into the basement of Chinatown CDC's Clayton Hotel. Al loved to bring me there to check out the Manilatown String Band, one of the best shows in town, with manongs in their seventies and eighties just "gettin' on down," just like they had for many years when they played at the I Hotel taxi dances. Take care, Brother Al.

On June 16, 2009, the Columbus United Cooperative officially opened its doors at 53 Columbus Avenue after an 11-year journey. A collaboration between the 21 families who lived there, the Asian Law Caucus, Asian Neighborhood Design (AND), the San Francisco Community Land Trust (CLT), and Chinatown CDC, Columbus United was the first affordable housing cooperative in Chinatown and the first community land trust cooperative in San Francisco.

While the Columbus cooperative was being negotiated and built, the revised proposal for a new City College campus was being developed in Chinatown. The 2003 Community College District and Chinatown Community College Advisory Committee study looked at facility needs and potential sites, raising one of the most challenging and complex land use issues to hit Chinatown in two decades. The need for a new Chinatown Community College had been evident for over 35 years, with Chinatown's community college classrooms spread over a dozen small facilities. City College had a high enrollment and lengthy waiting list of largely Chinese immigrant workers for English language, citizenship, and other vocational classes. A new Chinatown campus and a new Mission district campus had long been the highest priority needs in the San Francisco Community College system.

In 2003, the District purchased three sites on the International Hotel block–53 Columbus, the Columbo Building on Columbus Avenue, and Washingon corner and "Lot 5" on Washington St. adjacent to Columbo. The Friends of the Columbo Building (headed by activist Aaron Peskin, then president of the Telegraph Hill Dwellers) sued City College and reached an out-of-court settlement that preserved the building and also established design parameters limiting building on all three sites.

Then, in 2005, City College purchased the "Fantec" (named for its Taiwan-based owner) parking lot on the Northeast corner of Kearny and Washington Streets for the new campus. Chinatown CDC was very pleased with City College's decision, which saved the residents of 53 Columbus. During 2004–6, the District secured funding for the new Chinatown campus from both local and state bond issues.

The original City College plan in their draft EIR called for a 16-story, 255-foot high building. The EIR did not discuss alternatives in detail. Chinatown CDC submitted a seven-page response to the EIR, raising a number of questions and issues. Unfortunately, our letter was interpreted by some project supporters as "against City College," or giving comfort to the Hilton Hotel across the street from the proposed location, which they felt was out to kill the project.

The Friends of Economic Opportunity in Chinatown (FEOC), led by Chinese for Affirmative Action, was formed to mobilize support for the project and secured support from a range of Chinatown organizations, including the Chinese Six Companies and Chinese Progressive Association. An opposition coalition called Education Coalition for Responsible Development (ECRD) included the Hilton Hotel and state elected officials Leland Yee and Fiona Ma and argued that the proposed high-rise building was too tall, out of scale with the rest of Chinatown. Public debate, some of it very inflammatory, was all over the Chinese press, and there were dueling petition drives and press conferences.

While Chinatown CDC was very active in the 53 Columbus project, we initially did not participate in any of these City College efforts. From April through the summer of 2005, the public fight continued, and many feared that the project was headed for further litigation or delay, jeopardizing its bond funding, unless some compromise could be struck.

In September 2005, City College distributed a summary of design alternatives that included their original preferred 16-story building and two alternative scenarios in response to the Hilton calling for a two-building campus. One alternative was a 14-story building and a 4-story building, the other alternative was a 13-story/5-story pairing. The FEOC support coalition supported either the 16-story or the new 14/4 alternative, representing a departure from their original position, which had insisted only on the single site, 16-story project.

At that point, Chinatown CDC became more involved in direct discussions on the project. Our board of directors, then chaired by David Chiu, participated in meetings with City College at Chinese for Affirmative Action. Chinatown CDC took a position supporting the 13/5 alternative, feeling that it was good compromise to lower the high-rise building while adding more space to the smaller building. But City College later said this configuration was overly susceptible to litigation, and the 14/4 plan was finalized by the San Francisco Community College Board. Construction of the new Chinatown campus of City College broke ground on November 1, 2008, and the new campus was completed, at a total cost of $138 million, on September 26, 2012. The projected enrollment was for more than 7,500 students.

While I don't believe the community divisions over the City College project design could have been avoided, I do believe that City College (and the Chinatown community) lost five years in chasing the first project scenario predicated on demolition of the 53 Columbus and the Columbo building. Years were wasted explaining to City College that tenant relocation did not constitute replacement housing. That time and effort might have been better spent ensuring Chinatown community engagement in the planning of the new Chinatown campus.

The I Hotel Block, A Special Place

As described in Chapter 3, after the demolition of the I Hotel in 1978, various plans for the entire I Hotel block were developed by the International Hotel Citizens Advisory Committee, Chinatown CDC, and Asian Neighborhood Design seeking to create a special place whose sum is greater than its parts. Our challenge was to think bigger than just replacing the housing that was lost, to encompass a broader vision of community needs. The challenge was how to integrate housing, retail, and community service space, and to do so in a way that different uses could complement each other

As the I Hotel saga unfolded, it became clear that such grandiose, whole-block visions would not happen. There were too many ownership entities, too many players, too many needs that, while not incompatible, were not in sync in terms of interest or timing. And one could not even conceive of the magnitude of resources it would take to develop an entire block.

But, walk down Kearny and Jackson to the International Hotel Block today and look at everything that did eventually happen. It started off modestly enough with a new underground garage. Then, 104 new housing units were built for low-income seniors, including some original I Hotel tenants. A few years later, a new model tenant-owned cooperative housing was developed with a new home for a legal services organization. Chinatown's first new elementary school in decades opened its doors just a few years ago. And finally, a new community college opened for new immigrants and residents. It was never planned as one big master plan. Perhaps it had to happen organically. But Chinatown ended up with a block that is the home for many very important new institutions. They are indeed important as individual new buildings, but together they may be even more important, as neighbors on a block with a wonderful array of intergenerational services and constituents. This is what I see when I look at the International Hotel Block through the lens of planning.

I also see the I Hotel Block as someone who has spent a lot of my life on that corner of Jackson and Kearny, with many great people sharing many experiences, many good, some bad. When I look at that block today, I see not only what's there now, but I also see people from my past, and from Chinatown's past, that will always be there.

The I Hotel tenant leaders, Felix Ayson, Emil de Guzman, and Etta Moon, are all there. I can see them. And I can hear Bill Sorro and Al Robles calling out to me, "Hey, Brother," as they always did, wearing Hawaiian shirts like I was. The Kearny Street Workshop is there, a place where Asian American arts became a movement, and so is Everybody's Bookstore where I hung out with Steve ("Fey Doy") Wong. The International Hotel CAC is right there inside the I Hotel, too—Linda Wang, Dr. Lowe, Susie Wong—probably all having another meeting. And I can see Self-Help for the Elderly serving meals to the seniors upstairs, and youth slam, spoken word and poetry down at the Manilatown Center. Our rights are being fought for around the corner at the Asian Law Caucus, and looking at the new City College campus I can see Chinese for Affirmative Action, which fought for it. And of course, I can see the Chinese Chamber of Commerce (and hear Rose Pak) right in front on Kearny Street every year for the Chinese New Year Parade.

In the early morning or afternoon, I can see the hundreds of children playing in their nice blue and white St. Mary's uniforms, which my mom once wore. And I can see Dorothy with Phil Chin and Landy Dong at that first recruitment meeting for Chinese bus drivers at the Asian Community Center. And if I look down Jackson Street, I can see members of Team 40 shooting pool and nurturing young leaders at the Chinatown Youth Council with three friends, Albert Cheng, Alan Chin, and Stan Yee, who were executive directors in the basement of the old Hungry i.

4 mayors and ...
At a March 1975 photography exhibit at the International Hotel, photographer Chris Huie displayed two photos side-by-side. The first was an historic photo Chris had found of four San Francisco Mayors, (L to R) Elmer Robinson, George Christopher, John Shelley, and Joseph L. Alioto.

The International Hotel is a special place. And the whole International Hotel Block holds a special place in my heart because it encompasses so much of my life in Chinatown. Long live the I Hotel!

I Hotel Postscript: The Manongs and the Mayors

It must have been over 30 years ago when the Reverend Harry Chuck came by my office at Chinatown CDC, announcing that he had a gift for me. They were two photographs etched onto heavy Masonite slates, each about a foot and a half square. One depicted four former San Francisco Mayors—Elmer Robinson, George Christopher, John Shelley, and Joseph Alioto. The other was a photo of four manongs who were active tenant leaders in the International Hotel Tenant Association—Joe Bungayan, Andrew Toy, Claudio Domingo, and an unnamed manong. Harry told me he had salvaged the two slates a week or two after the August 4, 1977, eviction. The building was empty, the tenants had all been evicted, and there was sprinkler damage and debris strewn about the lobby. Harry said he just walked in and came upon the photos hidden away in a corner of the former lobby.

Harry gave me the photos for safekeeping, which I did for all those years, stashing them away in my office closet. I told myself that someday I would find out the real story of the photos, but it wasn't until I decided to write

4 manongs
The second was of four manong tenant leaders of the International Hotel, who Chris had posed to mirror the four mayors. They are (L to R) Joe Bungayan, Andrew Toy, Claudio Domingo, and a fourth unidentified manong. *(Photos courtesy of Chris Huie.)*

this book that I did some research. From Nancy Hom, former Executive Director of the Kearny Street Workshop, I found out that the photographer of the manongs was Chris Huie, who had been a key chronicler of I Hotel events through the entire decade-long struggle. Emil de Guzman, who was President of the International Hotel Tenants Association at the time of the eviction, helped to identify three of the manongs, and Chris graciously gave me use of the photos.

The photo of the four manongs, which was not titled, was taken in March 1975 in the offices of the International Hotel Tenants Association. Chris came across the photo of the four San Francisco mayors and then came up with the idea of having the four manong leaders pose to mirror the four mayors. The two photos were then displayed side-by-side at an exhibit at the I Hotel later in 1975. I don't know how long the exhibit was up, but the photos were then stored away until Harry Chuck found them after the eviction. To me, the juxtaposition of the two photos is a perfect and fascinating metaphor for what the I Hotel struggle was all about and what it meant to a generation of Asian American activists: the pairing of four symbols of official San Francisco power with the community power and leadership of those four manong leaders speaking truth to power in 1975.

CHAPTER 21

The Central Subway

THE CENTRAL SUBWAY has been a priority of Chinatown community organizations for more than three decades, identified as a potential new metro line in studies by the Municipal Transportation Agency in the 1960s. In their 1989 "Four Corridors Study," the MTA had identified key San Francisco areas for new transportation infrastructure, particularly to address expanded north-south transit service, to complement the MUNI metro, which primarily provides east-west service from the Financial District area to the City's western neighborhoods. The studies prioritized Chinatown/North Beach as one of four new transit corridors. These corridors were high priorities included in the City's Proposition B Sales Tax measure passed by San Francisco voters in November 1989 (three weeks after Loma Prieta). Proposition B established a County Transportation Authority to administer the program pursuant to its Four Corridors Plan.

Planning for the new T Third Street light-rail line serving Third Street in a 5.4 mile surface route from Bayview/Hunters Point to the South of Market area was completed in 2007. The Four Corridors Study, formally adopted by the City in 1995, recommended that the T Third Street light-rail line be extended via a new 1.7 mile underground subway to the San Francisco Convention Center, past Market Street to Union Square and ending in Chinatown. The Central Subway is essentially phase two of the T Third line.

The $1.6 billion Central Subway project will include three new underground metro stations at Yerba Buena Gardens, Union Square, and Chinatown and a new surface station at 4th and Brannan Streets. It would significantly reduce travel times and improve transit reliability between the southeast and northeast sectors of San Francisco, relieving pressure on existing surface bus lines, which are some of the most congested in the system. The MTA estimated that the Central Subway will provide direct service and reduce travel times from 51 minutes to 38 minutes for residents traveling to or from Visitation Valley and Chinatown.

The Central Subway has received near-unanimous support from San Francisco elected officials throughout its planning process. It has spanned five mayoral administrations, with much of the key project issues and funding challenges faced during Mayor Brown's tenure. There have been literally hundreds of public meetings, hearings, and approvals by the Board of Supervisors and various commissions (I think Rose Pak and the late Enid Lim went to almost all of them). And the project has gotten stalwart leadership from Congresswoman Pelosi and Senator Feinstein.

Some of the opponents to the Central Subway called the project "A Subway to Nowhere," (taking a cue from the Alaska Bridge to Nowhere that gained some notoriety for congressional earmark funding). This really upset a lot of folks in Chinatown who felt that the "nowhere" reflected disrespect, if not racism, directed at our community. For Chinatown, the Central Subway was the most important public infrastructure project proposed for our community since the construction of the Ping Yuen public housing projects in 1953. It will be a catalyst for further improvements to the Stockton Corridor and a stimulus for other economic activity. It will enhance Chinatown's important role in the tourism and visitor industry with a direct connection to the Union Square and Convention Center areas. Perhaps most importantly, the Central Subway will connect Chinatown and the northeast sector with the southeast sector, which is the major growth area in San Francisco.

The Central Subway was supported by every segment of the Chinatown community and Chinese Americans citywide. Chinatown CDC organized a petition drive that gathered 17,000 signatures in a two-week period. Citywide support also came from a broad spectrum of organizations, including SPUR, organized labor, senior organizations, and youth groups. Chinatown is the most transit dependent of any San Francisco neighborhood, with a high proportion of seniors and immigrant families very comfortable in subway systems. In a Transit-First city, it was surprising to many Chinatown residents that anyone could question a project that would reduce automobile dependency.

Many key issues arose during the planning phase of the Central Subway. Some suggested the construction of surface-level light rail, which would be less expensive than an underground subway. But Chinatown businesses and residents were adamant that this alternative would have had much more severe impacts on the environmental quality, health, and retail activity if Chinatown's major commercial street was dug up for the many years of construction.

Some opponents of the subway pushed an alternative Stockton Street Bus Rapid Transit Plan. The MTA and Chinatown rejected this alternative because the Stockton Corridor is very different from Geary or Van Ness, where BRT will be implemented. Stockton Street has only three moving lanes used by MUNI buses, cars, and commercial loading vehicles throughout the day. BRT would prohibit vehicles to service local merchants and impede Stockton's commercial activity. Despite the high frequency, buses are often full all day and cannot speed down the street.

The Central Subway, as with any large-scale public infrastructure project, has not been without impact and inconvenience to many people during its construction. Residents of South of Market have been inconvenienced, as have shoppers and visitors to Union Square. In Chinatown, 17 families and 9 neighborhood businesses had to be relocated for construction of the new Chinatown Central Subway Station. Dealing with relocation has been one of the most important roles that Chinatown CDC has played in recent years. We've helped find new locations for the businesses and new permanent housing for the residents.

The new Chinatown Station of the Central Subway will be an important connecting point for Chinatown with other parts of San Francisco. It will feature an underground metro station with retail services, an information kiosk, and community art on the street level and a wonderful new open space terrace on the terrace level. This new public plaza will be a place for residents, visitors, and subway patrons to rest—and a venue for community events.

Tense community concerns were voiced by North Beach restaurants and other businesses concerned about the extraction of the tunnel-boring machine on Columbus Avenue. The MTA has responded with the purchase of the former Pagoda Theater site and its demolition for the extraction of the machine. Someday, I hope this will be the site for an additional North Beach Station of the Central Subway. SPUR has convened a series of stakeholders to discuss the future transportation needs of the northeast sector, and there is great interest in an eventual extension of the T Line into North Beach and Fisherman's Wharf. The San Francisco Municipal Railway has completed a preliminary feasibility study, identifying possible routes for such an extension and a new community group, SF NexTstop, has been formed to advocate for the project, which will take another decade to implement. One can imagine a day when most of San Francisco's major visitor attractions—AT&T Park, the Moscone Convention Center, Market Street, Union Square, Chinatown, North Beach, and Fisherman's Wharf—are all connected by the T Line.

The final obstacle to the Central Subway was overcome when $942.2 million in federal funding was announced in October 2012. It has been a project that has been subject to countless studies and hundreds of public meetings. It's been affected by an earthquake and a freeway demolition. It has met funding challenges in the city, state, and federal levels. Its construction has touched many neighborhoods. It had seen five mayors and five MTA general managers. The Central Subway is a project that has spanned the three decades of Chinatown CDC.

I look forward to the day when the Central Subway is completed, which, last I heard, will be 2018. I'll be 70 then, and I hope my Senior Clipper card still only costs me 75 cents a ride.

CHAPTER 22

The New Era of Affordable Housing in San Francisco

THE FIRST DECADE of the millennium was a decade of great change and transitions in the affordable housing movement in San Francisco. The recession, the financial crisis, public sector deficits on both local and state levels, new administrations in Washington and Sacramento, three mayoral transitions, the demise of redevelopment in California, the continuing crisis of the San Francisco Housing Authority—these were all factors that affected San Francisco's affordable housing. During the decade, the leadership of San Francisco's affordable housing and Community Development Movements would lose some great San Francisco community activists and leaders—Bill Sorro, Mary Helen Rogers, Al Robles, Leroy Looper, Rene Cazenave, Eugene Coleman, Eric Quesada, Brother Kelly Cullen, to name a few, and I miss them all dearly.

Nonetheless, the decade would see Chinatown CDC continue to expand affordable housing serving low-income seniors, working families, and formerly homeless San Franciscans, with great support from San Francisco's Mayor's Office of Housing and the Redevelopment Agency, under the leadership of Executive Directors Marcia Rosen, Fred Blackwell, and Olson Lee. We did our first project in the new Mission Bay neighborhood, and we were proud to be involved in exciting new projects in partnership with the African American community and the homeless veterans community. However, by decade's end, the booming San Francisco real estate economy, spurred by a growing tech sector, led to record high rents for housing at all income levels and growing displacement of poor, working-class, and middle-class families. Affordable housing emerged in 2013 as San Francisco's most pressing issue, and one of the most important challenges for Mayor Lee and policy makers. And despite a major achievement in passing an historic Housing Trust Fund, nonprofit builders are challenged to produce sufficient new affordable housing to meet a skyrocketing demand and mitigate the loss of existing housing from displacement. It is a race against time, and Chinatown CDC and other nonprofit developers will seek to develop many more projects such as those developed in the past decade.

Parkview Senior Housing was developed by Chinatown CDC at 870 Turk Street under the auspices of the San Francisco Redevelopment Agency. The Chinatown CDC developed this 101-unit senior development in 2008 in partnership with AF Evans Company. Parkview is one of the sites that was formerly part of the demolished Central Freeway and identified in the Octavia Boulevard Plan for senior housing. Crescent Cove is a 236-unit apartment complex that Chinatown CDC developed in partnership with the Related Company and Union Bank in 2007, the largest affordable housing development in San Francisco's new Mission Bay.

In October 2013, Chinatown CDC dedicated the new Mary Helen Rogers Senior Community at 701 Golden Gate Avenue, another Octavia Boulevard freeway site we developed with the San Francisco Redevelopment Agency, the last parcel of the Western Addition A-2 Redevelopment Area. The project is named after famed Western Addition tenant advocate Mary Helen Rogers and was developed in a partnership with UrbanCore LLC and the faith-based Tabernacle Community Development Corporation, two leading African American community institutions. Financing was provided by the Redevelopment Agency, Neighborworks, and the Federal Home Loan Bank. The Mary Helen Rogers Senior Community has 100 affordable senior housing units, including 20 units set aside for formerly homeless seniors.

Veterans Commons is a partnership between Chinatown CDC and Swords to Plowshares, a highly-respected organization which since 1974 has served San Francisco's homeless veterans. Swords approached Chinatown CDC about doing a joint project on the site of a vacant lot at 150 Otis Street in the Mission District, a building that formerly housed the City's Social Services Department. Swords is providing a full range of mental health, drug dependency, and employment services for 75 formerly homeless veterans, and the project is a national model as the first such supportive housing project in the nation that includes on-site services from the Veterans Administration. House Speaker Nancy Pelosi has been a champion for Veterans Commons and joined in our ribbon cutting ceremony on January 30, 2013, when Swords Executive Director Michael Blecker said, "For Vietnam-era veterans who have suffered for decades, permanent supportive housing is the solution that will save their lives."

CALVIN WELCH

Calvin Welch led the Council of Community Housing Organizations for over four decades alongside Rene Cazenave. Calvin was one of the first community activists in San Francisco who took a young Chinatown CDC under his wing, as a teacher and advisor. He has been called the guru or theoretician of the San Francisco Community Development Movement, connecting the dots between affordable housing, land use policy, and politics. The San Francisco State University class he teaches is a virtual must-do for anyone who wants to learn how San Francisco policy and politics intersect. Calvin has led many important San Francisco ballot campaigns, including the 1976 District Elections Campaign, the 1986 Proposition M Growth Control measure, and the 1996 Affordable Housing Bond.

Calvin was greatly influenced by the San Francisco State Third World Student Strike. "It taught a lot of people a lot of lessons about politics and reality," he said. "And about the San Francisco Police Department and [Mayor] Joe Alioto, and about how it worked. That was the end of the '60s." Calvin has been a good friend and mentor for me for the past four decades. We have also shared a love of San Francisco sports teams through the good times and the bad. We both used to wear a San Francisco Giants satin Starter jacket, which, of course, neither of us can fit into today.

Leadership Transitions

The Council of Community Housing Organizations, long led by Calvin Welch and the late Rene Cazenave, transitioned to the new leadership of Peter Cohen and Fernando Marti, who brought new energy and creativity to the San Francisco Community Development Movement. Urban Idea, a new progressive policy institute, educates San Francisco about housing and community development policy. New organizations such as SF Rising, a coalition of San Francisco activist organizations representing communities of color, have also emerged, as have new leaders in many of the older community-based organizations.

The leadership over the third decade of Chinatown CDC in affordable housing policy continued in very capable hands. Deputy Director Malcolm Yeung and Policy Manager Gen Fujioka led the policy strategy along with Planning Manager Cindy Wu. The organization's housing development program continued under the leadership of Housing Director Whitney Jones, assisted by excellent project managers, including Thai An Ngo and

Kim Piechota. These leaders and every other community development organization in San Francisco are facing a very different affordable housing environment today.

The full impact of the end of redevelopment in California is only starting to be felt. Initiated by Governor Brown, the dismantling of redevelopment agencies has impacted communities and cities alike, taking away what has been a critical resource in the overall financing for affordable housing. The history of redevelopment, more popularly known as "urban renewal," is certainly associated with the displacement of thousands of low-income people in California, and the excesses of some local governments have abused redevelopment funding. But, the fact remains that redevelopment dollars, when used wisely as San Francisco has over the past decade, can be critical in the financing of affordable housing, especially in high-cost areas such as San Francisco.

San Francisco's passage of the Housing Trust Fund in 2012 is one such local resource that saw great leadership from Mayor Lee and many stakeholders, including private developers and the real estate industry, but nonprofit community developers led the way in crafting the measure and ensuring its passage. This will result in $1.5 billion of new funding for affordable housing over the next 30 years. However, even with this precedent-setting victory, it will not make up for what has been lost in redevelopment funding, which has financed over 10,000 affordable housing units since 1990.

I wish I could say that the Ping Yuen rent strike of 1978 resulted in making Ping Yuen a model public housing development, with adequate infrastructure, safe and decent living units, and social services to address the serious health, recreation, educational, and employment needs of its residents. But I cannot. Ping Yuen continues to have the same deteriorating physical and social conditions that plague most San Francisco public housing. The San Francisco Housing Authority is again in the headlines with yet another Housing Authority director and administration accused of a variety of misdeeds. It's a story that has recurred over the past four decades, with the Housing Authority repeatedly being placed on HUD's Troubled List, and at times it has been close to being placed under HUD receivership.

There have been signs of some hope, such as San Francisco's planning of new developments using the HUD HOPE VI program, created in the early 1990s to redevelop troubled public housing projects. In 2002, San Francisco crafted its own version, "HOPE SF," combining public and private investment to reconstruct the city's most-challenging public housing projects. The HOPE VI program awarded San Francisco a total of $118 million to redevelop five troubled public housing developments, including the North Beach projects on Bay Street, San Francisco's first public housing project and its most racially integrated with 229 units of Chinese, African American, and Caucasian residents. Unlike most HOPE VI projects in the nation, which cut total units and affordable units, the North Beach HOPE VI project added a net addition of 112 new affordable housing units. It became a model for new HOPE SF projects.

Mayor Lee has called for a major reinvention of San Francisco's public housing system, turning over development and management to private sector and nonprofit developers. The Mayor's ambitious plans received a boost on January 23, 2014, when HUD approved San Francisco's application for $180 million in Rental Assistance Demonstration funding earmarked for innovative public housing development. It was the largest RAD grant HUD approved, and HUD Secretary Shaun Donovan praised the City's "Innovative and cost-effective approach," which will affect 4,584 of the Housing Authority's 6,054 units, including Ping Yuen's 435 apartments.

In Chinatown, the revitalization of Ping Yuen will present both significant challenges and opportunities. As Ping Yuen represents 10% of Chinatown's entire land mass, RAD will be the most far-reaching physical development process that Chinatown has seen in over half a century (since the Ping Yuen projects were first built in the 1950s). The opportunity is to develop a new and better Ping Yuen with improved housing, outdoor recreation space, and services.

CHAPTER 23

Who Can Afford to Live in San Francisco?

IN RECENT YEARS, virtually all public opinion polls asking San Francisco residents what issues they believed were of most importance to the City cited housing affordability as the number one concern—not jobs, the environment, or crime, but affordability of housing. The robust San Francisco economy has given San Francisco a respite in recent years from the draconian budget cuts that once looked inevitable. Property taxes from the strongest real estate market in the nation, job growth in the tech sector, and an unprecedented number of market-rate housing developments have all contributed to a City that is in much greater financial health than most. But San Francisco has become the most expensive city in the nation for renters, with the median rent for a one-bedroom apartment over $3,100 per month.

Evictions in San Francisco increased 38% in the past three years, and Ellis Act evictions of lower-income San Franciscans increased by an astounding 170% during this same period. Evictions due to the Ellis Act, which first surfaced in Chinatown and North Beach a decade ago, have now exceeded 1,700 housing units citywide. One high-profile case that Chinatown CDC led was the Ellis Act eviction of the Lee Family at 1508 Jackson Street. Mr. Gum Gee Lee and his wife, Poon Heung Lee, both in their 70s, had lived in the building with their 48-year-old disabled daughter for 34 years, raising seven children there. Activists from all over the city led protests for weeks, but in the end, the family was evicted by the San Francisco Sheriff's Department in October 2013. On Dolores Street, near where I live, 98-year-old Mary Phillips was another sad example of an Ellis Act eviction.

San Francisco has certainly experienced previous periods of escalating rents and housing displacement (most recently during the past dot-com surge in the 1980s), but I think the San Francisco housing crisis today is unparalleled in its magnitude. It feels a lot like the 1960s and 1970s when we lost entire neighborhoods to redevelopment and thousands of existing housing units from evictions, SRO conversions, and demolitions. We've chronicled some of that history in this book, and I fear history may be repeating itself. What is happening today has fewer high-profile enemies such as the Redevelopment Agency or the owners of the I Hotel. As such, I think the current crisis is even more insidious. Its enemies are faceless, more amorphous, perhaps smarter than their predecessors.

The crisis in evictions and housing displacement today is much more widespread than it has been in any of the previous waves of displacement in San Francisco. The work of the Anti Eviction Mapping Project has depicted this very well, showing the hundreds of buildings that have been affected, most of them small apartment buildings. We simply must deal with the Ellis Act and its devastating impact on San Francisco's existing housing stock, and we need to deal with it both in Sacramento and with local strategies to stem real estate speculation. The loss of housing in Ellis Act buildings, the hundreds of additional units that have undergone some form of de facto conversion via Airbnb of permanent rental housing, or the practice of "tenants being bought out" by their apartment owners, have all resulted in a housing crisis of much greater breadth than previous periods of displacement. And it affects most neighborhoods in San Francisco.

Calvin Welch has always had a gift for using statistics to paint a picture. In an October 2014 interview in Tim Redmond's 48 Hills blog, Calvin cited the total number of housing units in San Francisco as 372,000. Of these, 9,661 were Section 8 Voucher units, 6,259 were public housing, 18,810 were residential hotel units, 18,810 were permanently affordable units built by nonprofits, and 172,000 were privately-owned rent-controlled apartment units. These types of housing, totaling roughly 237,000 units, are in one way or another under some form of government price regulation, the primary reason why residents earning less than $100,000 have been able to continue living in San Francisco today.

Supply Side Economics does not work in high-cost cities, particularly in cities those as San Francisco with limited new land to build on. While adding market-rate housing may create more choices, and more competitive pricing for ownership and rental housing for upper income and some middle-income households, it does little for low-income and working-class residents dependent on the existing rent-controlled housing stock to stay in the City. Even applying San Francisco inclusionary housing policies, some of the most progressive in the nation, does not create enough new affordable housing at rental levels that poor and service economy workers can afford, workers who live in those 172,000 rent-controlled apartments Calvin cited. We cannot simply build our way out of the housing affordability crisis in San Francisco.

Mayor Lee's "Housing for All" plan was unveiled in 2014 with the ambitious goal of building 30,000 new housing units over a six-year period, with one-third of those units affordable to those earning less than San Francisco's median income (up to $77,700 for a family of four). Building on the momentum of the Housing Trust Fund, the Mayor in his 2015 "Shared Prosperity" State of the City address also proposed a major expansion of local resources for affordable housing, including a new Affordable Housing General Obligation Bond Issue for the November 2015 ballot, new financing sources such as Infrastructure Financing Districts, a Private Investment Fund to attract private capital, and prioritizing publicly-owned land for new housing construction. If successful in passing a major new affordable housing bond in 2015, to complement the 2012 Housing Trust Fund, Mayor Lee can point to an expansion of local housing resources under his watch, greater than any mayoral administration in the past three decades.

But the context and the challenge today is different, as San Francisco faces its most severe affordable housing crisis in half a century, and such local resources will barely make up for the loss of redevelopment funding San Francisco has experienced at the hands of the State. This is why affordable housing advocates led by the Council of Community Housing Organizations have urged much more aggressive and comprehensive strategies—the targeting of publicly-owned land to build housing that is affordable to San Francisco families earning below 60% of area median income, the acquisition of existing small apartment buildings that currently contain an estimated 35,000 vacant units, earmarking city-owned land for development of low- and very-low-income housing, updating the City's Housing Linkage Program to include tech industry work spaces, and creating a new Workforce Housing Equity Fund. These are all important new measures, which San Francisco will need if it is to increase its affordable housing stock in the years to come.

It is interesting that Mayor Lee and New York City Mayor de Blasio both proposed major housing statregies in 2014. I happened to be in New York when the "Housing New York" plan was unveiled, calling for 200,000 new housing units over the next decade, with a mix of affordability, but with a high priority on affordability for working-class and lower-middle-class families earning below 60% of median income, a much more specific commitment to affordability than in San Francisco's plan. The Housing New

York plan also addresses the importance of preserving New York's existing housing stock in a much more direct manner, with the explicit targeting of new housing resources to housing preservation (60%) vs. new housing construction (40%). I have no idea how successful Mayor de Blasio's housing proposals will be, but it will be interesting to compare how San Francisco and New York are doing in meeting their housing goals in the years to come.

A Challenge to the Tech Sector

The tech sector has become the symbol, rightfully or not, of the displacement and income inequality that San Francisco faces, with the Google buses and their techie passengers behind those blacked-out windows the most prominent symbol of the crisis. But, we all know it isn't that simple, and I am given hope by the many attempts to foster greater dialogue with the tech community. While it may be unfair to blame individual tech workers for wanting to work and live in San Francisco, they are part of the real estate dynamic at work here in the City. And while that dynamic has made the Mission District ground zero of the tech-driven housing crisis in San Francisco, Chinatown has started to feel the effects of that crisis as well, exemplified by three high-profile issues in 2015.

On New Year's Day 2015, the Empress of China restaurant closed its doors. It was the anchor tenant in the China Trade Center, a five-story complex housing the two-story restaurant as well as many Chinatown retail businesses. As one of Chinatown's legacy restaurants, serving the community for over six decades, the demise of the Empress of China was decried by both Chinatown residents and San Franciscans throughout the City. The restaurant owners could not get their lease renewed by the building's owners, who had put the entire China Trade Center on the market for $25 million. The real estate advertisement promotion described the opportunity as an "ideal space to cater to creative, technology tenants," sparking fears throughout Chinatown that a new tech-centered complex would displace scores of community businesses and jobs.

In March 2015, 25 Chinese senior and family households at #2 Emery Lane, a 32-unit SRO hotel bordering Chinatown and North Beach, received eviction notices. The building's new owner, Paragon Real Estate, cited lease violations including the hanging of laundry and Chinese New Year decorations in the building's common space—dubious allegations at best. The owners had recently rented 5 of the 32 units to young professionals for $1,300 per month each, and it was obvious that they wanted to clear the building of long-standing Chinese tenants who were paying $500 each month. It was only after strong community protests, leading to Mayor Lee's intervention, that the eviction notices were withdrawn. The next month, in April, the second floor of a Chinatown building at 950 Grant Avenue was the site of a pop-up party celebrating a new, co-working tech space called 1920c. The space featured shared work space and SRO housing for tech workers, and was described ironically as "a collective space that incorporates wellness, sustainability, local community, and collaboration." The new co-working space was in clear violation of the 1986 Chinatown Rezoning Plan, which allowed commercial retail but not office uses on the second floors of Grant Avenue buildings—such tenants may need to vacate if the City takes enforcement action. *San Francisco Chronicle* reporter J. K. Dineen cited each of these three tech-related issues with the prediction that "Chinatown may be the next frontier of gentrification in San Francisco."

I've had a few informal conversations with tech leaders about affordable housing. A common theme I've heard from them is that they want to do something, but it's usually about ways to help their own workers to buy homes in this City. This is fine, but it is not enough. Most San Franciscans would say that tech workers are already at a competitive advantage over longtime residents in this overheated housing market. "Enlightened self-interest" is not in itself a bad thing, but *only* focusing on self-interest, as compared to the larger community interest, recalls to me the old industrial or agricultural "company towns," self-contained villages separated from the city and the world around them. Corporate leaders in other industries seem to get it better. The hotel and restaurant industry certainly understands the impact that the housing crisis has on their workers, due in large part to the leadership and advocacy from the Hotel and Restaurant Workers Union, Local Two, which has been a leading advocate for progressive housing policies. Banks seem to get it as well, encouraged by the Community Reinvestment Act and their experience in financing affordable housing as a way to "Do Well by Doing Good." Tech is here to stay in San Francisco as a leading force in our economy, but they need to start thinking about affordable housing as something that is both in their self-interest and in the larger community's interest.

My friends in the tech world have a few other refrains when the issue of affordable housing comes up. "We can't get involved in housing. It's too complex an issue, and we don't understand it." To which I would respond, you don't understand neurology either, but you have generously supported health care because you understand that health care is a basic need. A place to live is also a basic need for your neighbors, the waiters in the latest trendy restaurant, the child care worker who takes care of your children.

Yes, affordable housing can be complex, but you must work with people who have made it their life's work. There is no app that will solve the problem.

Another one I hear is "Housing seems so daunting. We can't solve the problem, so why try?" (I hear this one a lot from my friends in the philanthropic community as well). Well, yes, the magnitude of the problem seems big, but hey, you support food banks and health programs (as you should), and we still have hunger in this town and we still have sick people. You haven't "solved" hunger or disease, but you understand that we must work to address them, help as many people as possible, and there is a direct correlation between the lack of housing and health care, between housing and education, between housing and employment.

Salesforce CEO Marc Benioff has been one of the most generous tech leaders in San Francisco, making multimillion dollar donations to health care and education, and is the considered the moral conscience of the tech industry to "Give Back" to the City whose environment and culture, values and innovation have been so important to that industry's success. When asked about the civil disobedience that has been directed at the tech industry, he said "But we also need to take care of these other things: Regulate the buses, reform the Ellis Act, make sure we don't have broad gentrification. And then we need to make sure that the tech industry is giving back and supporting those efforts." Those were good sentiments that I thought reflected a real concern for tech's impact on San Francisco. Now is the time for tech to do something about it, with sufficient scale and commitment to help solve the problem of displacement and housing affordability in San Francisco. The Private Investment Fund, which Mayor Lee has proposed to attract business and corporate investment, particularly tech industry investment, is a good idea. The response from the private sector must be commensurate both to the magnitude of the housing need, and the significant level of resources that tech has in San Francisco.

We will see in the next few years whether San Francisco will be able to "have its cake, and eat it too"—growing a local economy anchored by the tech sector with new market-rate housing, while also protecting low-income, working-class and middle-class San Franciscans. While the first half of Mayor Lee's term was focused on his mantra of "Jobs, Jobs, Jobs," the issue of affordable housing looms as his greatest challenge for the remainder of his term and likely into his second term if reelected. Given Mayor Lee's roots as a Chinatown housing activist, it is perhaps quite fitting that affordable housing, both the building of new affordable housing and the preservation of existing affordable housing, is becoming his greatest challenge as mayor. *What goes around, comes around.*

Politics and Leadership, Chinatowns and the Asian American Movement

Section Five: Movements

My RETIREMENT FROM Chinatown CDC and Ed Lee's election as Mayor of San Francisco both occurred within a month of each other in October of 2011. While I am not suggesting that these two events were of equal importance, I thought it was interesting that as I was ending a career, Ed Lee was starting a new one. In the three years since my retirement, I've thought a lot about the larger contexts and social movements that permeated both of our careers—Asian American political leadership, the future of Chinatowns in this country, and the rapid growth of Asian American communities—and the connecting theme between all of them, leadership.

The story of San Francisco Chinatown as an important American neighborhood should be seen in the contexts of these larger social and political movements. The preservation of Chinatown over the past half century required not only sustained community organizing, but also political astuteness and growing political power. The planning vision that guided our work to plan for San Francisco Chinatown's future was informed by an understanding of all American Chinatowns and how they were dealing with similar issues of gentrification, small business retention, housing preservation, and environmental justice. The social justice lens through which we viewed so many of our local battles and strategies was empowered by seeing our work in the context of the larger Asian American Movement and learning from so many other Asian American communities. And our mission of preserving San Francisco's Chinatown was guided by a commitment to nurturing and growing community leadership, which was absolutely essential if we were to sustain that mission over the long term.

On January 8, 2012, Ed Lee was sworn in by Senator Dianne Feinstein as the first Chinese American Mayor of San Francisco. Pictured here are Mayor Lee with daughter Brianna, wife Anita, and daughter Tania. *(Photo courtesy of Sing Tao Daily.)*

The National Coalition for Asian Pacific American Community Development (National CA-PACD) demonstrated in our nation's capital in 2002 for civil and human rights after 9/11. L to R: Gordon Chin and Norman Fong; on the right is Lisa Hasegawa. *(Photo courtesy of National CAPACD.)*

CHAPTER 24

From Community Leadership
to Political Leadership

AMERICAN HISTORY WAS made on January 8, 2012, when Ed Lee was inaugurated as San Francisco's 43rd Mayor, the first Chinese American Mayor of the City of St. Francis. It was a proud day for Ed and his family, for the Chinese American community, for me, and I would like to think for most San Franciscans as well, whether they voted for Ed or not. The 2012 election for Mayor of San Francisco was unique. When former Mayor Gavin Newsom was elected as California Lieutenant Governor in November 2010, San Francisco needed an interim mayor to serve until the November 2012 election, and the decision on who should be interim mayor rested with the Board of Supervisors. It was an "only in San Francisco" show, with many interested candidates wanting to be the interim mayor, jockeying for position, and lining up support. Rumors were circulating all over town. Ed Lee, then the City Administrator, was a late entry in the sweepstakes, but at the end of the day, Ed Lee was elected by the Board of Supervisors by a vote of 10 to 1.

After Ed expressed his interest in the interim mayor role, he also stated that he did not intend to run for mayor for a four-year term in the 2012 election. By most accounts, Ed did a fine job in those early months of 2011 as interim mayor, getting high praise for his openness and desire to focus on "managing the city." The honeymoon was over on August 7th, when Ed announced his decision to run for a full term. This led to another little San Francisco political firestorm, with accusations that Ed had gone back on his word.

Among his encouragers were longtime friend Rose Pak, other Asian American leaders, community leaders from many neighborhoods, and colleagues who knew Ed from his work as Human Rights Director, DPW Director, or CAO. I was involved with a group of community leaders in the group "Run, Ed, Run," organizing petitions of San Franciscans asking Ed to run. Some of us involved in this effort to encourage Ed to run were also motivated by the fearful prospect of State Senator Leland Yee becoming mayor. Before Ed Lee's decision to enter the race, Senator Yee was perceived by many political observers to be the front-runner, or certainly one of the front-runners in the spring and summer of 2011. He had amassed a substantial campaign war chest and was working to develop a broad spectrum of support. The progressive *San Francisco Bay Guardian* newspaper even endorsed Senator Yee as its third choice (in San Francisco's ranked-choice voting system). Eventually, Senator Dianne Feinstein's strong appeal to Ed to enter the mayoral race—pulling him aside at the White House celebration of the San Francisco Giants winning the 2010 World Series Championship—was an important and timely factor in his decision to run. Pretty heady stuff.

Ed Lee's election as Mayor is symbolic of four decades of political growth and maturation of Chinese Americans in San Francisco, which was not merely an outgrowth of Chinese American population growth, voter registration, or increased political sophistication. Ed's election, in my view, came out of the community leaders nurtured in Chinatown and other neighborhoods through their involvement in both community and citywide activism, people who learned about the importance of civic and political participation through their engagement and commitment to community issues—housing, recreation, health, transportation, youth, and education. Ed Lee was one of these Chinatown leaders who found himself in a unique moment in San Francisco history, seizing the opportunity to play a larger leadership role.

A New Generation of Chinese American Political Leadership

Chinatown no longer monopolizes the political power of Chinese Americans in San Francisco as it once did, though it continues to combine symbolic political power and serves as a source of significant community leadership, fundraising, and Chinese media attention. For decades, Chinatown was the place where all the politicians went to take photos to fundraise and to seek endorsements for their campaigns, candidates for local office, state office, and Congress. Chinatown was the "capital" of the San Francisco Chinese community, where all the Chinese organizations were based and where the power was.

For many years, the voting strength of the Chinese American community citywide was in Chinatown and in Supervisorial District Three, the northeast sector of the City. Historically, Chinatown and District Three as a whole have voted more liberally than the Chinese American electorate

ED LEE

Ed started at the Asian Law Caucus early in 1978 after graduating from UC Berkeley Law School. He didn't have much time to acclimate himself to a new organization and a new community before he was thrown into the public spotlight, representing the Ping Yuen Tenants Association in their rent strike. It was a role for which he was a natural fit—articulate, bilingual, patient, qualities that Ed would display many times in his eleven-year career with the Caucus. He was one of four law school roommates who went on to outstanding careers—Ed Chen, who was appointed by President Obama in 2012 as US District Judge for Northern California; Alan Yee, partner in the firm of Siegel & Yee and an Oakland Port Commissioner; David Louie, Attorney General of Hawaii; and Ed Lee, who would become Mayor of San Francisco.

I will always know Ed as the same regular good guy I first met in 1978. Back then, most folks meeting Ed were surprised he was a lawyer (it must have been his clothes, which I would charitably characterize as "affordable"). I used to take Ed to Oakland Raiders football games. I knew this was one sweet guy when the only food he would bring was a paper bag filled with candy bars. Ed always wanted to go to the game when his hometown Seattle Seahawks were visiting, and there was this one game when Ed came dressed in Seattle gear, with T-shirt and hat. I told Ed, "Man, are you trying to get us killed? Take that stuff off!" He had the good sense to do as I said, and I am pleased to have taught Ed a little bit about the importance of self-preservation, a quality that has served him well ever since.

citywide, reflecting not so much its ethnic composition, but more so the high renter population. In terms of the Chinese vote in District Three, a more liberal voting history also reflects the fact that Chinatown residents are lower-income renters, who vote more liberally than renters overall.

However, Chinese American voting power outgrew Chinatown well over two decades ago. The total Chinese population and number of registered Chinese voters in the Richmond District (Supervisorial District One) and the Outer Sunset District (District Four) have been growing steadily, and each of those "Westside" districts bypassed District Three in terms of aggregate numbers of potential Chinese votes by the time of the 2002 election. It has been fascinating to observe the evolution of Chinese American and Asian American political leadership in these neighborhoods outside of Chinatown.

San Francisco District Six is perhaps San Francisco's most diverse supervisorial district in San Francisco. It encompasses a wide range of neighborhoods, including Union Square, the new Mission Bay area, Treasure Island, and Civic Center. The Asian American population in the district grew in the last decade to 28%, including a Tenderloin District with a near majority Southeast Asian population and a South of Market area with a large concentration of Filipino families. The district has been represented since 2010 by Supervisor Jane Kim, who was the Youth Program Coordinator with the Chinatown CDC from 2000 to 2006. Jane has had to deal with a broad spectrum of complex issues since her election in 2010 as the first Korean American elected official in San Francisco history. District Six has been the primary battleground for new growth in San Francisco, office and commercial growth and major public infrastructure developments. It is also ground zero for the expanding tech industry and its displacement impacts, and Jane has had to balance her positions to mitigate such growth through strategies including community benefit agreements. I think Jane epitomizes the emergence of a new generation of Asian American political leadership, with her broad interests and experience with many neighborhoods and in many issues—youth, education, the arts, affordable housing. This diversity of background and expertise has served her well in dealing with the complex issues of District Six.

Eric Mar was first elected as Richmond District Supervisor in 2008. Eric was a longtime leader of the Chinese Progressive Association. His leadership on issues such as healthy foods for children gained him some unexpected notoriety nationally (on Conan O'Brien's show) for his proposal to ban McDonald's Happy Meals.

When Eric was up for reelection in 2012, his primary opponent was David Lee, head of Chinese American Voter Education, who was supported by most of the downtown business and real estate industry, and who outspent Eric by a margin of 4 to 1. Nonetheless, Eric Mar was reelected by a broad coalition of residents and youth, activists and labor, tenants and homeowners, a racially diverse base that extended much beyond Asian Americans. This election was not about race. It was about different ideologies and values of two Chinese Americans and, as such, was an important symbol of the maturation of electoral politics in San Francisco.

The November 2013 election was also a watershed election for Asian American politics in San Francisco's Sunset District, which has come to symbolize the larger Westside of San Francisco politics. Carmen Chu, previously appointed by Mayor Newsom as District Four Supervisor, was elected as San Francisco Assessor. Carmen's former Supervisorial Aide, Katy Tang (who was appointed by Mayor Lee to serve out the remainder of Carmen's term) was elected in her own right as the new District Four Supervisor. And Norman Yee, an old friend and Board of Education Commissioner, was elected in a very close race in District Seven, which includes the Inner Sunset.

Carmen Chu and Katy Tang are certainly more conservative than I am, but they represent their constituencies with integrity and honesty. Frankly, I was pleasantly surprised that the progressive *San Francisco Bay Guardian* endorsed both Carmen and Katy for the 2013 election—both ran unopposed—and got some flack from some progressives for doing so. The Sunset, like the Richmond district and other San Francisco neighborhoods, is changing. The Chinese American political profile and future in San Francisco is changing as well, as the City has experienced in the last decade, a critical mass of new generation Asian American political leaders who represent a wide range of political ideologies, neighborhoods, and styles.

San Francisco Values

I've often wondered whether growing up or living in San Francisco leads people to change their political thinking and orientation over time. Do "San Francisco values" for tolerance, individualism, cultural diversity, or compassion rub off on newcomers who move here? I remember an episode in 1990 when the San Francisco Public Health Department wanted to open a new AIDS hospice in the Visitation Valley neighborhood, which was predominantly Chinese and Filipino. The proposal was met with controversy, and an evangelical Chinese church led the opposition. It took many Chinese American physicians and health professionals (from Chinatown) devoting their own time, going door-to-door and talking to people over months, before the hysteria died down. Those Chinese residents were scared, but they learned to accept, and they changed. They live in San Francisco.

San Francisco is truly a city of immigrants who have not only enriched our cultural diversity, but also added vitality to our economic and political leadership. San Francisco is a city that also has attracted immigrants from other parts of the country, progressive people who have gravitated to this town. And it is this convergence of different types of leadership—homegrown families who can claim five or six generations as San Franciscans, recent immigrants—which has, over time, contributed to Asian American political success, including the election of Mayor Lee.

For me, community leadership is the foundation of political leadership.

JANE KIM

Jane Kim represents District Six on the San Francisco Board of Supervisors. She was first elected to the board in 2010 and reelected in 2014. Jane was not only the first Korean American elected to any office in San Francisco, but also the first Korean American supervisor in America. Jane brought to her political career a great deal of experience in a variety of leadership roles—as a consumer advocate for the Greenlining Institute, as a co-founder of the Lotus Arts gallery, and with Chinatown CDC as Youth Program Coordinator from 2000 to 2006. In 2006, I was amazed that Jane was able to continue her excellent job with Chinatown CDC, pass the State Bar to become an attorney, and get elected to the San Francisco Board of Education. Jane is a wonderful example of smart, young Asian American political leadership, especially women leadership, both in San Francisco and nationwide.

Norman Yee was a community child care activist and education specialist long before he decided to run for office. Jane Kim's career as a Youth Coordinator with Chinatown CDC, combined with her other community leadership roles in the arts and education, influenced her decision to seek elected office. They, like Ed Lee, are not career politicians. They started out in the community, and the values that they brought to City Hall were formed in those communities. Phil Ting and David Chiu, elected to the California State Assembly in 2012 and 2014 respectively, both understood the importance of a community track record, serving on numerous nonprofit boards before entering politics.

The election of these Chinese American leaders didn't just happen overnight. Their success in the electoral arena can be traced back to the foundation these leaders built in the Chinese American community. The electoral success can also be attributed to the growing organization and maturity of the Chinese American community and the impulse to work on political campaigns and make our voices heard in the electoral arena.

Asian Americans Are Becoming More Progressive

The evolution of Chinese American political perspectives in San Francisco should also be understood in the context of trends for all Chinese Americans and Asian Americans nationally. In the 2012 Presidential election, 72% of Asian Americans supported President Obama (vs. 26% for Mitt Romney), according to exit polls conducted by the Asian American Legal Defense and Education Fund (AALDEF) and National CAPACD. The Asian American vote was likely an important factor in many swing states such as Nevada. Asian Americans across the country are becoming more liberal on major social and economic issues. The National Asian American Survey, conducted by the University of California in 2008, reported that 60% of Asian Americans and Pacific Islanders (AAPIs) believe the government should provide health care for all Americans. The survey further showed

- 57% support immigration reform and a path to citizenship for the undocumented

- 68% supported expansion of federal housing programs for the poor

- 67% favored higher taxes for households earning over $250,000 a year

- 58% supported same-sex marriage

The UC study concludes that Asian Americans are much more supportive of an activist government to protect the disadvantaged, human rights, and the environment. And the UC study cites as a critical factor Asian Americans' belief that the Republican Party has rejected science in their policy positions on global warming and the environment, turning off many Asian American professionals in science, technology, and engineering.

San Francisco's national reputation as a center of progressive politics often makes it difficult to put easy labels on our elected officials. What is considered liberal or progressive in Des Moines or Cleveland may be merely moderate (or even conservative) in San Francisco. I find it fascinating that San Francisco's four Asian American Supervisors represent not only a broad political spectrum—Jane Kim and Eric Mar as progressives, Katy Tang as conservative/moderate, and Norman Yee as moderate/progressive—but also a broad generational span with Jane and Katy as younger leaders, with Eric and Norman more from my generation. Watching them interact and debate each other on issues at City Hall sometimes feels like a big Asian American family arguing at the dinner table.

Rose, Ed, and Me

David Talbot's book *Season of the Witch* has a chapter titled "The Empress of Chinatown," which includes Rose Pak, Ed Lee, and myself. The three of us have a relationship approaching half a century, a relationship that has evolved given our career paths and the decisions we have made along the way. There can be no discussion of politics in the Chinese American community or San Francisco without talking about Rose Pak, who has been a close friend for nearly four decades. More has been written about Rose than any other Chinese American in San Francisco, including Mayor Lee. She has been described in recent lengthy articles as a "One Woman Tammany Hall" and "Chinatown's Champion." I once surmised that the term Political Action Committee (PAC) was named after Rose.

Leaders in the public spotlight (or quarterbacks on a football team) often get more credit and more blame than we deserve. In the political world, Rose has certainly been the most out-front leader advocating Chinese American political empowerment, but not the only one. She has been a catalyst for a lot of leadership in our community and that leadership will grow, no longer needing Rose's help or mine. In the last couple of years (since my retirement), when I have hung out with Rose, I think we spend much less time talking about politics and more of our time talking about family, about food, and about our respective physical ailments. That's what friends do.

It's been said that "All politics are local." With Rose, all politics are indeed local, but I think Rose would also say that "All politics are personal" and that politics is all about relationships and honest communication, which in Rose's case can be somewhat blunt. As she has said, "You can't be afraid to fight with your friends, if that's what's best for the community," and I saw this played out when she expressed that Mayor Agnos, whom she and much of Chinatown supported, was disrespectful of Chinatown's needs during the Embarcadero Freeway fight.

While Rose has certainly been a major supporter of Mayor Lee, she has not shied away from publicly sharing criticism of the Mayor's decisions or policies if she believes they are not in the best interest of her constituencies and community. A case in point was Mayor Lee's decision on January 8, 2015, not to appoint Cindy Wu to the District Three Supervisorial seat, left vacant by David Chiu's election to the State Assembly. Apparently, Cindy's progressive views and strong tenant advocacy did not achieve a comfort level with the Mayor. I shared Rose's deep disappointment over the Mayor's decision to bypass Cindy, who as Planning Manager for Chinatown CDC as well as President of the City Planning Commission would have brought great expertise in planning and land use to the Board to help address San Francisco's housing affordability crisis.

Rose, Ed, and I remain old friends. But, friends can and do disagree, and we cannot let old relationships prevent us from standing up for our beliefs when such disagreements might arise over appointments or issues such as affordable housing policy. As I heard Calvin Welch say many times, "In politics, there are no permanent friends or enemies, there are only permanent interests." And while the historic importance of Ed Lee's election as San Francisco's first Chinese American mayor and the recent electoral success of Chinese and Asian Americans in San Francisco represents our community's political growth and maturation, we must not define our community only through the lens of elected representation. Politics to me is merely a means to an end to improve the lives of the people and communities we care about, and we should never be afraid to speak truth to power.

San Francisco has been one of the key national laboratories (others include New York, Los Angeles, and Seattle) of how Asian Americans respond to progressive policy issues—preserving affordable housing, progressive taxation, labor and worker rights, environmental regulation, etc. Equally important is how such issues are framed to Asian Americans and how successful progressive movements will be in attracting the active involvement of Asian American youth and younger adults in particular. Community-based organizations such as the Chinatown CDC and others around the country are key facilitators to growing our young indigenous Asian American leaders to move beyond our own neighborhoods and become leaders in our cities and larger American social movements.

CHAPTER 25

Chinatown, USA

A FEW YEARS ago, my good friends at Asian Americans for Equality in New York City subtitled a recent Chinatown Master Plan as "A Plan for America's Chinatown." We in San Francisco all had a real good laugh over that one (just as 49er fans do when the Dallas Cowboys called themselves "America's Team"). We shrugged it off as just typical New York attitude. New York Chinatown is certainly the largest Chinatown in the country, but San Francisco Chinatown has always been the First Chinatown in America. As New Yorkers and San Franciscans continue to debate biggest Chinatown vs. first Chinatown, we need to understand both of these communities in the context of all American Chinatowns, historically and today, and the commonality all American Chinatowns have shared in their fights for survival and fights for land and place in their cities and regions.

Chinatowns have existed in America for over 170 years, since the first Chinese settlements in San Francisco and California, which served as support systems for Chinese immigrants working in the California Gold Rush and the building of the railroads in the 1860s. It was no accident of history that since the turn of the last century, particularly in the post-war 1950s, many inner-city Asian American communities were faced with displacement of low-income residents and small businesses caused by private development or government-sponsored development. These urban communities shared the common evolution of having been started by Asian immigrants who located near waterfronts or railroads, reflecting the type of work they did. But, they had neighbors in central business districts that also formed and grew adjacent to ports and railroads, as they were essential distribution resources for economic growth. The growth of central business districts has resulted in the development of valuable lands that once were American Chinatowns in New Orleans, in Phoenix (see U.S. Airways Arena), in Detroit (see MGM

Grand), and in Washington D.C. (see Verizon Center). This doesn't even include historic communities such as Denver's old Chinatown, which was burned down in anti-Chinese rioting in the 1880s. So many of our historic Asian American places have been impacted by development of downtowns, freeways, casinos, sports stadiums, prisons and detention facilities, often part and parcel with official "master plans" and redevelopment areas, such as the fate of San Francisco's Japantown in the grand vision for the Western Addition area.

Chinatowns in Oakland, Los Angeles, Philadelphia, Chicago, Boston, and Seattle's International District all lost major portions of their neighborhoods due to freeway or public infrastructure expansion in the 1950s and 1960s. Oakland Chinatown after WWII lost hundreds of homes and businesses from a succession of publicly-sponsored developments—the Nimitz Freeway, the Bay Area Rapid Transit (BART) system, a new Laney College, and a new Oakland Museum of California. Los Angeles lost parts of its older Chinatown for construction of the Hollywood Freeway in the 1950s. In the early 1960s, construction of the Stevens Expressway in Chicago claimed hundreds of Chinese-owned and Italian-owned homes as well as Harden Park next to Chicago's Chinatown.

Chinatowns and Asian American communities did not go down without a fight. In the late 1960s and early 1970s, these fights would be galvanized by younger Asian American activists who brought energy and some political savvy. Tenant revolts sprang up in all of these cities, fighting off evictions created by downtown expansion, or in the case of Boston Chinatown, institutional expansion from Tufts University. In 1974, activists in Little Tokyo in Los Angeles protested the eviction of tenants at the Sun Hotel by the Los Angeles Redevelopment Agency, and in Seattle's International District activists such as "Uncle Bob" Santos occupied the Milwaukee Hotel for many months. The Committee Against Nihonmachi Evictions (CANE) formed in San Francisco's Japantown and People Against Chinatown Evictions (PACE) formed in Honolulu Chinatown.

In 1974, Asian Americans for Equal Employment (AAFE) led mass demonstrations in New York Chinatown with protests against the construction of the 764-unit Confucius Plaza Apartment project on the edge of Chinatown. They were not against the housing itself, but demonstrated in the thousands against the virtual absence of any Chinese or local residents in the construction workforce. On April 26, 1975, Peter Yew, an engineer, was severely beaten by New York police, and AAFE organized 10,000 Chinatown residents to march on New York City Hall. I remember being simply amazed when I heard about this. "Man, 10,000 people! Those New Yorkers are taking care of business."

In 1966, Philadelphia Chinatown residents and activists protested a proposal to turn Chinatown's major street, Vine Street, into an expressway to connect with the Ben Franklin Bridge, beginning a two-decade battle that the community finally won in 1986 when the City decided to put the expressway underground. Led by parishioners of the Holy Redeemer Catholic Church (which was slated for demolition in the plan), Philadelphia Chinatown organized demonstrations and formed coalitions citywide. They fought, they learned, and they stayed. The early activism in Philadelphia Chinatown led to the creation of the Philadelphia Chinatown Development Corporation (PCDC), headed by an old friend, Cecilia Moy Yep, becoming the first Asian American Community Development Corporation in the country.

In 1971, the Seattle King County Council approved a new Kingdome Stadium on the edge of Seattle's primary Asian American neighborhood, the International District. Activists led by newly-named Executive Director Bob Santos and the International District Improvement Association (INTERIM) led community demonstrations against the stadium's impact on traffic and local businesses, and potential for gentrification.

The fights over land in and around Asian American neighborhoods are not a thing of the past; they continue with equal intensity today. In 2012, Philadelphia Chinatown had to fight again, this time against the building of Philadelphia's first casino three blocks from Chinatown. They achieved a partial victory in forcing the city to move the casino to another site a mile away. Seattle's International District today still faces threats and pressures from development and public infrastructure with a plan for a new basketball arena a few blocks from the Kingdome. Los Angeles Chinatown currently is in an intense struggle over a proposal to build a Walmart and has united organized labor and Chinatown small businesses in opposition.

All these Asian American community struggles had two important things in common. They had community leadership that cared deeply about place and about land. This place was where they lived and where their families lived, in some cases going back five or six generations and over a century. This land to them was symbolic of their history and sense of belonging in America. These Asian American communities also shared the energy and passion that young people brought into their lives and communities. It was a passion that young activists felt whether or not they had a personal or family history in the community. They shared the feelings of residents that these places and this land represented something important not only to themselves, but to all Asian Americans and to all Americans.

Chinatown USA Convocation

The common experiences of many urban American Chinatowns in con-
fronting displacement and battling major public and private development
led many Chinatown leaders around the country to reach out to each other
to compare strategies and offer mutual support. But, we were all so embed-
ded in our own communities that we usually concluded these visits with
the promise that "Someday, we should bring together our Chinatowns to
form a permanent coalition." That opportunity finally came in 1990 with
the Chinatown USA Convocation. It included a proposal I wrote to the Ford
Foundation to sponsor what we called "The Chinatown USA" project. Ford
provided a $50,000 grant to support research and a convening of eleven
Chinatown-based organizations.

It was an enriching event sharing experiences and strategies on many
important common issues—housing preservation, dealing with private
developments, economic development, historic preservation, satellite Chinatowns, and interracial relations. The latter topic was an emotional one for
all of us, especially for Debbie Ching from the Chinatown Service Center,
as the Convocation occurred just days after the Los Angeles uprising, which
highlighted, among many issues, the growing tensions between the African
American and Korean American communities.

The Chinatown USA Convocation was not the start of the Asian American Community Development Movement; that actually started with local
activism at the International Hotel in San Francisco, the Milwaukee Hotel
and Kingdome in Seattle, Philadelphia Chinatown's fight against a freeway,
and many other struggles. But, the significance of the Convocation was that
it was the first formal gathering of many established organizations and veteran community development leaders. I consider these leaders to be some
of the most outstanding people I have ever met and have the honor to call
friends.

The Convocation reinforced the notion that we were not isolated in our
local community challenges; we were all part of larger movements for social and racial justice in America. One of the main conclusions we reached
was there was a great need to have a formal national coalition or network.
Moreover, any such coalition should not be limited to Chinatown-based
organizations, but should bring together community-based organizations
from all Asian American communities. As such, Chinatown USA was a
forerunner to the establishment in 2001 of the National Coalition for Asian
Pacific American Community Development (National CAPACD).

The End of Chinatown?

In December 2011, the *Atlantic Monthly* contained an article by Bonnie Tsui with the provocative title "The End of Chinatown?" While I enjoyed Tsui's earlier book *American Chinatown*, I was surprised by Bonnie's *Atlantic Monthly* article, particularly its dramatic title, which spawned a mini firestorm in the blogosphere. Subtitled "Does China's rise mean the decline of America's most storied ethnic enclaves?," Tsui's premise was that American Chinatowns were depopulating due to reduced immigration from China and the growth of Chinese ethnoburbs. Many critics questioned Bonnie's methodology—census data showing declining Chinatown populations—and they questioned her suggestions that China's economic climate would lower future immigration into Chinatowns or trend to a dispersed immigration pattern to other ethnic enclaves.

While some core Chinatown census tracts do show declining population, this may indicate increased residential displacement and overcrowding that is underreported, particularly among the undocumented. Also, significant growth in Chinese population in areas adjacent to Chinatowns is not counted by many cities as part of Chinatown. For example, there has been steady and well-documented Chinese American population growth in the New York City's Lower East Side, the Bowery, and even Downtown, which are not considered Chinatown, not to mention the explosion of Chinese population in Flushing, Queens, and all other New York boroughs.

Some of the drama over Bonnie's article has subsided (her title caused a lot of it), but the ensuing debate over the article was important. The fact is that major American Chinatowns may not be on their deathbeds, but all are certainly undergoing rapid change, affected by local, regional, and economic trends that have not been adequately researched, disseminated, or debated—much less understood for their significance to local and national public policy.

In October 2013, the Asian American Legal Defense and Education Fund (AALDEF) released a preliminary report from their yearlong study of Chinatowns in New York City, Boston, and Philadelphia. Titled "Chinatown: Then and Now, A Snapshot of New York's Chinatown," the report warns that "Chinatowns are becoming increasingly destabilized as their future as sustainable low-income immigrant communities is threatened." And contrary to Tsui's supposition that Chinatowns are dying because of decreasing immigration from China and the growth of Chinese ethnoburbs, the report cites real estate trends and city planning policies that have promoted high-end housing and business development and the resulting displacement as the primary causes of declining population in New York Chinatown.

The AALDEF report highlights an important trend that many Chinatown activists have observed—that while decreasing overall population is a concern, the decrease in Chinatown family and children population is most dramatic. New luxury condominiums near New York Chinatown, targeted to single professionals, have had a spillover effect on adjacent Chinatown housing and small businesses. With fewer rental alternatives, families pursue better options in outlying boroughs. In San Francisco, we have seen displacement of low-income seniors and families not only in the Chinatown core, but also in adjacent areas such as North Beach and Nob Hill, where Chinatown families have historically moved from Chinatown.

The decline in family population in American Chinatowns is a trend seen not only in Chinatowns in the AALDEF report—New York, Boston, and Philadelphia—but also in San Francisco, Oakland, Chicago, and Honolulu. We may be seeing a second wave of declining family population. The first wave was in the 1960s and 1970s when major public infrastructure developments, particularly freeway expansion, wiped out entire sections of Chinatowns. This second wave may be more complex. Indeed, Chinatowns have played a "way station" role, giving new immigrants an initial home— as crowded and inadequate as those homes may be—with the hope that they may save up and buy a home or move to better rental apartments. And some families do want to raise their children outside Chinatowns. But increasingly, the housing markets in and around our Chinatowns have forced relocation of families who otherwise want to stay. This is why Chinatown CDC has prioritized affordable family housing in its two new developments on the Broadway Corridor, and why strong rent control, tenant protections, and new strategies dealing with the Ellis Act are very important.

That people still want to live in Chinatown is reflected in the record numbers of people who apply for new affordable housing there. They are people from all over—from other San Francisco neighborhoods and the Bay Area, not necessarily from China. I don't know how many calls I have gotten from professional friends in wealthy Bay Area cities who tell me that their mom or grandmother would like to move out of their luxurious four-bedroom villa (with swimming pool) and come "back to Chinatown," even though it means living in a studio or residential hotel. Housing is not the same as community, and many Chinese seniors feel isolated out in the 'burbs, no matter how nice the home is, because they have no community there. The situation might be a little less isolating in ethnoburbs with Chinese markets and services, but it is still not the same as the Chinatown community they knew so well.

San Francisco Chinatown and San Francisco hold special meaning for many Chinese Americans in the Bay Area. Chinatown's core population may change over time, with fewer families, perhaps with greater ethnic diversity. But, it's also about San Francisco as a city with special significance for Chinese Americans, a city where the Chinese population has grown steadily, as it has in New York. San Francisco, for Chinese Americans as for the LGBT community, is special. Chinatown is our "first place," a place of comfort and familiarity, where our family history lies, a safe place of refuge.

Historic Chinatowns, New Chinatowns, and "Ethnoburbs"

Chinatowns aren't dying, but they are changing. Immigration patterns into Chinatowns are diversifying. Immigrants, historically coming from Guandong Province into San Francisco Chinatown, have diversified to encompass many regions in China, Taiwan, Vietnam, Southeast Asia, Malaysia, and Singapore. And the extent of undocumented Chinese populating Chinatowns and other Chinese ethnic enclaves has not been sufficiently analyzed for their impact on local housing and economies. As we have seen, the value of Chinatown land and adjacency to downtown areas is a major contributing factor in the gentrification of Chinatown economies and displacement of longtime residents.

Chinatown economies are in transition. The impact of 9/11 on New York Chinatown's economy has been severe and needs attention and planning. Other Chinatowns that have not experienced surges of immigration struggle to redefine or diversify their economies in ways that are not susceptible to public rationales for casinos (or Walmarts). Chinatowns in Los Angeles and Honolulu are becoming trendy-hipster-artsy hangouts, challenging local Chinatown merchants and residents attempting to balance increased economic attraction with diminishing ethnic cultural identity. In San Francisco, many historic large banquet restaurants have closed due in part to competition from suburban Chinese American restaurants. In their place, proposed new upscale restaurants are seeking to appeal to a wealthier clientele. In the midst of these changes, Sam Wo Restaurant, one of Chinatown's most historic restaurants, known for its good, inexpensive food and colorful waiter Edsel Ford Fung, has fought to survive. Founded in 1912, the restaurant was closed in 2012 for code violations and an impasse in their lease negotiations, causing an outpouring of both outrage and nostalgia from its customers. But, with great support from the community and new investor partners, Sam Wo announced that it will be reopening in a new location in July 2015.

Chinatowns and other Asian American communities in San Francisco, Seattle, Los Angeles, St. Paul, Honolulu, and Oakland are all experiencing the impacts and future implications of major light-rail transportation projects, in many cases the largest such infrastructure projects occurring in those cities. While the local Chinatown reaction to such developments has ranged from support to opposition, the impact they will have on these Chinatowns will be significant.

The future of historic core Chinatowns will likely be most impacted by the rapid growth of the Chinese American population in other neighborhoods and cities in our regions. The demographic and geographic growth started with "Satellite Chinatowns" or "New Chinatowns" within a city (i.e., San Francisco's Richmond or Sunset Districts, or Oakland's Eastlake area). In New York, both Flushing, Queens, and Sunset Park in Brooklyn have larger Chinese American populations than Chinatown and in San Francisco, and the Chinese population of the Richmond and Sunset Districts both surpassed Chinatown over a decade ago.

"Chinese Ethnoburbs" have flourished in Southern California's San Gabriel Valley, the Bay Area's South Bay (Silicon Valley), and most major metropolitan areas. Newer Chinatowns have formed around Chinese-themed shopping malls in Sunbelt cities such as Las Vegas, Atlanta, and Orlando. And Houston is planning to redevelop its historic Chinatown, which has long been surpassed by its new Chinatown as the center for Chinese American community. Professor Peter Kwong of Hunter College notes, "The recognizable pattern of Chinese settlement in this country is not exactly disappearing. Rather it is being reconstituted in a much more complex, dispersed way." While the growth of suburban Chinese American ethnoburbs is usually characterized as competition to historic Chinatowns or as alternative housing and settlement options, the relationship between historic Chinatowns and these newer places can be synergistic. Newer enclaves may be bedroom communities for immigrants who still work or do business in the older Chinatown. Or, they may be places for expanding a business that is still headquartered in Chinatown.

Charlie Lai of the New York Chinese History Museum notes the growing trend of Chinese immigrant workers who live in New York City, but travel to other East Coast or even Midwest cities for work (often in Chinese restaurants) for weeks or even months at a time. I also had a conversation with Michael Byun of Asian Services in Action, based in Cleveland, Ohio, which "completed the loop" of my conversation with Charlie, telling me about the terrible temporary housing conditions these New York Chinese workers suffered in Cleveland and other places. In some ways, this "workforce exporting role" of New York City mirrors the historic role that San Francisco Chinatown played over a century and a half ago, when it was a home base for Chinese immigrants who worked on California's railroads, mines, or agricultural fields and temporarily lived in squalid company-owned shanty towns. Is history repeating itself?

All of these trends are affecting America's Chinatowns, for better or worse, in different degrees of magnitude. Understanding changing Chinatown demographic, economic, and political contexts can help guide strategy, advocacy, and public policy development for local leadership challenged by these fundamental and provocative questions:

"How are Chinatowns perceived?"

"Are Chinatowns valued in America?"

"Does America need Chinatowns?"

"What can America learn from its Chinatowns?"

One of the "Top Ten Great Neighborhoods in America"

In October 2013, the American Planning Association selected San Francisco Chinatown as one of the "Top Ten Great Neighborhoods in America." In APA's three major criteria for the Great Neighborhood designation, APA cited Chinatown's rich cultural capital exemplified by the Chinese New Year Parade and other celebrations, unique architecture and street art; its planning milestones, such as the Chinatown Rezoning Plan, Alleyway Plan, Broadway Streetscape Plan; and most of all for its community activism and leadership from individuals, families, and strong network of active community organizations.

Frankly, I had never thought of Chinatown as a "great" neighborhood, since it still has many challenges—overcrowded housing, struggling small businesses, underemployment, public safety—which won't be solved in the near future. But if great neighborhoods are defined as places with no problems, then I guess only wealthy neighborhoods would qualify. The APA award recognizes the importance of leadership in a community that cares deeply about place despite the problems it faces.

In his book *Cool, Gray City of Love*, San Francisco writer Gary Kamiya observes,

Yes, Chinatown is a ghetto. But it is a ghetto that works.... Chinatown is a living demonstration that crowded and squalid conditions
cannot defeat determined and hard-working people. In that sense,
its 16 blocks contain nothing less than the entire American immigrant experience, played out anew with each generation... Like
many other immigrants, more than most, the Chinese have faced
racism and prejudice. But, also like other immigrants, they have
overcome them to make a better life for their children. By night,
the streets of Chinatown are magical; by day, they are crowded and
dirty. But to walk them, by day or by night, is to walk the history
of America.

The real story of San Francisco Chinatown is a story about leadership
sustained by Chinatown families across generations. I have met so many
great Chinatown families over the past four decades. Wayne Hu, a founding
board member of the Chinatown CDC ran the Chinese New Year Parade for
30 years, carrying on for his father, Jackson Hu, who ran it 30 years before
Wayne. Or Allan Low, an attorney who has given much to the Chinatown
and Chinatown YMCA with the same values of civic participation exemplified by his dad, retired Superior Court Judge Harry Low. Or Kari Lee, who
became Executive Director of the Chinatown YMCA after her dad, Ford Lee,
dedicated his life to the institution, and Joanna Tom who followed her father
Harvey Wong's leadership as President of the Chinese American Citizens
Alliance. Chinatown has been blessed with hundreds of such families.

Leadership is not something that is passed on from generation to generation. Each new generation must earn that leadership role if they aspire to it.
What can be passed on are values about giving back and loving this place
we call Chinatown. For me and for so many others it is very personal, the
idea of sharing a place that was also my mother's place, and her mother's
before her.

CHAPTER 26

The National
Asian American Community
Development Movement

MY FOUR DECADES of visiting and learning about other Asian American
neighborhoods throughout the country has helped me better understand
my own community, putting our local work into a broader historical context
of the Asian American experience. Looking through the lens of community development history, it is no longer only about America's historic
Chinatowns and Little Tokyos. The emergence of hundreds of newer Asian
American places is much more dynamic and at times much more complex
in the factors that led to their creation.

Asian Americans and Pacific Islanders are the fastest growing population in the country—15 million strong in 2010, representing almost 5% of
the U.S. population, and growing at a rate that is four times the national
average. While this growth is spread across all regions, it is strongest in the
West (California in particular) and in the South.

Historically, settlement patterns of particular Asian American communities have been quite varied. San Francisco's Tenderloin evolved as the
place for Vietnamese immigrants, in part because of the lack of housing in
Chinatown. Contrast this to Honolulu Chinatown, which is rapidly becoming more Vietnamese than Chinese. Seattle's growing Vietnamese district
settled in an area adjacent to its historic International District. Oakland was
"chosen" by Korean businesses as a much more affordable place than San
Francisco. Hmong Americans migrated in the 1970s within the U.S., from
Fresno and the Central Valley of California to Minneapolis/St. Paul, seeking
better job prospects and a more welcoming local environment.

Las Vegas and Henderson, Nevada, experienced an explosion of Asian
Americans seeking work, starting in the late 1990s, that included a large
number of Filipino Americans and native Hawaiians leaving a stagnant
Hawaiian economy. Las Vegas officials, led by their colorful Mayor Oscar

SECTION FIVE: MOVEMENTS   267

Goodman, conducted a "Housing Study Tour," visiting Chinatown CDC's Tenderloin Family Apartments seeking solutions to the growing housing crisis in Las Vegas. I enjoyed my talk with Mayor Goodman, though he was not enamored with some of my suggestions for rent control, inclusionary zoning, and imposing a housing impact fee on casinos.

In June 2013, the National Coalition for Asian American Community Development (National CAPACD) produced an important new report entitled "Spotlight: Asian American and Pacific Islander Poverty." The report highlights a fact that may be surprising to most Americans: more than *two million* Asian Americans, native Hawaiians, and Pacific Islanders live in poverty. The report explores the dimensions of poverty in our diverse communities based on 2010 Census data:

- The rate of poverty in the Asian American community grew in the last decade by 37%, compared to the U.S. rate of 27%.

- Over 50% of the Asian American/Pacific Islander poor population live in ten (10) metropolitan areas: New York, Los Angeles, Chicago, Honolulu, Seattle, San Francisco, San Jose, Houston, Sacramento, and Philadelphia.

- The Asian American/Pacific Islander poor reflect the ethnic diversity of the total AAPI population: Chinese (450,000), Asian Indian (245,000), and Vietnamese (230,000) with the Hmong and native Hawaiian populations experiencing the fastest growing rates of poverty and the deepest rates of poverty.

Poverty in many Asian American communities may not be as visible as it is in other populations. While not a large proportion of the homeless in most cities, Asian Americans suffer from a much higher degree of overcrowding, most graphically seen in the increase in families living in single residential hotel rooms in San Francisco. In New York, many high-profile stories have exposed unscrupulous Chinatown property owners renting out their apartments in three 8-hour shifts each day to immigrant Chinese workers who have no better alternative.

While New York Chinatown may not be "America's Chinatown," it certainly is the biggest Chinatown in the country, and now it has many new Chinatowns in Brooklyn and Queens serving New York's nearly half million Chinese Americans. In California, eight of the top ten cities with over 30% Chinese population are in Southern California, five in the San Gabriel Valley alone. Our work in San Francisco must be informed by an understanding of what is happening not only in other American Chinatowns, but also in other Asian American neighborhoods. That understanding, for me, has been greatly enhanced by a national organization that I am proud to have helped form in 1999, the National Coalition for Asian American Community Development (National CAPACD).

Starting National CAPACD

In the half decade after Chinatown-based leaders met in San Francisco for the Chinatown USA Convocation in 1992, the interest of Asian American groups to form a national organization grew with each new national issue—anti-immigrant legislation, welfare reform, HUD devolution. Other national Asian American membership organizations existed, such as the Japanese American Citizens League (JACL) and the Organization of Chinese Americans (OCA), which have advocated for civil rights over many decades. But there was no national organization that was place-based—a strong national Asian American voice to speak out on how federal policy was impacting our communities from a community development perspective. The time was right as strong, experienced Asian American community development organizations matured in most major cities. Under the interim banner of "The National Partnership for Asian American Community Development," we called a summit planning meeting in Seattle on June 4–5, 1999, with 40 leaders from 16 Asian American organizations.

The early years of National CAPACD were a time of great energy and excitement. It was the coming together of not only leaders, but Asian American communities as well, forming something bigger, a national movement. To veteran activists like me, it had the spirit of the 1960s with high ideals and a growing sense of community, but this time on a national level. Though some of us were involved in other national networks and trade associations, National CAPACD was different. It reflected the newness of many of our Asian American communities, and hence we had to build a national infrastructure that was inclusive of a much broader array of organizations, such as community centers, social service agencies, arts groups, and youth groups. The Chinatown groups that had been around for two decades or more needed to be careful not to dominate the discourse and agenda simply because we had existed longer.

Of course, any national coalition worth its salt knows how to party, and folks like me, Uncle Bob Santos, and Kerry Doi rationalized the partying as critical to building a strong national network of relationships. At the first planning meeting of National CAPACD in Seattle, we hung out a lot at the Hurricane Bar near the Holiday Inn where we were staying. We renamed it "Hurricane Aley" after Aleyamma Matthew, a dynamic young South Asian organizer who worked for AAFE and served as our first and only staff person during that first year or so. Aleyamma and Seema Agnani from Chhaya CDC also inducted me as the first male member of the South Asian Women's Creative Collective, because they thought I had South Asian eyebrows in serious need of threading. National CAPACD hired its first Executive Director, Lisa Hasegawa, in 2000. She had headed the White House Initiative on Asian Americans and Pacific Islanders, started by an Executive Order by President Clinton.

Early National CAPACD conventions provided opportunities for emerging communities to convene as well. The Filipino Caucus and a South Asian Task Force were both created, in part to ensure that their voices were heard as National CAPACD developed programs and policy platforms with strong values of inclusion from younger American communities—Korean, Vietnamese, South Asian, Hmong, Cambodian—and native Hawaiians and Pacific Islanders. They developed partnerships with other national networks.

National CAPACD's early programs reflected this value of inclusion and movement building with a Peer-to-Peer Technical Assistance, pairing more experienced member organizations with newer and smaller organizations. "Community in the Capitol" brought staff from emerging organizations for a week-long training in D.C. to learn about the federal system and federal policy processes. "Next Gen" focused on bringing younger leaders together. National CAPACD has been a wonderful part of my life and a constant source of inspiration and learning. These are just a few examples of that inspiration. But they may also help paint a picture of the breadth of National CAPACD's view of the Community Development Movement.

National CAPACD held its second national conference in Washington, D.C., in May 2002, eight months after the horrific events of 9/11. A highlight of the conference for me was a March to the Capitol in advance of our testimony before Congressional hearings to discuss federal policy affecting Asian Americans and Pacific Islanders and our concerns—federal affordable housing policy, economic development, small business lending, and community reinvestment.

But, our chants and picket signs in our March on the Capitol reflected other issues that our members and our communities were experiencing on a very personal and emotional level—the unlawful detentions of hundreds of Muslim and South Asian Americans in the months following 9/11 and the unjustified dismissal of scores of Filipino screeners in many American airports. These civil and human rights issues were important for National

CAPACD to support, every bit as important as the more traditional community development policy agenda. Another important policy priority for National CAPACD in those formative years was support for native Hawaiian sovereignty rights (seeking similar status as afforded Native Americans and Native Alaskans), and our March on Washington in 2002 was a graphic symbol of this support as well.

Later that year, some friends of mine, longtime veterans in community development, asked me why our new national Asian American organization seemed to be losing focus, emphasizing civil rights over community development. "What does native Hawaiian sovereignty have to do with community development?" one of them asked. I responded that native Hawaiian sovereignty and social and racial justice were indeed community development issues, because our communities are deeply affected by them. We cannot just go about our business building new housing and providing services when local and federal public policies are hurting our residents and our communities.

What National CAPACD's March on the Capitol taught me was that it is all about "place." Some of our struggles have been decidedly "place-based"— the International Hotel, the fights to save our neighborhoods from freeways, prisons, casinos. But the human rights issues we marched for were about a broader sense of place, our sense of place in America, our legitimacy as Americans, our rights as Americans. It taught me that as Asian Americans and Pacific Islanders, our collective voices are stronger than our individual voices.

Thai Town, Los Angeles

Ernesto Vigoreaux from the Thai CDC in Los Angeles tells the story of getting their community in East L.A. renamed as Thai Town. This eight-year effort, led by the Thai CDC and business leaders, established the first Thai Town in America, which is a home base for the 80,000 Thai Americans living in Los Angeles, a city that shares with Bangkok a name meaning "City of Angels." They wanted a visible symbol not only for the Thai community, but also as a strategy for neighborhood revitalization. They achieved official designation by the City Council, and later a Preserve America designation in 2009.

Ernesto said the initial opposition to the idea came from older residents of the neighborhood, particularly the Armenian community that comprised the largest part of the population. They had settled in that same East Los Angeles neighborhood in the 1970s and considered it "Little Armenia," the largest Armenian community outside of Armenia, and felt the name change was disrespectful to their history. Armenians owned most of the property in the area. Both communities worked it out, recognizing the importance of collaboration, and today the two neighborhoods overlap in visitor maps and guidebooks.

The story of Thai Town made me think about how important place names are and how they are intertwined with our feelings about both race and place. After all, the name "Chinatown," which has been around a couple of centuries, may foster positive or negative impressions depending on whose opinion you ask. America has hundreds of historic ethnic neighborhoods named after European immigrants—our Little Italy's, Little Warsaws, Germantowns, Greek Towns, and Little Armenias—alongside Chinatowns, Little Tokyo's and Japantowns, Little Manilas, Korea Towns, and Thai Towns. Some have been around for centuries, others only the last couple of decades. The names of our places represent not only pride in our ethnic identity, but also a sense of belonging and security that we have a place in this country.

The story of Thai Town taught me that how we identify and promote our Asian American neighborhoods is important, as is our relationship and interaction with the neighbors and neighborhoods around us. In the community development work we do, issues of race and place are integrally linked, whether those places have been here for 160 years like San Francisco Chinatown or only a few decades like Thai Town.

Kukui Gardens, Honolulu

Built in 1970, Kukui Gardens was an 857-unit affordable housing complex on North King and Vineyard Streets in Honolulu, threatened in 2006 with conversion to market-rate housing. The complex was purchased for $131 million by Carmel Partners, a California developer who announced its plan to demolish the 22-acre complex and build 3,700 luxury housing units. It was the single largest "at risk" affordable housing project proposed for displacement and conversion in the United States. The demolition would have displaced 2,500 residents, most of them low-income families. The issue became front page news in Honolulu for many months, and there was great sympathy for the residents across the political spectrum, with Republican Governor Linda Lingle even urging eminent domain to save the housing.

Carol Anzai and her family had lived at Kukui Gardens for 38 years. As the president of the Kukui Gardens Resident Association, and as a labor organizer, she knew that they needed broad community support. She called

Faith, Action for Community Equity (FACE). FACE was an activist faith-based coalition, founded in 1996, with a membership of 38 churches on Oahu and Maui that had gained a reputation for activism.

In the summer of 2006, National CAPACD held its annual convention in Hawaii and used the occasion to visit Kukui Gardens in order to help brainstorm strategies to save it. The issue was a personal one for many National CAPACD board members who had roots in Hawaii. I think our half-day session with the tenant leaders and FACE was helpful at least in providing some moral support from friends who understood from experience that winning this battle would require multiple strategies in innovative housing financing, public education, advocacy, and organizing.

The issue raged on, with the State Legislature awarding an unprecedented $55 million appropriation towards the preservation of Kukui Gardens. We were elated to hear later that year that a deal had been cut with Carmel to sell half of the complex to a nonprofit developer for affordable housing. The Ecumenical Association for Housing (EAH), a Marin, California–based affordable housing developer, and San Francisco–based Devine and Gong, purchased the 11-acre site at the end of 2006 to renovate 389 units and build 200 to 400 new units. The new Kukui Gardens officially celebrated with a ribbon cutting ceremony in July 2011.

The fight for Kukui Gardens reinforced for me the critical importance of preserving housing for families as a core source of a community's social capital, a value that Chinatown CDC has embraced. Kukui Gardens also taught me that the support and involvement from the religious community is very important to our work. After all, "You can never have enough faith, and you can never have enough faith-based leadership."

Transportation

In 2011, National CAPACD convened a meeting in St. Paul to talk about transportation. Led by Policy Director Gen Fujioka, this historic meeting brought together community leaders from five Asian American neighborhoods that were dealing with a major public transportation project—St. Paul, San Francisco, Seattle, Los Angeles, and Honolulu. While older Chinatowns in New York, Boston, Chicago, and Philadelphia all have local subway stations developed when these cities invested in mass transit at the turn of the last century, a commitment to new transportation infrastructure in Western and Midwestern cities is a more recent phenomenon, supported primarily by federal funding for smart growth.

The projects in each of the five cities spanned a spectrum of type, scope, and community impact. Seattle's International District is located at the nexus of a King County regional transit strategy including new light-rail, Amtrak, and future high-speed rail to link Seattle and Portland. This convergence of rail lines and downtown growth led Seattle to "upzone" for new high-rise, high-density housing in and around the ID, which ID advocates believe will cause displacement without sufficient new affordable housing.

New light-rail lines and stations in Los Angeles have spurred an increase in residential displacement in the Boyle Heights neighborhood and new mixed-use development in Chinatown, reflecting the mixed bag of both adverse and positive impacts that transit projects can generate.

Honolulu is planning its most ambitious transit expansion in its history, a 20-mile elevated light-rail system with 21 stations from the airport into Ala Moana Center near Waikiki. The Honolulu Rail Transit Project has been one of the most controversial issues in Hawaii in the past decade.

National CAPACD was most involved in St. Paul, assisting the Hmong American Partnership and other groups in the Frogtown and Rondo neighborhoods deal with the impacts of St. Paul's Central Corridor Light Rail Transit project, which was designed to connect the Twin Cities of St. Paul and Minneapolis. The two neighborhoods have a population largely of Hmong and African Americans, who protested both the construction impacts and the inadequate number of new proposed stations serving their communities. In an historic collaboration, the Hmong organizations joined with the NAACP to file a formal complaint with the Federal Transportation Agency in 2010, leading eventually to the addition of three new stations (bringing the total number of stations to 18) serving the Central Corridor and the Hmong and African American communities.

National CAPACD's Transportation Convening taught me that transportation has become perhaps the key public infrastructure issue impacting many Asian American communities, with outcomes both good and bad. New light-rail and subway systems have been generally supported by these local neighborhoods, as the Central Subway has certainly been in San Francisco. Historically, inner-city Asian American neighborhoods suffered great displacement from the build out of the American freeway system, and expanding public transit (as an alternative to automobiles) is a very good thing. But adverse impacts from the projects have to be mitigated. Local leadership must be poised with sound neighborhood planning and community organizing to make sure our voices are heard in the planning process.

New Orleans East: A Village Called Versailles

Most Americans will never forget the horrific images in August 2005 of Hurricane Katrina's impact on low-income neighborhoods such as the Ninth Ward in New Orleans. Less well known is the story of another neighborhood, New Orleans East, which did not suffer the total devastation of the Ninth Ward, but found most of its structures underwater and experienced the relocation of an entire community. New Orleans East was the primary area where the Vietnamese community emigrated in the mid 1970s, a neighborhood of 8,000 people, about half Vietnamese and half African American. Called "Versailles" by many of its Vietnamese residents (after the Versailles Arms public housing projects) it was the first neighborhood in the city to rebuild after Katrina and the spirit and commitment of the Vietnamese community to this was a significant reason.

A cornerstone institution in New Orleans East is the Mary Queen of Vietnam Catholic Church, pastored by Father Vien Nguyen. While most of the Vietnamese community fled to Houston and other Gulf Coast cities after Katrina, only 400 stayed behind. Six weeks after Katrina, Father Vien called for a mass, and 300 residents came. A week later, the mass attracted 800. And by the third week, 2,200 "came home." The church developed a plan to rebuild, with visions of new senior housing, a new cultural center, and a community farm. Then word came that Mayor Ray Nagin was using his emergency powers to locate a new landfill a mile from New Orleans East. The Chef Menteur Landfill was to be operated by one of the largest garbage companies, Waste Management Company, and would be the repository for all the waste from Katrina. No environmental impact statement. No studies on waste containment and water treatment. No input from the community. Led by Father Vien, New Orleans East fought back, Vietnamese and African Americans working together in a way they had never done before. Their incredible campaign became the subject of the Emmy-nominated documentary titled *A Village Called Versailles*.

In May 2006, National CAPACD held its annual convention in Houston, which housed the largest number of New Orleans East refugees. We invited Father Vien to speak, and he brought along many of his young leaders. It was a moving experience for all of us to hear his story of heartbreak and resilience, of hope and fear. I was really proud that National CAPACD seized the moment and turned the convention into an impromptu mobilization to help New Orleans East defeat the landfill. Groups from all over the country formed a working group, developed an online petition, contacted our connections in national environmental organizations, and talked with our elected officials, all lending our voices to New Orleans East.

New Orleans East taught me the power of an engaged national network working for a local cause, helping to shine a national light, and mobilize national connections. It was a cause we could all relate to. It was their "I Hotel," and they were fighting to save their home. New Orleans East also taught me that our Asian American communities have always had to fight for survival, whether from public infrastructure, private development, or natural disaster.

The Cambodian American Heritage Museum, Chicago

One the most powerful examples I have seen of the merging of arts and culture with community development is the Cambodian American Heritage Museum, located in the Albany Park neighborhood on Chicago's Northside where Korean, Vietnamese, and Cambodian Americans have settled over the past three decades. I visited the museum with the National CAPACD Board of Directors, first when the museum was under construction and again in September 2012 after it was completed. We were all greatly moved by the very idea of this place, which combines a multipurpose community center serving the Cambodian community with a museum dedicated to the history and lessons of the "Killing Fields."

Dary Mien, Executive Director of the Cambodian Association of Illinois, which developed the museum, told her story of growing up as a child in Cambodia during the Killing Fields era. Dary also spoke of the challenges to the museum project, starting with the consensus building needed in her own community, many of whom just wanted to forget and didn't understand initially why the story needed to be told, not only for future generations of Cambodian Americans, but for all Americans. It took time for a family and community dialogue to take place across generations and for the idea for the museum to take hold and become real as a place for services and for learning. Dary also spoke about how much she valued her relationships with leaders of the Holocaust Museum, who understood that their museum was not only about a people's history or contributions, but about genocide and survival.

Our neighborhoods need places that help build community. These places can be museums like the Cambodian American Heritage Museum, Chinese history museums in San Francisco or New York, Chicago, or Honolulu, or the Wing Luke Museum in Seattle. They can be community centers like the Betty Ann Ong Center in San Francisco or libraries like the ones built in Los Angeles Chinatown or built in conjunction with affordable housing as with Village Square in Seattle. Increasingly, Asian American communities have embraced community centers as centerpieces for their community development strategies. The Lo Lu Mien community is building a new cultural center in Oakland, and Chhaya CDC is planning a new multipurpose center in Jackson Heights, Queens. The Little Tokyo Service Center in Los Angeles is planning the Budokan, a comprehensive sports complex with basketball, swimming, and martial arts.

The Cambodian American Heritage Museum was a powerful reminder to me that community development is about much more than affordable housing or successful businesses, good parks and safe environments, as important as these needs are. It is also about culture and history, and weaving these values into the physical institutions we build in the places we care about. And in so doing, we not only strengthen these places, we strengthen our sense of community, our shared humanity with other places, even thousands of miles away.

A Broader Vision of Community Development

Marching on the Capitol; the stories of Thai Town, Kukui Gardens, and New Orleans East; the critical transportation issues in Asian American communities; and the Cambodian American Heritage Museum are just a few of the wonderful experiences I have had with National CAPACD. National CA-PACD did not lead these local struggles, but it has helped give voice to them nationally, spreading those compelling human stories that describe who we are as Americans.

They are experiences that represent the broad lens through which we have embraced community development. It's not only about being housing developers, as the examples above all reflect broader, place-based challenges. They reflect issues such as neighborhood identity in the contexts of both race and place, and the importance of inter-neighborhood communication and collaboration. The experiences teach us that housing preservation remains an essential part of our strategies, and the importance of keeping families in our neighborhoods. And that neighborhood planning for natural disasters can be a context for community unity and empowerment.

The stories teach us that many of our inner-city communities face common challenges from major public infrastructure projects that may have both adverse and positive impacts on our neighborhoods. Further, they teach us that arts and culture must be inherently integrated into our neighborhood strategies, and that community facilities of all types serve as cornerstones not only for services, but for social justice as well.

The Community Development Movement in America is currently undergoing some serious evaluation about how it must change for the future, particularly in the context of shrinking housing resources on all levels of government. I am not suggesting that the stories above represent some new paradigm for the Community Development Movement, but I do think they suggest some broader roles, new challenges, and opportunities that can be elements of our community development strategies in the future.

CHAPTER 27

You Can Never
Have Enough Leadership...
or Hawaiian Shirts

LEADERS ARE NEITHER born nor made. I believe leaders arise when circumstances bring out abilities and courage that they may have not realized they had. Chinatown leaders have come in all shapes and forms—church leaders, small businessmen and women, youth and students, bus drivers—motivated by different circumstances, different challenges. They may have been motivated by a sense of survival, as was Mrs. Bao Yan Chan when her home at Notre Dame senior housing was threatened, or as were the tenants of the International Hotel when faced with eviction. They may have been inspired by a sense of service as the Reverend Harry Chuck, Linda Wang, and Cynthia Joe were in the two-decade struggle to build Mei Lun Yuen. Or, by a passionate sense of justice exemplified by a Rose Pak, an Enid Lim, or a Norman Fong when they feel Chinatown is being threatened.

Other leaders have had a quieter sense of courage, a Carol Cheung fighting cancer or a Betty Ann Ong giving her life to awaken this country. Young leaders may be moved by their search for personal identity in Chinatown, the Chinatown Adopt-An-Alleyway youth or young '60s activists, including myself and Ed Lee, who discovered Chinatown as a special place in our lives. What these leaders share is Chinatown—a respect for Chinatown's place in history, a commitment to improving Chinatown today, and a passion for protecting Chinatown's future as an important place in America.

Many years ago, I had the privilege of meeting Bill Shore, who founded Share Our Strength, which was dedicated to ending global hunger. Bill wrote a book titled *The Cathedral Within* that describes the commitment of workers who worked on building the great cathedrals of Europe, knowing that they would not see the fruits of their labor during their lifetimes, but also knowing that they were part of something much bigger than themselves. I have often viewed my work from the perspective that we were all part of a historic continuum of Chinatown leadership, from the Chinatown leaders who stopped the City from moving Chinatown after the 1906 Earthquake and Fire to our young Chinatown leaders today.

I believe that the people who were actively involved in these episodes of Chinatown's past are the best people to tell these stories. Some already have. Sabrina Gee wrote the story of the Mei Lun Yuen housing project as her bachelors thesis, as did Fei Tsen on the International Hotel, long before they became professionals. Linda Wang was passionate that the International Hotel Citizens Committee must compile a chronology and history of the I Hotel, post demolition. Ford Lee wrote a wonderful book about the history of the Chinatown YMCA, and Self-Help for the Elderly told their story in "Eternal Spring" commemorating their 30th anniversary. The Asian Women's Resource Center is currently working on a history of the Gum Moon residence hall. And Doreen Der in her retirement has taken on the awesome task of organizing a century's worth of archives from Cameron House.

None of these people are professional writers, but they knew that these stories, these histories, needed to be documented. They also knew that *no one else was going to do it*. The stories of so many other important Chinatown institutions, such as the Chinese Hospital, need to be written as well. We don't have a lot of time. The leaders who know that history because they helped make it are getting older every day. Memory does fade with age, if we don't translate our memories into histories, over time they will become just folklore. I wrote this book to help tell some of the stories of San Francisco Chinatown. I have often been asked, "How can you have stayed at the same place for so long?" At my retirement dinner, staff divulged their Top Ten Reasons Why Gordon Waited So Long to Retire. Among my favorites were "No tech support at home," "Frequent Flyer Miles from Work Travel," "Terrified of Dorothy's To-Do List," "Couldn't Leave Until the Giants won the World Series."

There is a grain of truth to all of these reasons why I lasted 34 years in the same job, and I have been asked about my longevity by both younger leaders and by many of my own peers who have had multiple careers. For me, it is all about *place*. And those places have been San Francisco's Chinatown and Chinatown CDC. In many ways, I feel that I have had many different jobs over the 34 years of leading Chinatown CDC—from heading a "start up" and the challenge of starting something new, to guiding an organization through some challenging issues, to managing periods of growth and transition to new leadership—and have been able to "age in place" in one place.

Executive Directors of nonprofit organizations have to be pretty good actors, stretching beyond our personalities, playing any role that the organization needs us to play. We put on our suits to meet with bankers and elected officials. We put on our jeans to do grunt work. We have to be outspoken leaders and behind-the-scenes directors. We have to be "all things to all people," which can be quite challenging, and a lot of fun. I have enjoyed the challenge of stretching myself over the years, and it has helped keep me fresh and engaged, and less prone to burn-out.

One of my messages to young leaders has been to be whatever you want to be and don't feel you need to choose your lifelong career path too early. You can change your mind and you can explore many paths, as I did in 17 jobs before I became Executive Director of the Chinatown CDC when I was 29. And my message to older leaders, Boomer Directors like me but who may feel stuck in a rut, is to shake things up a little. Play a different role in your organization (or another organization). It's OK to move on.

Vision

Along with an ability to act, another useful trait for someone managing an organization is vision. I don't have a formal theory, but I think it is important to see an issue or manage an organization from as many vantage points as possible. Vision is forward looking, imagining how an issue may play out, defining possible scenarios. This is not the same as trying to predict the future, and leaders make no claim to clairvoyance. But they do need to imagine possible outcomes and plan for how to react to each one. I think leaders of organizations also need a sense of hindsight to recall situations from the past that might be helpful in meeting a challenge today.

In complex challenges, one needs a form of X-ray vision, not in a Superman sense, but cutting to the heart of an issue. What is really going on here? Who is fighting, and why? Leaders need to look at issues with peripheral vision too, in order to see what might be happening outside of the immediate picture that might be affecting that issue, might involve other players or other issues. As many of us age, our optometrists may recommend switching to bifocal glasses (or contact lenses), which help us see both near and far with equal capability. When I got my first bifocal glasses, I thought they looked kinda goofy, but they have served me well in maintaining my vision, both near and far.

I think I have learned a lot from how others see the world, how they interpret what they see, sometimes in very unexpected ways. Listening to how children describe something they see has always been a joy for me. A few years ago, I was hanging out at a local mall, waiting with a bunch of packages as I usually am, bored and standing next to one of those kiosks with the map of the mall and the red dot showing that "You Are Here." Standing next to me were a young mother and her little girl, probably four or five, who seemed as bored as I was. All of a sudden, the cute little blonde girl points to that little red dot and chirps, "Mommie, Mommie... How do they know we are here?" I think her mom and I laughed for two minutes straight, until I froze and asked myself, "Yeah, how *do* they know we are here?"

I have been blessed with many experiences that have helped me form my approach to leadership. Of course, I have learned most from the many mentors and associates you have met in this book. I learned from listening to them talk and watching their styles of leadership. I have also benefited from so many wonderful leadership training opportunities, some formal and others informal. The Evelyn and Walter Haas Jr. Foundation's Flexible Leadership Award supported dialogue among Executive Directors about the challenge of leadership for ourselves and our organizations. It made me think about leadership with much more intentionality. About a decade ago, Dr. Rolland Lowe, an early mentor and board member of the San Francisco Foundation, convened some of the most senior Executive Directors serving the Asian American community—myself, Anni Chung (Self-Help for the Elderly), Sherry Hirota (Asian Health Services), Maurice Lim Miller (Asian Neighborhood Design), Jennie Chin Hansen (On Lok), and Lynette Lee (EBALDC) —for a series of conversations held at his house, quarterly for a two-year period. These honest talks about our leadership, about grooming the next generation of leadership, and about succession planning, really helped each of us to think about our futures and prepare our organizations for our eventual departures. I have always felt that one can learn so much by listening to other leaders talk about their challenges and by offering whatever lessons we can share with other leaders of smaller or newer organizations.

Books on Leadership

I have read a few books about leadership by recognized leaders in the field, like Peter Drucker, but I think I have learned the most about leadership and strategy from two books in particular that you won't find in the management section of your bookstore. George Woo turned many of us young activists on to Sun Tzu's *The Art of War* at one of our visits to his house, telling how Mao Tse Tung based his military strategy on the teachings of Sun Tzu and this book in particular. The book is a classic on military strategy and has been used in corporate planning and political campaign strategy. Community organizations who are engaged in advocacy, waging campaigns as "issue wars," have also cited Sun Tzu's teachings. Some of my personal favorites from the book:

> He will win who knows when to fight, and when not to fight.

> Strategy without tactics is the slowest route to victory. Tactics without strategy is the noise before defeat.

> Do not repeat the tactics which have gained you one victory, but let your method be regulated by the infinite varieties of circumstances.

> And my favorite one word teaching... Provisions.

Timing, strategy, and tactics were all critical elements in many issues Chinatown CDC has dealt with, particularly in the 10-year struggle to achieve the rezoning of Chinatown. In the early years of the organization, we knew that we would not win a Chinatown zoning fight, and it took a decade to build up community support and political capital before the opportunity arose to implement the rezoning.

Bill Walsh and Bruce Bochy

I've learned a lot from being a lifelong Bay Area sports fan—Niners and Giants, A's and Raiders. My buddy Mike Yep and I used to take Chinatown Police Athletic League kids to Kezar Stadium, admiring how the Morabito family, who owned the Niners, "gave back to the community" with free tickets for hundreds of inner-city youth. Strong leadership and good management are not only about teamwork. They are also about the importance of team chemistry and having clear organizational roles, about strategic game planning and building a strong organizational foundation

The late Forty-Niners coach Bill Walsh was often called a "football genius." I have a copy of his book *Finding the Winning Edge,* which has come to be regarded as a bible of pro football strategy, and his cerebral approach to the game resonated with me. He was a great motivator, leader, and manager, and his book talks about how to integrate leadership and management, how to wage campaigns, how to think strategically about challenges, and how to improvise variants of those strategies when circumstances change. Bill Walsh was known for his "scripting" of the first 25 plays the 49er offense would run at the beginning of each game, but he was also ready to improvise if the assumptions your plan was based on did not materialize. I've always been a firm believer that preparation and planning, scenario playing and improvisation were essential tools in the work I did. The community development world often presents us with complex issues with many dimensions and variables, whether you are trying to develop affordable housing or starting an advocacy campaign. And as our initial assumptions about funding sources, neighborhood impacts, or political support may change, we need to be able to adapt our strategies, improvise new plays. We usually don't have the luxury of time to chart out these changes because the "game has already started."

Bruce Bochy, in managing the San Francisco Giants to three World Series Championships, exemplifies the type of calm, even-tempered leadership and management that I have aspired to. Like Bill Walsh, "Boch" always seems to think two or three steps ahead when making key decisions in a game, when to change pitchers, how to utilize his bench players, etc. Further, the San Francisco Giants have gained a reputation for understanding the importance of team chemistry, valuing character as well as talent in building a team that starts with a strong leadership core and then balances that core by bringing in the right mix of young rookie talent and older veterans. I think those abilities are also important in running any organization, and I've learned a lot about both leadership and management from observing local heroes like Bill Walsh and Bruce Bochy.

What I've Learned from Jazz

I'm a huge jazz fan. I think the only material possession I have that I really value is my jazz record collection (4,000 and still growing). Listening to jazz giants like Bill Evans, Sonny Rollins, John Coltrane, or Miles Davis, I have a great appreciation and passion for one of America's great art forms, a passion that has taught me a great deal about leadership, whether it's the value of periods of introspection in one's life, like Sonny Rollins spending all those lonely nights on the Brooklyn Bridge just blowing his horn, or the beauty of ensemble arrangement in hundreds of Ellington compositions. From jazz, I've learned that improvisation not only makes life interesting, but can be valuable in community work. That one always needs to have a personal interpretation of the work we are engaged in, open to different arrangements, able to read the "changes" that will inevitably happen in the sometimes complex issues we have to deal with.

And I've learned that whether you are listening to a solo piano piece, a small jazz ensemble, or a big band (or running a small organization, a growing organization, or a large Community Development Corporation), the same basic principles are important—connecting melody and harmony, understanding tempo and rhythm, arrangement and improvisation, having a vision for what you are doing and doing it with a sense of integrity.

Jazz is the one of the best learning contexts about the African American struggle in this country, and Leroi Jones's eloquent *Blues People* was the first book I read that taught me the importance of African American artists, or any indigenous artists, having control over their art form, and how powerful that art could be in the larger struggle of people and communities, much as Jon Jang and others have done in the Asian American jazz community.

What Goes Around, Comes Around

I've used this phrase, *What goes around, comes around,* a few times in this book. I don't know if it's my sense of irony, déjà vu, or serendipity, but I have always felt that things have a way of connecting back to something I've experienced earlier in my life. A sense of events coming full circle. Whether it's being born in Chinese Hospital and then being involved in the new hospital project half a century later. Or meeting Dr. David Louis at the first ethnic studies class in the nation and finding out that he was a busboy in my dad's restaurant, then years later a loving physician for my mom and dad. Or discovering a similar connection between my work and my family in the Chinatown CDC's project to improve Ross Alley where my mother spent her youth. As Reverend Norman Fong often says, "The Lord works in mysterious ways." It was either fate (or the Lord) that brought Norman and me together, many years after Norman's mom worked together with my aunts in Chinatown gift shops. And now I'm seeing Ed Lee, who started out as a housing activist, facing affordable housing as one of his primary challenges as Mayor.

I'm not sure what all this has to do with leadership, but for me I think it has something to do with patience and the belief that one needs to be committed to the long haul of one's life work, guided by an abiding optimism that despite the struggles along the way, things will have a way of working out. Experiencing Loma Prieta at the 1989 World Series, I never imagined then how that event and our recovery thereafter would so profoundly change the landscape of San Francisco, or that the Giants would win three World Series Championships a quarter century later. We Giants fans know patience.

EPILOGUE

THE REV. NORMAN Fong was appointed as Executive Director on October 1, 2011. Norman has been a great friend and ally in Chinatown and in the Movement for the past three decades, and his passion and spirit have inspired so many activists in Chinatown, San Francisco, and nationally. The future of Chinatown CDC is in great hands under Norman's leadership and the team he has around him. I told Norman I would continue to help in any way I can, if only he would stop calling me "Founding Father," which sounds so old, in a George Washington sort of way.

One thing I have taken great pride in throughout my career at Chinatown CDC is attracting and retaining great staff, and I have been blessed with the privilege of working with so many dedicated people during my 34 years there. Back in the day, before computers, I hand-wrote all my memos, which then had to be deciphered by my assistants. I entitled one of my early strategy memos "The Stuff That Dreams Are Made Of" (Bogart's line from *The Maltese Falcon*), but my assistant typed it up as "The Staff That Dreams Are Made Of." I decided to let it stand, given its many possible interpretations

A number of years ago, a local political leader urged me to run for City Supervisor. When I declined, that person said that maybe I was too satisfied by being a "Big fish in a little pond," afraid or unwilling to leave Chinatown to become more of a citywide leader. I thought about this a lot afterwards, asking myself whether being at City Hall was really that big of a pond compared to Chinatown. I wasn't insecure or in fear of "going to City Hall," but my heart just wasn't in it. Plus, there was so much more that needed to be done in Chinatown.

I viewed my role as helping to nurture the great young leadership that was emerging in our community, leadership that will take over the helm of Chinatown organizations, becoming leaders on the many issues facing our community and our City or seeking elective office if the spirit so moved them. Mayor Ed Lee has made this decision, as has District Six Supervisor Jane Kim. They join many other community leaders whose stories I have shared in this book, people who have dedicated their lives to their community, celebrating its successes and struggling over its challenges. Yet, they all share one thing in common, a love for this special place we call Chinatown. In October 2013, the American Planning Association selected San Francisco Chinatown as one of the Top Ten Great Neighborhoods in America, citing Chinatown's rich cultural and social fabric, its creativity in planning for its future, and its resident and institutional leadership. The Chinatown CDC and individuals who have been a part of the organization have received many wonderful awards over its three-and-half decade history, but I don't think there has been an award that moved me as much as the APA award. That is because it was an award not to any one organization or to any one individual. It was an award that honored an entire community, San Francisco Chinatown.

I have more than a hundred Hawaiian shirts. They are comfortable, colorful, and casual, a reflection of my values. They also reflect an attitude represented by another of my more common sayings, "We shouldn't take ourselves too seriously, but we should take our work very seriously." Whenever I saw my old buddies Al Robles and Bill Sorro, both of whom I dearly miss, hanging out near the I Hotel, it was always comfortable, always colorful, and most certainly casual. We shared an attitude about life that was about the Hawaiian concept of Ohana, or "family." And family in this sense means no one is left behind. Ohana applies not only to one's immediate family, but also embraces the broader network of relationships we share as a community. I have learned a lot from this sense of communal sharing from my visits to Hawaii. It is a sharing based on respect, an intergenerational sense of respect for the many generations who came before us and who will continue on after we are gone. And it's this respect for the land and places where we live that teaches us that we don't really own this land, but are merely its stewards for future generations. These teachings have guided my work in Chinatown and San Francisco. This book was written in the spirit of Ohana.

At the Chinatown CDC "Aloha" Retirement dinner for me on October 1, 2011, I brought a couple dozen of my old Hawaiian shirts for guests to wear, in case they forgot to bring their own. It was a blast to see all those Hawaiian shirts as I was being roasted by Norman Fong, Supervisor David Chiu,

Mayor Ed Lee, and Speaker Nancy Pelosi. October 1st was also my mom's 93rd birthday. After the dinner, most of the shirts I had brought were not returned (I guess it wasn't clear that they were not giveaways), but I didn't care much since most of them didn't fit me too well anymore. In the three years since that night, an occasional smile comes over my face when I think of the many leaders I have had the privilege of working with, and from the image of my Hawaiian shirts roaming all over San Francisco. After all, *You Can Never Have Enough Leadership, or Hawaiian Shirts.*

Aloha

Gordon Chin
December 2014

NOTES

Preface

My knowledge about Chinatown was aided tremendously by a number of important books and films:

Him Mark Lai, Genny Lim, and Judy Yung, *Island*. Seattle: University of Washington Press, 1991.

C. Y. Lee, *Flower Drum Song*. Film: Universal Pictures, 1961; novel, 1957.

William Poy Lee, *The Eighth Promise: An American Son's Tribute to His Toisanese Mother*. Emmaus, PA: Rodale Books, 2007.

Wayne Wang, *Chan Is Missing*. New Yorker Films, 1982.

Judy Yung, *San Francisco's Chinatown (Images of America)*. Mount Pleasant, SC: Arcadia Publishing, 2006.

Judy Yung, *Unbound Feet: A Social History of Chinese Women in San Francisco*. Berkeley: UC Press, 1995.

See also:

Yong Chen, *Chinese San Francisco, 1850–1943: A Trans-Pacific Community*. Palo Alto: Stanford University Press, 2000.

Thomas W. Chinn, *Bridging the Pacific: San Francisco Chinatown and Its People*. San Francisco: Chinese Historical Society of America, 1989.

Philip P. Choy, *San Francisco Chinatown: A Guide to Its History and Architecture*. San Francisco: City Lights Publishers, 2012.

Chalsa Loo, *Chinatown: Most Time, Hard Time*. Santa Barbara, CA: Praeger, 1991.

Victor Nee, *Longtime Californ': A Documentary Study of an American Chinatown*. Palo Alto: Stanford University Press, 1986.

Faye Myenne Ng, *Bone*. New York: Hyperion, 2008.

San Francisco State Third World Student Strike:

Margaret Leahy, "On Strike, We're Gonna Shut It Down." In *Ten Years That Shook the City 1968–1978*, edited by Chris Carlsson and LisaRuth Elliot. San Francisco: City Lights Publishers, 2011.

Chapter 1: Ten Years That Woke Up Chinatown

1968 Chinatown protest quote:

"Demonstration Ends Chinatown Passivity: Days of Silence Over." *East West*, 28 August 1968.

Foo Hum quote:

Bill Moore, "One Chinatown View." *San Francisco Chronicle*, 15 August 1969

Other groups for youths:

Another group was "Leways" (for Legitimate Ways), which was formed by American-born Chinatown youth and young adults to help keep kids out of trouble.

Chinese Culture Center:

The Chinese Culture Center obtained a lease with Justice Enterprises, the prime developer of the new Holiday Inn, the first redevelopment project in Chinatown. The newly incorporated Chinese Culture Center in 1967 signed a 60-year lease with Justice Enterprises for $1 for the 20,000-square-foot space. The ensuing protests, led by young attorney Gordon Lau and others, later helped spark the creation of Chinese for Affirmative Action. The late historian Him Mark Lai wrote a comprehensive history and analysis of the history of the Chinese Culture Center in 2005 that detailed the chronology and political dynamics of the Center in its early period.

Two important 1969 Chinatown studies:

"Chinatown, An Analysis of Population and Housing," principal author: Alice Barkley. Published by Community Design Center, University of California Extension, San Francisco, June 1969.

"San Francisco Chinese Community Citizens Survey and Fact Finding Committee Report," Alessandro Baccari. Published by Bank of Canton, San Francisco, 15 August 1969. The Chinatown Citizens Survey and Fact Finding Committee was co-chaired by businessman Albert Lim, artist H. K. Wong, and attorney Lim P. Lee.

See also:

"That Chinatown Population Boom: Broad S.F. Study." *San Francisco Chronicle*, 25 May 1968.

"The Threat to Chinatown." *San Francisco Chronicle*, 4 November 1968.

Baccari quote:

"The Threat to Chinatown." *San Francisco Chronicle*, 4 November 1968.

Chapter 2. Fighting for San Francisco Neighborhoods

Community Development Corporations:

In their heyday, CDCs in America numbered in the thousands, assisted by a growing infrastructure of national intermediary organizations such as the Local Initiatives Support Corporation (LISC), the Enterprise Foundation, National Reinvestment Corporation, and the Center for Community Change, as well as statewide associations of community developers such as the California Community Economic Development Association and the Northern California Non Profit Housing Association, with varying support from local governments and foundations.

Redevelopment in the Western Addition:

After the displacement and devastation caused by the first phase of redevelopment in the Western Addition, WACO gained more influence over the planning for the second phase, which extended redevelopment east to Van Ness Avenue, aided in no small part by a lawsuit over inadequate relocation provisions filed on behalf of WACO by the San Francisco Neighborhood Legal Assistance Foundation.

Yerba Buena:

The plan for the new Yerba Buena Center (YBC) was initially opposed by organized labor given the many blue-collar retirees and unionized industries in the area, and the historic distrust of downtown "financial types." However, in the end, labor, led by the building trades, supported Yerba Buena for the new construction jobs it would bring.

TOOR lawsuit:

The TOOR lawsuit was brought with the assistance of the San Francisco Neighborhood Legal Assistance Foundation (SFNLAF), seeking adequate relocation prior to any demolition of their homes. In April 1970, TOOR won an historic victory when Federal District Court Judge Stanley Wiegel ordered an injunction against the Yerba Buena project, requiring a satisfactory relocation plan before any release of federal funding for the project.

San Francisco redevelopment:

For a comprehensive history and analysis of the story of redevelopment in San Francisco, see Chester Hartman's excellent *City for Sale: The Transformation of San Francisco* (Berkeley: UC Press, 2002), and for the story of the Western Addition, see Rachel Brahinsky's "Hush Puppies, Communalist Politics and Demolition Governance: The Rise of the Black Fillmore," in *Ten Years That Shook the City* (San Francisco: City Lights Publishers, 2011)

Harvey Milk quote:

The complete quote: "Let us make no mistake about this: The American Dream starts with the neighborhoods. If we wish to rebuild our cities, we must first rebuild our neighborhood. And to do that, we must understand that the quality of life is more important than the standard of living. To sit on the front steps—whether it's a veranda in a small town, or a concrete stoop in a big city—and to talk about neighborhoods is infinitely more important than to huddle on the living room lounger and watch a make-believe world in not quite living color."

Chapter 3. The Fall of the I Hotel

Estella Habal, *San Francisco's International Hotel: Mobilizing the Filipino American Community in the Anti-Eviction Movement.* Philadelphia: Temple University Press, 2006.

I am indebted to Estella Habal, a former I Hotel resident and activist, whose book is the most comprehensive narrative, history, and chronology of the I Hotel fight. For heartfelt memories about the I Hotel from a range of participants, see "Remembering the I Hotel Eviction," KALW *Crosscurrents,* 4 August 2010. http://blog.sfgate.com/kalw/2010/08/04/remembering-the-i-hotel-evictions/

San Francisco Neighborhood Legal Assistance Foundation (SFNLAF):

This group was headed by Sid Wolinski and had a long relationship representing the I Hotel tenants. SFNLAF was a great resource for community movements nationwide in the 1960s and early 1970s before the Nixon administration ultimately defunded the Legal Services Corporation. SFNLAF was later joined by many great private attorneys—Gil Graham, Bill Carpenter, Bob Thompson, Sue Hestor, and Alice Barkley to name a few—and attorneys with the Asian Law Caucus (including now Mayor Edwin Lee), who all worked pro bono on behalf of the I Hotel.

Chapter 4: Saving Chinese Playground

Committee for Better Parks and Recreation in Chinatown:

CBPR leadership in the 1980s and 1990s included Terry Ow-Wing and Gary Wong, who co-chaired the Committee for many years, and Camille Shih, Jerry Lee, and Bernie Lee. Community Planners Jennie Lew, Wai Ching Kwan, and Jasmine Kaw, along with Doreen Der and Norman Fong, worked on numerous open-space projects.

Chapter 5: The Mei Lun Yuen Affordable Housing Project

Mei Lun Yuen:

I am indebted to Sabrina Gee and her thesis paper, "Shaking Up Chinatown: The Democratic Moment of San Francisco Chinatown: The Story of Mei Lun Yuen." The thesis is also the source of the quotations about CCBH from Harry Chuck and Linda Wang, and from Cynthia Joe. Sabrina grew up as a Cameron House kid in San Francisco and attended UC Santa Cruz, where she wrote this as her senior B.A. thesis. She became a successful realtor, deacon in the Presbyterian Church, and a board member of Chinatown CDC.

Arcon/Pacific decision:

Todd Carrel, "Jee Bows Out as Developer: It May Be Soon for Mei Lun Yuen Housing." *East West,* 19 July 1978.

Mei Lun Yuen hearings:

In April 1972, the Planning Commission surprised its staff by rejecting the boundaries for the Mei Lun Yuen development, after the department had worked on the proposal for 18 months, with some commissioners saying it was too dense. Then a week later, the Commission voted to pass the boundaries. A month after that, several hundred Chinese packed a hearing to push for the passage of the preliminary plans, which were approved. Said one elderly Chinese woman at the hearing, "You can live anywhere, but not us... We cannot go outside of Chinatown because it is there we find our necessities, and we do not speak English. When you force us to continue living like this we are just waiting for our death."

"The Day Chinatown Went to City Hall." *San Francisco Chronicle*, 19 May 1972.

"Alioto Asks Speedy Aid on Chinatown Housing." *San Francisco Chronicle*, 15 September 1972.

Phil Chin and Harry Chuck quotations:

Sheri Tan, "Mei Lun Yuen Opens After Years of Work." *AsianWeek*, 16 September 1982.

Section Two: Preservation

Chapter 7: Starting an Organization

United front coalition:

We received plenty of help. Friends such as Chris Yee, who was Director of the Chinatown YWCA at the time, helped put a proposal together for discussion and eventual buy-in from the five volunteer groups, and leaders including Rev. Harry Chuck and Linda Wang from CCBH, Sister Beverly Karnatz and Doreen Der from CBPR, George Lee and Mrs. Chang Jok Lee of the Ping Yuen Residents Improvement Association.

615 Grant Avenue office:

On the fourth floor of 615 Grant Avenue was a nonprofit employment training program, the Chinatown Resource Development Center (CRDC), and you can imagine some of the name confusion a lot of people had with both our organizations.

CDBG funding:

Mayor Moscone appointed a new 15-member Citizens Committee for Community Development, including Dorothy Yee from Chinatown and many other neighborhood leaders—Bennie Stewart from WAPAC, Jeff Mori from the Japanese Community Youth Council, Toby Levine from the Mission Planning Council, Paulie Baugh and Mabel Sheen from Bayview/Hunters Point. Jim Jacquet was the first Director of the Mayors Office of Community Development, and Jim Johnson was the Community Relations Officer.

CCC relationships:

If there is one thing I took away from meeting CCC leaders, it was their great courage. President Pablo Eisenberg was the community conscience, urging the foundations to support community advocacy and organizing. The courage of Julian Bond in the Civil Rights Movement is well known. President of the National Council of La Raza, Raul Yzaguirre was an important voice in teaching and reminding America that race is not a black and white issue. These guys had guts and spoke "truth to power." Meeting people like them was a great inspiration to this young leader in the 1980s.

Chapter 8: Becoming Housing Developers

"As a result of distrust of City housing agencies...":

CCBH's disappointment in public agencies was partly due to the Redevelopment Agency's recommendation in January 1978 for a new two-block Chinatown— "Stockton/Washington Redevelopment Area." Chinatown property owners were outraged to see their buildings included in fancy plans by a City agency that had the power of eminent domain. The plan was eventually unanimously rejected by CCBH and all Chinatown organizations. The #701 Study had actually recommended that Chinatown consider forming either a community development corporation with a broad mission and scope or a Housing Development Corporation (HDC), which would focus only on affordable housing. CCBH decided that an HDC would be more viable given the momentum of Mei Lun Yuen and the fact that the Chinatown Resource Center had just been formed with a broader community development agenda.

District elections of supervisors:

Prior to 1976, San Francisco Supervisors were elected citywide. The passage of the district elections system in 1976 created 11 supervisorial districts. District elections was repealed by San Francisco voters in 1980, and reinstated in 1996.

Chapter 9: The Ping Yuen Rent Strike

This chapter was greatly informed by the Ping Yuen rent strike case study, which Sue Lee prepared for the Chinatown Resource Center as part of our HUD Neighborhood Development program in 1979. The case study provided a detailed chronicle of the events leading up to, during, and after the rent strike.

The Ping Yuen projects' population in the early 1960s was estimated at more than 3,000 residents, with a large number of children and youth. Designed by architects John Bolles and J. Francis Ward, the Ping Yuen projects were the highest density apartments in San Francisco at the time, with 89 units per acre.

Other Ping Yuen improvement projects in our early days, led by Program Director Sue Lee and Community Organizer Agnes Lee and supported by planners Jennie Lew and Babette Jee, were outdoor playground projects and organizing support for long-needed interior improvements, including new doors, window screens, and lighting. We advocated for CDBG funding on behalf of both the Ping Yuen Tenants Association and the San Francisco Housing Authority, whose own capital improvement budget was virtually nonexistent.

Ed Lee quote:
Chinatown CDC Newsletter, winter 1978.

Chapter 10: Saving Residential Hotels

Carol Cheung quote:
Chinatown CDC Newsletter, summer 2000.

Movement to preserve residential hotels:
The Burnside Consortium in Portland was a leader in this new movement. New organizations sprang up, including the Skid Row Housing Trust to preserve SRO housing in Los Angeles's Skid Row and INTERIM in Seattle's International District, sparked by their fight to save the Milwaukee Hotel.

Residential hotels and local strategies:
In recent years, there has been a movement toward "supportive housing" as a key strategy to deal with homelessness. This movement has brought together hundreds of nonprofit housing developers with social service, health, and mental health agencies to develop comprehensive service-rich environments.

Professor Liu quote:
John K. C. Liu, "San Francisco Chinatown Residential Hotels." San Francisco: Chinatown Neighborhood Improvement Resource Center, 1980.

Chapter 11: Chinatown Alleyways

Chinatown study:
Mui Ho's 1980 study was co-sponsored by Chinatown CDC and the Chinatown Park Rec Committee, and supported by a National Endowment for the Arts grant. It chronicled the development of Chinatown alleys (from China to Chinatown) and researched design guidelines for three Chinatown alleyway prototypes: 1) alleys as primarily residential thoroughfares, 2) mixed residential/commercial thoroughfares, and 3) dead-end alleyways. The detailed guidelines with design drawings included alleyway barriers, bollards, delivery zones, garbage bin locations, gateways, murals, paving, play areas, rest areas, lighting, and landscaping. The study concluded with specific recommendations for three Chinatown alleyways (representing each of the types): Ross Alley, Trenton Alley, and St. Louis Alley.

Chinese Six Companies:
The presidency of the Chinese Six Companies (Chinese Consolidated Benevolent Association) rotated among the eight district associations every two months.

Chapter 12: Chinatown Land Use Wars

1000 Montgomery:
The 1000 Montgomery Tenants Association received great legal assistance from attorneys Tim Lee and Larry Yee of San Francisco Neighborhood Legal Assistance Foundation and Steve Schectman of West Bay Law Collective.

Macris quote:
Letter from Dean Macris to Tom LaLanne, 25 August 1981.

Planning Commission vote on Pineview:
The policy item before the Commission was a zoning change for the Pineview site, but it was effectively a vote of support for both Jackson Court and Pineview.

Commissioner Nakashima quote:
Transcripts of City Planning Commission meeting, 15 November 1984.

See also:
"Ning Yung Assoc Plans 12-Story C-town Condo," *AsianWeek*, 11 November 1982.

Rose Pak quotes from interview, 13 August 2013.

Chapter 13: Rezoning Chinatown

Maximum build out
Planners refer to "maximum build out" as the amount of new development allowed for a particular site given the density allowed by the zoning. Density is measured by Floor Area Ratio (FAR). For example, a 2,000 sq. ft. site with an allowable FAR of 3.0 would be able to "build out" to a maximum of up to 6,000 feet, assuming the existing height limits would allow for it.

The planning efforts of other San Francisco neighborhoods:
Other groups working to rezone their neighborhoods were included in the Council of Community Housing Organizations and San Franciscans for Reasonable Growth, an umbrella environmental coalition. Most of the ring neighborhoods were advised by, and in some cases represented by, land use attorney Sue Hestor.

Section Three: Revitalization

Local Initiatives Support Corporation:
LISC was founded in 1979 to support community development corporations nationwide, providing grants and loans, technical and management assistance, policy support for affordable housing development, commercial and facility development, and neighborhood planning.

Neighborhood Preservation Initiative:
NPI aided efforts in the 1990s to create what was known as "Concentrated Community Initiatives"—foundation-led initiatives with multi-year funding to particular neighborhoods, often requiring a collaboration of neighborhood organizations and in some cases, local government agencies.

Chapter 14: The Loma Prieta Earthquake

Nonprofits receiving advance grants:

The Non Profit Sector Research Fund, under the auspices of the Aspen Institute, published an excellent report in 2006 entitled "Weathering the Storm: The Role of Local Non Profits in the Hurricane Katrina Relief Effort." Recommendations included calls for greater coordination of nonprofit efforts, increased and more flexible funding for preparedness, and proposed federal legislation mandating that the American Red Cross contribute at least 5% of its overall fund-raising to local nonprofits and faith-based groups.

Housing stock damaged by the Loma Prieta Earthquake:

Mary Comerio, "Housing Repair and Reconstruction After Loma Prieta." NISEE, U.C. Berkeley, 1997.

UMB Bond:

The UMB Seismic Retrofit Ordinance came after a lengthy and contentious debate involving numerous stakeholders—the City, the structural engineering community, tenant advocates, and property owner associations. The result was an ordinance that required a lower standard of seismic retrofit, which became known as "Bolts Plus," that involved tying together all walls and floors to maintain the structural integrity and allow residents to escape after a seismic event.

"Soft story" buildings:

Before and after Loma Prieta, low-income neighborhoods in Chinatown and the Tenderloin had long heard from real estate developers and politicians that UMB buildings and residential hotels were unsafe and should be demolished or converted to other more lucrative uses as a way to finance their retrofit, a position that tenant and community activists strongly opposed. Chinatown CDC learned from Loma Prieta that the issues of seismic safety and affordable housing preservation were integrally linked, and we dedicated our efforts in Chinatown not only to support seismic safety, but also to create programs to ensure adequate fire and life safety building code compliance, and educate both tenants and owners on fire and earthquake safety.

Rebecca Solnit quotes:

Rebecca Solnit, *A Paradise Built in Hell: The Extraordinary Communities That Arise in Disasters.* New York: Viking, 2009.

Chapter 16: Preserving Housing, Preserving Neighborhoods

Citywide Families in SROs Collaborative:

The member organizations included Mission SRO Collaborative (Mission Agenda, Mission Housing Development Corporation, and St. Peters Housing Committee), Chinatown SRO Collaborative (Chinatown CDC, Chinese Progressive Association, and Community Tenants Association), the Coalition on Homelessness, Hogares Sin Barreras, and the Homeless Prenatal Program.

Census of SROs:

The census of SROs methodology utilized 16 census workers speaking a total of six languages and conducting an on-site count in over 400 SRO buildings in target neighborhoods and 195 family interviews over an eight-week period. Their findings were shocking: over 40% of all San Francisco SROs have at least one child living in them. The majority of families live in Chinatown (62%), followed by the Tenderloin (13%), Mission (11%), South of Market (4%), and other San Francisco areas (11%). The average SRO family has 3.4 people and has lived in their SRO rooms for over four years.

Housing Tax Credit:

The federal Low-Income Housing Tax Credit program was created in the 1986 Tax Reform Act, allowing private investors and corporations to invest in affordable housing projects in exchange for federal tax write-offs. The LIHTC has been the primary federal source of affordable housing funding since it was created.

Post Office:

The Larkin/Pine building is actually a new single-room occupancy development with shared kitchens and baths. On Lok helped advise on a design that clustered four rooms together.

Chapter 18: Building Community, Chinatown Style

"Many great youth agencies":

Many Chinatown youth, particularly those growing up in the '50s and '60s, were identified (or self-identified) as either a "Cameron House kid" or a "YMCA kid." Having capable and successful youth organizations is essential to the social fabric of all American communities, and San Francisco Chinatown is no different.

AAA quotes:

Bonnie Tsui, *American Chinatown: A People's History of Five Neighborhoods*. New York: Free Press, 2010. In the chapter "Alleyway Kids."

Sharing stories of community leaders with a wider audience:

The personal stories of Mr. Wing Hoo Leung and Wing Pak Tse, two tenant leaders who fought the Ellis Act eviction in their building on Jasper Place in 2009. "Jasper Tenants Hope for a New Beginning." *Beyond Chron*, 4 May 2010. http://www.beyondchron.org/news/index.php?itemid=8080

Chinese history museums:

Chinese American history museums have been valuable educational resources and environments for progressive change in Chinatowns nationwide—in New York City, Chicago, Honolulu, Los Angeles, Seattle, and other cities. For example, the Museum of Chinese in America (founded in 1980 as the New York Chinatown History Project) led by activists Jack Tchen and Charley Lai, and New York–based artists, historians, and students, developed its new museum in 2009 in a greatly expanded facility designed by Maya Lin. MOCA has been a creative resource in planning for neighborhood change in New York Chinatown.

Intergenerational leadership:
A version of this section first appeared in the LISC-sponsored Institute for Comprehensive Community Development journal on December 2011.

SECTION FOUR: TRANSITIONS

The San Francisco Giants won their third World Series of the decade in 2014!

Chapter 19: The Rise of the I Hotel

For a detailed chronology and history of the International Hotel, from the 1978 demolition to the new International Hotel in 2006, see "A History of the International Hotel Citizens Advisory Committee / Kearny Street Housing Corporation, 1979–2006."

Chapter 22: The New Era of Affordable Housing in San Francisco

San Francisco affordable housing policy:
For an excellent overview of the history from 1978 to 2012, see Marcia Rosen and Wendy Sullivan's report for the National Housing Law Project, "From Urban Renewal and Displacement to Economic Inclusion," November 2012.

San Francisco Housing Authority in the headlines:
Chris Roberts, "Discrimination Not Proven Against Ousted SF Housing Authority Director." *San Francisco Examiner,* 8 May 2013.

Chapter 23: Who Can Afford to Live in San Francisco?

Marc Benioff quote:
"The Benioff Doctrine." Interview with Jon Steinberg, *San Francisco Magazine,* May 2014.

SECTION FIVE: MOVEMENTS

Chinatown CDC leadership transitions:
I am always proud to see many former Chinatown CDC staff take on leadership positions throughout the community development field: Margaret Gee at Bay Area LISC, Joanne Lee at the Northern California Loan Fund, Peggy Lee at the Northern California Association for Non Profit Housing, Joshua Simon with EBALDC, Jane

Duong with National CAPACD, to name just a few. Others have gone into government: Jasmine Kaw with DPW, Helen Kwan with the Municipal Transportation Agency, Daryl Higashi with the Health Department, and Supervisor Jane Kim at City Hall.

Chapter 24: From Community Leadership to Political Leadership

Chinese American political leadership:

Not all Chinese American politics was progressive. Westside Chinese Julie Lee and Rose Tsai also hosted a Chinese radio show that claimed to give voice to the "silent majority" of Chinese American homeowners who were diametrically opposed to most progressive San Francisco land use policies, including rent control, condominium controls, and tenant eviction protections. Tenant advocates, including Chinatown CDC and the Community Tenants Association, were frequent targets of the SF Neighborhood Association radio show. Lee and Tsai captured the attention of the San Francisco media as an up-and-coming force to be reckoned with, symbolizing the emergence of the more conservative "Westside Chinese" in counterpoint to Rose Pak and other Chinatown leaders.

Chapter 25: Chinatown, USA

Chinatowns worldwide:

Virtually every major city in the world has a Chinatown—London and Paris, Johannesburg and Buenos Aires, Melbourne and Sydney. The first known Chinatown was founded in Manila in 1504.

Chinatown, USA proposal:

Organizations participating: Chinatown CDC, San Francisco; East Bay Asian Local Development Corporation, Oakland; Asian Americans for Equality, New York; Philadelphia Chinatown Development Corporation, Philadelphia; International District Improvement Association, Seattle; Seattle Chinatown/International District Preservation and Development Authority, Seattle; Asian Community Development Corporation, Boston; Chinese American Planning Council, New York; Chinese American Service League, Chicago; Chinatown Service Center, Los Angeles; Hawaii Chinese History Center, Honolulu.

Peter Kwong quote:

Peter Kwong and Dusanka Miscevic, *Chinese America: The Untold Story of America's Oldest New Community*. New York: The New Press, 2005.

Gary Kamiya quote:

Gary Kamiya, *Cool Gray City of Love: 49 Views of San Francisco*. New York: Bloomsbury USA, 2014.

Chapter 26: The National Asian American Community Development Movement

Starting National CAPACD:

I drafted an initial concept paper and facilitated the summit. Chris Kuo from AAFE was elected as our first chairperson, and AAFE committed to house the new organization. Bill Watanabe came up with the new name, "National Coalition for Asian American Community Development" or National CAPACD for short. (We all thought this was a cool acronym, but we always have to stop people from calling us "Incapacity.") The organizations that participated in the founding meeting on June 4–5, 1999, were Asian Neighborhood Design (SF), Chinatown CDC (SF), Indo Chinese Housing Project (SF), EBALDC (Oakland), Lao Family (Oakland), INTERIM (Seattle), Seattle Community Improvement Public Development Authority (Seattle), Little Tokyo Service Center (LA), Pacific Asian Consortium in Employment (LA), Search to Involve Pilipino Americans (LA), Thai CDC (LA), Chinatown Service Center (LA), Asian Americans for Equality (NYC), Asian Community Development Corp. (Boston), Asian Development Corp. (St. Paul).

Newer National CAPACD communities:

These included Hmong National Development, Southeast Asia Resource Action Center (SEARAC), and the National Korean American Service and Education Consortium (NAKASEC), and formed a strong relationship with the Council of Native Hawaiian Advancement, itself an organization with 80 member organizations.

Chef Menteur Landfill:

It was officially closed and capped in August 2006. New Orleans East had won, but the battle continues to this day, as even a closed landfill still contains a tremendous amount of accumulated waste.

INDEX

Page numbers in italics indicate photos.

Bank of America National Advisory
Council, 212

Barcelon, Wayne, 27

Barkley, Alice, 27–28, 37, 38, 41–43, 47,
56, 57, 64, 69, 72, 92, 99, 292

Barkley, Dick, 43, 69

BART. *See* Bay Area Rapid Transit

Baskin Robbins, 144

Baugh, Paulie, 293

Bay Area Rapid Transit (BART), 49, 258

Bay Bridge, 163, 170, 173

Bayside Senior Housing, 185

Becker, Bill, 29

Bell Hotel, 54, 145, 217

Benioff, Marc, 244, 299

Bennedetti, Dante, 115

Betty Ann Ong Chinese Recreation
Center, *162*, 209–10, 277

Bierman, Sue, 122, 128, 136

Bilingual education, 43

Bing, Bernice, 45

Black Panther Party, 21

Black Student Union (BSU), 22, 24

Blackwell, Fred, 234

Blecker, Michael, 235

Bochy, Bruce, 284

Bolles, John, 294

Bond, Julian, 97, 294

Bosselman, Peter, 130

Brady, James, 116

Brandolino, Frances, 125

Bridges, Harry, 78

Broadway Corridor, 125–26, 185–88

Broadway Family Apartments, *159*, 187

Broadway/Sansome Apartments, 187

Broadway Tunnel, 65

Brown, Jerry, 237

Brown, Willie, 28, 29, 71, 113, 155, *159*,
175–77, 187, 212, 215, 220, 221, 231

Brown v. Board of Education, 44

Bruce, Lenny, 53, 85, 116

BSU. *See* Black Student Union

Budokan, 277

Building Movement Project, 203

Bungayan, Joe, 228, *229*

Burton, John, 55

Burton, Phillip, 29–30

Bus drivers, Chinese, 77–82

Bush, Barbara, 156

Busing protests, 44

C

CAA. *See* Chinese for Affirmative Action

CACA. *See* Chinese American Citizens
Alliance

Cadillac Hotel, 113, 117

Caen, Herb, 127

California Community Economic
Development Association, 155, 291

CalTRANS, 171, 173

Cambodian American Heritage
Museum, 276–77

Cambridge Hotel, 116

Cameron, Donaldina, 69

Cameron House, 27, 40, 42, 45, 46, 63,
65, 67, 69, 71, 100, 109, 155, 193, 205,
208, 280, 298

Campaign Academy, 195–96

CANE. *See* Committee Against
Nihonmachi Evictions

Canton Bazaar, 19, 155

Canton Flower Shop, 120

Capone, Al, 17, 18

Carmel Partners, 272, 273

Carpenter, Aleta Dwyer, 21, 183

Carpenter, Bill, 60, 292

Cathay Mortuary, 94, 207

CATS. *See* Chinatown Alleyway Tours

Cayton, Revels, 24

Cazenave, Rene, 52, 103, 234, 236

CBPRC. *See* Committee for Better Parks
and Recreation in Chinatown

Community Development Block Grant (CDBG) program, 30, 93, 94, 97, 98, 103–4, 107, 108, 117, 122, 293, 294

Community Development Corporations (CDCs), 49, 291

Community Development Movement, 49–53, 104, 206, 234, 236, 267–78

Community Reinvestment Act, 243

Community Tenants Association (CTA), 71, 190–93, 199, 200

Concentrated Employment and Training Program (CETA), 30

Concerned Chinese Nob Hill Citizens, 74–75

Concerned Chinese Parents, 44

Cosby, Bill, 53

Council of Community Housing Organizations (CCHO), 52, 102–4, 236, 241, 296

CRDC. *See* Chinatown Resource Development Center

Crescent Cove, 235

Cross Cultural Child Care Center, 182

Cruise Terminal, 188

Crutchfield, Nesbitt, 24

CTA. *See* Community Tenants Association

Culbertson Hall, 69

Cullen, Kelly, 234

Cypress Freeway, 163, 170

D

Dang, Ted, 99, 101

Dante Hotel, 145

Davis, Miles, 50, 284

Dean, Tim, 98

De Blasio, Bill, 241–42

De Guzman, Emil, 57–59, 221, 227, 229

Delacruz, Ed, 24, 26

Denman, James, 56

Der, Doreen, 64, 93, 280, 292, 293

Der, Henry, 41

Development Training Institute (DTI), 97

Devine and Gong, 273

Dick, Ilene, 154

Dientsfrey, Ted, 217

DiMaggio, Joe, 163

Din, Wil, 79, 80

Dineen, J. K., 243

Dionnes, Joe, 57

Displaced Persons Act, 40

Doi, Kerry, 269

Domingo, Claudio, 228, 229

Dong, Jim, 204, 206

Dong, Landy, 27, 78–81, 227

Donovan, Shaun, 238

Downtown Plan, 145, 152

Drucker, Peter, 282

DTI. *See* Development Training Institute

Duong, Jane, 299–300

E

EAH. *See* Ecumenical Association for Housing

East West newspaper, 37–38

Eckbo, Dean, Austin, and Williams, 64

Economic Opportunity Council (EOC), 38, 40–42, 45

ECRD. *See* Education Coalition for Responsible Development

Ecumenical Association for Housing (EAH), 273

Education Coalition for Responsible Development (ECRD), 225

868 Associates, 218

Eisenberg, Pablo, 294

Elberling, John, 51, 152

Ellington, Duke, 50, 284

Ellis Act, 160, 179, 180, 191, 239–40, 244

Embarcadero Freeway, 157, 170–76, 185–87, 255

Empress Bazaar, 19

Empress of China restaurant, 242

San Francisco Community Land Trust (CLT), 214, 223–24

San Francisco Department of Public Works (DPW), 121, 122, 186

San Francisco Exploratorium, 188

San Francisco Federal Savings, 101, 102

San Francisco Forty-Niners, 257, 283

San Francisco Foundation, 88–89, 156, 165

San Francisco General Strike of 1934, 78

San Francisco Giants, 163, 212, 236, 249, 283–85, 299

San Francisco Hall of Justice, 44–45

San Francisco Housing Authority, 57, 58, 68, 84, 98, 107–10, 234, 237, 294

San Francisco Human Rights Commission, 24, 29, 57, 92

San Francisco Merchants Association, 168

San Francisco Neighborhood Association (SFNA), 174–75

San Francisco Neighborhood Legal Assistance Foundation (SFNLAF), 43, 107–9, 112, 134, 291, 292

San Francisco Oriental School, 222–23

San Francisco Parking Authority, 176, 218

San Francisco Planning and Urban Research (SPUR), 103, 156, 231, 232

San Francisco Planning Commission, 63, 64, 70, 71, 74, 100, 126–28, 130–31, 135–36, 139, 154, 186, 293, 296

San Francisco Planning Department, 67–76, 131, 132, 137, 140, 141, 143, 144–46, 148–49, 152

San Francisco Public Health Department, 181, 252

San Francisco Public Housing Tenants Association, 109

San Francisco Recreation and Parks Commission, 63, 155

San Francisco Recreation and Parks Department, 94, 162, 209

San Francisco Redevelopment Agency, 41, 50, 68, 69, 98, 103, 159, 178–79, 198, 234, 235, 294

San Francisco State Third World Student Strike, 22–25, 34, 35, 37, 38, 196, 201, 236

San Francisco Unified School District, 44, 132, 167, 196

Sanger, John M., 61

Sanger Study. See Chinatown Block Study

Sang Wo, 120, 144

Santos, "Uncle Bob," 14, 258, 259, 269

Sarsfield, Ed, 30

Save North Beach, 126, 128

Schectman, Steve, 295

Schmitz, Eugene, 168

School desegregation, 44

Schwartz, Laura, 134

Scott, Lois, 216

Scott, Walter, 108

Seale, Bobby, 21

Self-Help for the Elderly, 36, 41, 55, 68, 70, 73, 76, 79, 93, 107, 109, 132–34, 137, 218, 219, 224, 227, 280

Senior Escort Service, 79

SFNA. See San Francisco Neighborhood Association

SF NexTstop, 232

SFNLAF. See San Francisco Neighborhood Legal Assistance Foundation

SF Rising, 236

Shaheen, Thomas, 44

Shao, Chi Hsin, 80

Share Our Strength, 279

Shaw, Randy, 112, 113, *160*, 180

Sheen, Mabel, 293

Shelley, John, *228*

Shelley, Kevin, 175

Shifting Sands Initiative, 206

Shih, Camille, 292

Gordon Chin in 2015, in one of his 100 Hawaiian shirts. *(Photo courtesy of Gordon Chin.)*

About the Author

Gordon Chin is the former Executive Director of San Francisco's Chinatown Community Development Center, which he co-founded and ran for 34 years before retiring in October 2011. Recognized nationally as a leader in community development and affordable housing, and as a pioneering Asian American activist, he led Chinatown CDC in developing thousands of units of affordable housing for low-income seniors, working families, and formerly homeless residents. From the beginning of the Asian American Movement in the turbulent 1960s, he has devoted himself to building community, organizing tenants and immigrant families, and developing youth leaders. Mr. Chin lives in San Francisco, where he continues to be involved in community issues and is an avid Giants fan.

CPSIA information can be obtained
at www.ICGtesting.com
Printed in the USA
FSHW022215240419
57549FS